Trees in the Urban Landscape

OTHER TITLES FROM E & FN SPON

For more information on these and other titles please contact:
The Promotion Department, E & FN Spon,
2–6 Boundary Row, London SE1 8HN.
Telephone 071 865 0066

Trees in the Urban Landscape

PRINCIPLES AND PRACTICE

Anthony Bradshaw, Ben Hunt and Tim Walmsley
University of Liverpool, UK

E & FN SPON
An Imprint of Chapman & Hall

London · Glasgow · Weinheim · New York · Tokyo · Melbourne · Madras

Published by E & FN Spon, an imprint of Chapman & Hall, 2–6 Boundary Row, London SE1 8HN, UK

Chapman & Hall, 2–6 Boundary Row, London SE1 8HN, UK

Blackie Academic & Professional, Wester Cleddens Road, Bishopbriggs, Glasgow G64 2NZ, UK

Chapman & Hall GmbH, Pappelallee 3, 69469 Weinheim, Germany

Chapman & Hall USA, One Penn Plaza, 41st Floor, New York NY 10119, USA

Chapman & Hall Japan, ITP-Japan, Kyowa Building, 3F, 2-2-1 Hirakawacho, Chiyoda-ku, Tokyo 102, Japan

Chapman & Hall Australia, Thomas Nelson Australia, 102 Dodds Street, South Melbourne, Victoria 3205, Australia

Chapman & Hall India, R. Seshadri, 32 Second Main Road, CIT East, Madras 600 035, India

First edition 1995

© 1995 Anthony Bradshaw, Ben Hunt and Tim Walmsley

Designed and typeset in 10/12pt Times by John Saunders Design & Production

Printed in Great Britain at the University Press, Cambridge

ISBN 0 419 20100 9

A catalogue record for this book is available from the British Library
Library of Congress Catalog Card Number: 94–68795

♾ Printed on acid-free text paper, manufactured in accordance with ANSI/NISO Z39.48–1992 (Permanence of Paper).

Contents

Acknowledgements

This book is based on the accumulated experience of many people, including the excellent work of the Forestry Commission, and the work on urban trees carried out at the University of Liverpool, supported by the Joint Committee of the Science and Engineering and the Education and Social Research Councils, and particularly by the Department of the Environment under contract PECD/2/89, for which the authors are much indebted. They would like to acknowledge particularly the continued support of John Peters and John Angell (Department of the Environment) and Derek Patch (Arboricultural Advisory and Information Service), and the kindness of John Capel, Peter Gilbertson, Tony Kendle and Richmond Dutton (all previously of Liverpool University) in allowing the free use of their data, and Nerys Jones (Black Country Urban Forestry Unit), Grant Luscombe (Landlife) and the staff of Nottinghamshire CC Forestry Team for reading the final draft and making many useful comments on it, and Betty and Rachel for all their support while the book took shape.

We are also very grateful to the following. For lending photographs: E.W. Ambrose Ltd (Figure 6.2), Martin Glyn (Figure 6.5), Forestry Commission (Figures 15.2a, d, e and 15.3), Margaret Game (Figure 1.5), John Mills (Figure 1.3), Philip Putwain (Figure 9.1), Chris Baines (Figure 16.8); for providing drawings: Penny Bradshaw (Figures 3.1, 4.1, 4.9, 6.1, 6.4, 9.9, 10.10, 12.1, 12.6, 12.7 and 12.15), David Prescott (Figures 1.9, 4.2, 6.9, 9.12 and 10.14); for permission to use already published copyright material as source for figures: AB Academic (Figures 2.2, 2.3, 2.4, 2.6, 5.1, 6.11, 7.6, 7.8, 8.1, 8.8 and 11.9), Blackwell Scientific (Figure 17.19), Butterworth Architecture (Figure 10.10), Elsevier (Figures 1.9 and 1.11), Forestry Commission (Figures 7.9 and 11.1), HMSO (Figures 1.7, 3.3, 4.5, 4.8, 5.4, 5.7, 6.6, 7.10, 9.12, 9.13, 10.1, 10.3, 10.4, 10.6, 10.7, 10.8, 11.2, 11.4, 12.13, 13.3, 13.4 and 14.4), National House Building Council (Figure 9.11).

Introduction

Aims of this book

In 1987 and 1988 Britain experienced two unusually violent storms. They caused a great deal of damage to property, and they destroyed thousands of trees in towns and cities as well as in the countryside. Trees that had been growing for 100 years were uprooted; trees that were a familiar part of the landscape suddenly were no more. It is easy to take trees for granted and forget their contribution to our surroundings. When one morning they have disappeared, we are given a rude reminder of their importance, and how much we value them.

Great changes have been taking place over the last 20 years in our towns and cities. Areas of old and obsolete housing have been torn down and replaced by new. Whole industries have disappeared and new industries in new buildings have come in their place, often in elegant 'science-park' layouts. Whole new towns have been created.

All this has brought about a new interest and concern for 'greening'. People expect the storm-thrown trees to be replaced. But they are also expecting new developments to be green, with substantial numbers of trees and open spaces; and they are planting more trees in their own gardens. As a result, millions of trees are being planted every year, no longer just in traditional forest areas but in the much more artificial areas of towns and cities. With this has come a series of problems, because these areas are unnatural and much more difficult for tree growth. Yet, because of their concern for greening, people expect these trees not only to grow well, but also to provide an instant contribution to the landscape.

To achieve good growth of trees in cities is difficult; to achieve an instant effect is more difficult. Unfortunately, present-day levels of success in tree planting are not good, although better in some places than others. In one London Borough immediately after the Great Storm of 1987 it was possible to count as many newly planted trees standing dead as old trees blown over. An average death rate for newly-planted trees in cities is about 10% per year; and many of the trees that do not actually die grow badly. All this represents money wasted. It also means that landscape schemes do not achieve the performance that was intended. In the end it is the public which suffers from this poor state of affairs.

Trees have been planted successfully in cities for many centuries, so what is going wrong? Much must be due to changes in the way trees are managed, particularly in the way the labour force involved acquires its expertise. In the past the workers in parks and gardens went through long apprenticeships, working with older people. In this way the accumulated experience of generations was collected and passed on. Now the apprenticeship system has gone, and little formal training on the handling of trees has replaced it. Few books are available. Even the training of managers involves little about trees; landscape architects, who are responsible for many of the major tree planting schemes, learn little about trees in their training. There are excellent well-trained arboriculturalists, but far too few of them.

When people with some knowledge of trees read this book, they may keep thinking 'but I know that'. It is possible that they will feel that little within these pages is completely new. What is so disappointing, however, is how much was learnt in the past and is now forgotten or not paid attention to. It is forgotten, otherwise trees would not now be planted and treated so badly. For evidence that it was once learnt, the quotes which follow may be of interest. There is a great need for everyone to remember old wisdom as well as to discover new.

This book is therefore aimed at all those people who have to deal with trees, whether as designers, managers, operators, teachers or garden owners. It sets out to re-state established methodology, because it has been forgotten, or has not been included in training programmes. It makes this restatement in the light of the recent research, in this country and elsewhere, by which methods have been refined and modified. Modern research has not only to be able to develop new techniques, but also to show what happens if established techniques are not carried out properly, and to indicate why. In this respect it provides the scientific justification for operations and techniques which, without this evidence and with the decline of experience, become forgotten or overlooked.

Good practice depends on understanding. In the case of trees, this means understanding the biology of the whole tree, the way it works and the way it responds to treatment; so details of tree biology are included to give both a general background and an understanding to good practice . It also means understanding the evidence which has shown how trees should be handled; so details are given of some of the experiments that have been carried out.

Lessons from the past

A symposium was held not long ago on tree establishment which was forward looking and dealt with many of the problems which are treated in this book. In the beginning of the published proceedings *(Tree Establishment*, University of Bath, 1983), P. R. Thoday quotes from a dissertation by James Justice FRS published in 1759, to remind us of how much has been known for so long, and how much of this has been forgotten or ignored. What James Justice wrote over 200 years ago is totally applicable today, and we have further good evidence to support what he says, some of which will be given in this book.

Planting in heavy (compacted) soils (Chapter 6).

If your soil is stiff, and has never been ploughed, it will be extremely proper in the winter preceding the spring when you intend to plant or sow, to cast up pits three feet deep, throw out the earth above the surface, to get the benefit of the winter weather; and when you plant or sow, you may fill up the pits again: this will be of very great service to your plants, when they come to shoot out their tender fibres, as by the freeness of the earth, which has been exposed, they will have full play to run into it, to become woody and strong, and will enable them to thrust themselves through the neighbouring earth, which may be perhaps of a harder contexture.

Care when lifting and root pruning bare-rooted transplants (Chapter 7).

When you are to transplant them, before you draw them, you must loosen them with the spade: for as they emit a strong radical deep into the ground, they would be in hazard of breaking if they were not thus loosened. When you have taken them up, you may shorten the strong radical, or top root: but be very sparing in pruning their lateral fibres. After their removal, plant them, thrusting down the earth to their roots.

Disadvantage of planting old stock (Chapter 7).

Twenty-two years ago, I made a considerable plantation of several kinds of trees, such as Ashes, Elms, Planes (i.e., Sycamore), etc. which I transplanted when they were pretty old. The first year after they were transplanted, those which held pushed pretty vigorously, the second year they grew weakly, and the third year they languished very much. The trees that suffered most, were those that were oldest when transplanted. I now perceived that their roots had not strength enough to support their heads, nor the shoots they had made the first year after transplanting.

The advantage of autumn planting (Chapter 9).

In dry land there is this advantage in planting early (autumn), that the trees will have made good fibres before Winter, and will not be so apt to be injured by Summer's drought, as when they are planted in the Spring; for often it comes to be extremely expensive to give due water to them in the Summer months.

The value of water and mulch, particularly for spring transplants (Chapters 10 and 13).

(In spring) rather than lose the opportunity of the season, if the ground and weather be dry, dig pits where you intend to plant, make a strong pap of the earth, and when you plant your trees, cover the roots with mulch or straw, to prevent the sun and air from drying them too much.

Weed control (Chapter 13).

In summer they (first year transplants) must be kept quite free from weeds; and the year after they are planted, if the weather is very parching, you must give them water, which will promote their growth.

Effect of good husbandry on the growth rate of young trees (Chapters 13 and 17).

I caused sow in my garden some seeds, of the same trees that I sowed in my woods. The first I left to nature, but these in my garden were cultivated with the greatest care and art possible: the effect was, that the Oaks I sowed in my gardens had stems eight feet high and two and a half inches diameter at the bottom: while those in the fields had stems about the bigness of my finger, and were but three feet high; and the Oaks in my gardens had heads in eight years which served as a sufficient cover to their roots, but those in the fields has no heads to cover their roots.

Established practices of more than 200 years ago (Chapter 17).

I would not be understood to insinuate that what I am to lay down is quite new, or what was never before practised by the public: on the contrary, I have known them practiced by many, and their success, as well as my own for forty years and upwards, engages me to recommend it to all. I have given what I apprehend to be sufficient directions concerning the planting of forest or barren trees from the nursery to planting them out where they were to remain for ornament in vistas, avenues, and even to protect your gardens from the inclemency of the weather.

Writers in the past were not only sources of practical advice but also of understanding. Because this book lays stress on the importance of root systems in both the establishment and maintenance of trees in urban landscapes, it is interesting to go back to the Greek plant scientist, Theophrastus (371–287 BC), for his comments. Because Theophrastus was translated into Latin and then English in the sixteenth century, his observations were read and quoted by John Evelyn in his own well-known book *Sylva* (1678).

Take great caution in planting, to preserve the roots, and especially the earth adhering to the smallest fibrills, which should by no means be shaken off .... Not at all considering, that those tender hairs are the very mouths, and vehicles which suck in the nutriment, and transfuse it into all the parts of the tree, and that these once perishing, the thicker and larger roots, hard and less spungy, signifie little but to establish the tree.

Theophrastus: de Causis Plantarum, Third Book, Ch. 7

Much of the knowledge needed for successful planting and maintenance of amenity trees is not difficult or abstruse. Nor is it all new, although a great deal has added to our understanding. We cannot expect to plant trees successfully if this knowledge is disregarded. Trees are living organisms. They have requirements for growth. If these are understood and respected, trees will grow well and soon provide rewards.

The authors hope that this book will not only be of value to those interested in trees and be helpful for training purposes, but will also show that we now have a properly established technology for urban trees, based on scientific principles, which can lead to both reduced costs and better performance. The latter in particular is badly needed. What would happen to a motor vehicle or washing machine manufacturer whose product had the same failure rate as urban trees? Yet despite all the concern for green issues we seem to accept failure in trees as the norm. The authors hope that this book will go some way to change this.

For all these reasons the sub-title for this book is 'Principles and Practice', because it sets out not only to provide the principles but also the practical answers to the problems involved in growing trees, especially in towns.

Costs

A recurrent theme of this book is not only how to achieve a satisfactory level of success in tree establishment but how to achieve it with economy. It should always be possible to obtain success if sufficiently elaborate steps are taken. The critical point is to achieve success at minimum cost. The costs of operations and prime costs are therefore given wherever appropriate. Since the aim is to place all costs in perspective, and because prices can vary on account of suppliers and materials as well as inflation, the costs are given in relation to the average cost of supplying, but not planting, a standard tree, termed a tree unit. At the time of writing this is approximately equal to £10. Further details of both prime costs and labour can be obtained from *Spon's Landscape and External Works Price Book,* which is updated annually.

Tony Bradshaw
Department of Environmental and Evolutionary Biology,
University of Liverpool, UK

Ben Hunt
Department of Transport and Planning, Nottingham County Council, UK

Tim Walmsley
Groundwork Trust, St Helens, UK

1 *The value of trees*

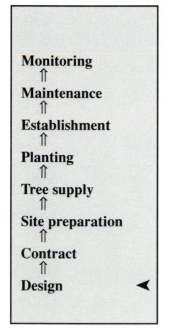

Monitoring
⇑
Maintenance
⇑
Establishment
⇑
Planting
⇑
Tree supply
⇑
Site preparation
⇑
Contract
⇑
Design ◄

- Trees have been an integral part of city landscapes for many centuries.
- Once they were restricted to the properties of the rich.
- Now, with greater wealth, and as their contribution to the environment has been appreciated, their presence in cities has become almost universal.
- Their presence involves space being set aside for them, as well as planting and maintenance costs.
- If these costs are used as a measure of their value, in the UK, in terms of the space they occupy, their value is about £200 000 million, while the salaries of those who tend them is about £10 million per year.
- They make major aesthetic contributions to our surroundings which are well understood; this means that individual trees can be valued in terms of thousands of pounds.
- Their environmental contributions, in terms of reducing air pollution, noise, wind and other factors, are equally important although difficult to quantify.
- Planted correctly and well cared for, trees have a crucial contribution to make to towns and cities.
- This is now widely recognized by Government, local authorities, developers and individuals.

Most people take it for granted that trees are an essential part of the cities of this country. Almost every advertisement for a new house has a carefully drawn tree somewhere in the picture; one well-known house builder has an oak tree as their emblem. Yet few trees are to be found in the middle of old cities, whether it is London, York or Chester. It seems that, whatever the present, in the past we did not much care for them.

But is that really true? Anyone who knows a city well realizes that trees are to be found almost everywhere, although in the hearts of old cities they tend to be confined to formal squares and parks, or are lodged in odd small corners, sometimes occupying rather large parts of very small back gardens. Some of the finest trees in this country grow in city squares.

We seem to have an ambivalence towards trees. Where there is room we like

Figure 1.1
St James' Park. The monarchs of Britain made sure their lands were well planted with trees.

to have them, but where there are pressures on space, we will do without them. There are few in the City of London; but in the Inns of Court, Buckingham Palace or similar places, trees abound. City dwellers who had money made sure that they had trees. Most parks in London were started by our Kings and Queens; in other cities they began as the estates of rich landowners (Figure 1.1).

1.1   *A history of trees in cities*

All this suggests that we are not so ambivalent after all, and that we do like to have trees if we can. What has changed is our means and ability to possess them. Although the nobility could ensure they had trees and parks in the fifteenth and sixteenth centuries, the development of trees in cities is bound up with increasing affluence in the eighteenth and nineteenth centuries, firstly of successful merchants and subsequently of the general population. It was the appearance of an affluent middle class in Britain which led to the development of city squares. Clever developers realized that these people would like to see trees out of their windows when they lived in town and could afford it. The best place for the trees was in a central square, by which everyone could enjoy the same trees and the same open space beneath them (Figure 1.2).

However, squares and parks were not the only places where trees were being

Figure 1.2
London squares were a clever piece of design by land developers to make sure that all the surrounding houses had views of trees.

Figure 1.3 Princes Avenue in Liverpool was laid down in the last century so that the rich ship owners and merchants could enter Liverpool from Princes Park, where they lived, along a pleasant boulevard.

Figure 1.4
Toxteth, Liverpool. In the last century while the rich had trees round their houses the poor were made to do without.

planted. Originally, when streets were narrow, there was no place for trees. But as money became more freely available, the roads became wider, with pavements into which trees could be planted. In some places, such as Paris, grand boulevards were constructed by pulling down old buildings. There are not so many places in Britain where this happened, because there was more democracy and more land was in private hands. But where new roads were built, grand avenues were sometimes constructed (Figure 1.3), and where land was bought and cleared by city councils for large new civic developments, space was nearly always provided for trees.

However, the poor could only enjoy the trees and open spaces provided by the rich. Their houses were closely packed to make maximum use of the land, built by developers trying to extract as much housing as possible from each acre (Figure 1.4). No room was provided for trees, whether it was Toxteth, Liverpool, Chapeltown, Leeds or other places, unless the cities themselves began to buy land for genuinely public parks. Sometimes there were great arguments when landowners wanted to use the right that they believed was theirs to develop land as they wanted it. Hampstead Heath in London was bought for the public in 1872 as a result of such a conflict, so that it could be a public park in perpetuity; it already had magnificent trees (Figure 1.5).

Then at the beginning of the twentieth century, people began to realize that it was no longer acceptable that there should be two cultures, of the haves and the have-nots, of trees and open space in cities. New developments should be carried out so that trees and open space would be an integral part of cities, as they always had been of the country districts from where the city dwellers had once come. In 1902 Ebenezer Howard produced the idea of the garden city. As

Figure 1.5 (opposite)
In 1872 Hampstead Heath, already full of great trees and much loved, was bought for the public to enjoy in perpetuity.

Figure 1.6
An estate in outer Liverpool. In between the two world wars great strides were made to provide pleasant housing with trees for ordinary people.

originally undertaken, at Letchworth and subsequently at Welwyn, the idea was interpreted in a rather splendid manner, extravagant in both land and money, and therefore not entirely appropriate for ordinary people.

But from that time, cities in Britain changed. Ebenezer Howard realized that industrial workers must be given better conditions, and that the extra amount of land required was a worthwhile cost which should be born by society. Although subsequent developments, carried out by local authorities and private developers, have often been meaner, the incorporation of a green element in cities has become an integral part of our expectations (Figure 1.6). The green influence spread into private gardens, as these became larger and more able to carry trees as well as flowers. There was a new interest in ornamental trees and shrubs, aided by the influx of new material brought in from far off places such Tibet, China and Japan by plant hunters – George Forrest, Kingdom-Ward and others – often supported by the new rich merchants.

Now, the combination of all the experience of the past, the wealth of species, and higher standards of living, should mean that urban trees and landscapes are better than ever before. Sadly this is not always the case. In the inner areas of our older cities much has had to be replaced. Roads have been replanned, houses have been rebuilt, old industries have disappeared and been replaced. If this had been an orderly and high-quality process, there would have been no problems.

But in many cities the pace of change has left large areas of derelict land crying out for temporary, or permanent, landscape treatment. Despite special allocations of government money, there is still almost as much urban wasteland as there was 20 years ago.

Yet at the same time a series of new towns with sensitive, high-class tree and shrub planting, using ecological principles, such as at Warrington, have come into being. Community forests are being established around many big cities. The intelligent use of ecological principles is being advocated and used widely. The present is an age of the best and the worst in urban landscape treatment.

1.2   *The numbers of trees and their value*

In new towns and new suburbs, trees are taken for granted. In the first 10 years of Warrington New Town 300 000 trees were planted, for a population of 100 000; in Washington New Town 250 000. But there are 65 000 trees in the longer established London borough of Wandsworth, and 970 000 in Edinburgh. A recent survey shows that there are about 25 trees per hectare in town centres and about 55 trees per hectare in residential areas, and 80% are privately owned. Amenity tree cover varies from about 5% in inner city areas to more than 25% in parks and along transport corridors (Figure 1.7). There are probably 100 million trees in Britain as a whole, grown just for amenity.

These trees have a considerable value with which we are intuitively familiar. The problem is to determine this value in any sort of precise, monetary terms. One method is to look at present capital expenditure, such as recurring expenditure on new planting. The value of the hardy nursery stock being sold, at wholesale prices, is currently over £120 million per year. Unfortunately this only covers the cost of the stock and not its planting, and such material could either be replacements or for new schemes. Another approach is through maintenance costs. Leaving on one side the unpaid work of private individuals, there are about 1000 arboriculturalists in the UK who tend amenity trees, paid at least £10

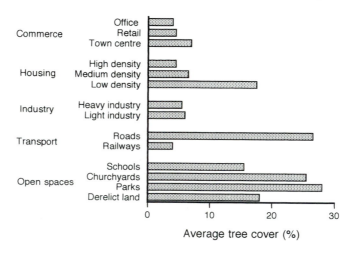

Figure 1.7
The cover of amenity trees in different situations. They are a major component of urban landscapes (redrawn from Land Use Consultants, 1993).

million per year in salaries, with at least an equivalent amount in support costs. There are only twice as many foresters tending forest trees. As an aside, when trees reach the ends of their lives and have to be removed, they can cost over £200 each, although small specimens will cost less.

However this only gives a valuation in terms of what we are prepared to pay at present to have trees. It does not indicate what all these trees might really be worth to us. To some people, nature is beyond price and trees possess an infinite value. This can hardly be true. But when some mature trees were damaged recently, a court of law decided that they were worth £2000 each. In the USA it is customary to value street trees at between $200 and $400 each. It is difficult to know how these figures are arrived at, but they must include the perceived benefits and the replacement cost. This approach has recently been developed into a systematized valuation by the Arboricultural Association, where different attributes of a tree are scored and the points gained are multiplied together to obtain an assessment of the the value of the tree (Table 1.1). This is converted into a monetary value by a conversion factor, at present recommended to be £10 per point. From this the value of an average urban tree could lie between about £400 and £4000. The method is now used widely, even though it is somewhat subjective.

Economists attempt more direct measures of value by asking the consumer what he or she is already implicitly paying for trees, or is willing to pay should a price ever be demanded. But this can be done in all sorts of ways. One method is to consider the value of the land put aside for trees, which might be used for other purposes. If an average urban tree occupies about 50 m² and urban land is worth about £400 000 per hectare, the land occupied by amenity trees is worth about £200 000 million. However, much of the land under these trees has a second use, so that this figure may be an overestimate.

Perhaps the most interesting approach is to compare the value of houses without trees with that of comparable houses with trees, the hedonic price method. Some work suggests that the proximity of woodland can raise house prices by 7%. In the USA it is normal for $500–$1000 to be added onto house

Table 1.1 *An evaluation method for trees: a practicable system produced by the Arboricultural Association (1990) (reproduced by their kind permission)*

Factor	Points			
	1	2	3	4
Size of tree	small	medium	large	very large
Useful life expectancy (years)	2–5	5–40	40–100	100+
Importance of position in landscape	little	some	considerable	great
Presence of other trees	many	some	few	none
Relation to the setting	barely suitable	fairly suitable	very suitable	especially suitable
Form	poor	fair	good	especially good
Special factors	none	one	two	three

To obtain a value for a tree the individual point scores should be multiplied together: this final amenity value can be converted to a monetary £ value by multiplying by a factor of 10 (1994 recommendation).

prices where there is a sound street-tree programme (1975 prices). If we really want to know the value we set on trees there is much more research to be done. But it is clear that the total value of our urban trees must be measured in hundreds of millions of pounds.

1.3 *The contribution of trees to our environment*

Against such costs and overall expenditure, it could be surprising that we have any trees at all. It would be simpler and much cheaper if we did away with them, or at least gave up planting any new ones. But we have not, and tree planting continues unabated. When our trees were damaged in the storms of 1987 and 1988, there was a great outcry and £25 million was immediately put aside by the Government to ensure what was lost is replaced.

Figure 1.8
Euston Road, London. Large trees are a foil for the built environment.

So what is it that we value? What are the special qualities of trees that we cherish and appreciate? There is no doubt that the primary quality is that they are alive and growing, that they change with the seasons, that they show us when it is spring and when it is autumn, and they show and remind us of the nature which ultimately supports us. But they offer more than this. In particular they have their own beauty, and can provide a foil for the built environment (Figure 1.8). Architects have, for centuries, used trees to enhance buildings, to add grandeur to vistas, to soften the harshness of roads. Houses without trees are hard and even relentless. Trees break their monotony and tie them back to the landscape. Trees are sometimes used to punctuate or sharpen a view, to contribute to it what might equally have been given to it by a building. But the contribution is softer than a building, more natural and changing, and it may, at certain seasons, when the tree is breaking bud or flowering, be a contribution of unashamed prettiness. A modern road or highway is a particularly bleak environment. Trees can be used to soften their harshness, as well as to define and clarify the line of the road at bends for the benefit of drivers.

This visual, aesthetic, contribution of trees does not need stressing because it is so familiar. Since time immemorial human beings have valued and used trees for other purposes – for shelter and protection. Trees lower wind speeds, provide protection from hot sun, and remove dust and pollutants, better than other plants (Table 1.2). Some people may feel that they can achieve all this in other ways, but there is nothing else which can provide shelter so readily (Figure 1.9). Trees significantly reduce wind speeds over a distance 20 times their height. Buildings only produce greater winds, as the air is forced around them. When elm disease removed our old elms, people discovered the protection they had lost. In reducing wind speeds trees have an important cumulative effect, so that a scattering of tall trees within a housing estate benefits everyone in the area.

Trees are very important providers of shade, particularly in high summer. This has been an important reason why trees have for centuries been planted along roadsides and in city squares in sunny climates. At the same time, by the evaporation of water from their leaves, trees can cool and freshen the air around them (Figure 1.10). However their leaves have an important role as absorbers of pollutants such as SO_2 and NO_x, and particularly by taking up CO_2 and releasing oxygen. Recently we have heard a great deal about the greenhouse effect produced by increasing amounts of CO_2 in the atmosphere. It is not

Table 1.2 *The potential environmental contributions of trees, shrubs and grass: trees can have the greatest effect*

	Trees	Shrubs	Grass
Air pollutants	• •	•	•
Dust	• •	• •	• •
Oxygen	• • •	•	•
Heat	• • •	•	•
Wind	• • •		
Noise	• •	•	

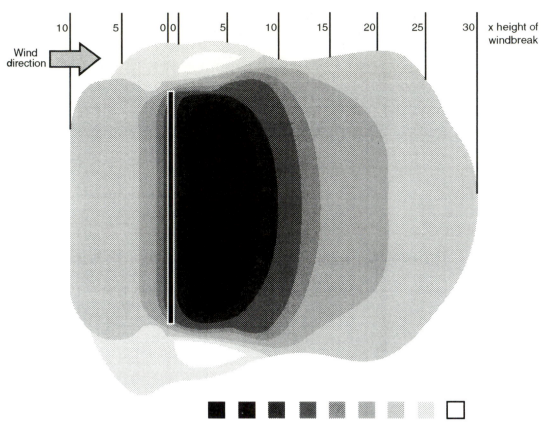

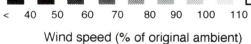

Figure 1.9
Wind speed reduction by a small block of trees (redrawn from Caborn in Bernatsky, 1978). The effect is appreciable for a distance equal to 20 times the height of the trees.

Wind speed (% of original ambient)

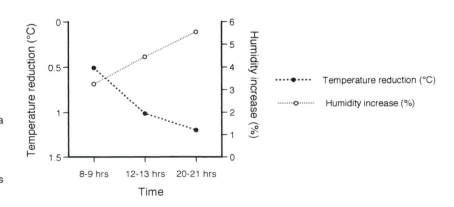

Figure 1.10
The mean reduction in temperature and increase in humidity in a 50–100 m wide tree belt in Frankfurt, from measurements made on eight different occasions over the summer (Bernatsky, 1978). Areas of trees can cool and freshen city air.

Table 1.3 *The absorbtion of CO_2 by amenity trees. Trees can make a major contribution to controlling global warming although not enough to cope with the extravagance of modern car drivers*

A mature oak tree weighs at least 1.5 tonnes and contains about 0.5 tonnes of carbon which is equal to about 1.8 tonnes of CO_2

The growth rate of a mature tree is about 1% per annum
The tree would therefore fix about 18 kg of CO_2 per year

A gallon of petrol produces about 10 kg of CO_2

An average driver travels about 10 000 miles per year and uses at least 250 gallons of petrol per year

To fix the CO_2 from this amount of driving therefore requires about 140 trees

difficult to calculate the amount of CO_2 that a tree such as an oak will absorb during its lifetime (Table 1.3); a faster growing tree such as a conifer will absorb more. Unfortunately we are so profligate with fossil fuels that many trees are necessary even to equal one car. But this is no reason not to begin, even if large forests are really what is necessary. Of course, in the end, when the tree dies and decomposes, the stored carbon will be released. But before this, the standing crop of timber represents an important way in which our excessive CO_2 can be captured.

Trees can be absorbers of noise (Table 1.4). Specially designed solid walls may be more effective, but they are far more expensive and very ugly. Traffic is a major source of noise in our modern society. A well-designed deep tree belt beside a roadway can absorb a great deal of noise for a small outlay of capital,

Table 1.4 *Examples of noise reduction by broadleaved trees and shrubs (from Beck, 1967, in Bernatsky, 1978): a reduction of 8 dB cuts down noise substantially*

Noise reduction of 4–6 dB

Acer negundo	*Pterocarya fraxinifolia*
Betula pendula	*Populus x canadensis*
Corylus avellana	*Sambucus nigra*
Crataegus x prunifolia	*Tilia cordata*

Noise reduction of 6–8 dB

Carpinus betulus	*Quercus robur*
Fagus sylvatica	*Rhododendron* spp.
Ilex aquifolium	

Noise reduction of 8–10 dB

Viburnum lantana

Noise reduction of 10–12 dB

Acer pseudoplatanus	*Tilia platyphyllos*

Figure 1.11
The distribution of lead away from a road in relation to different plant barriers (redrawn from Keller in Bernatsky, 1978). Trees are very effective in trapping and absorbing pollutants.

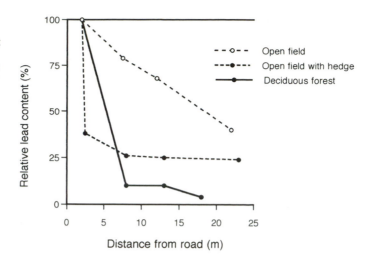

and at the same time be an important trap for dust and pollutants such as lead and NO_x (Figure 1.11). Heavy leaved evergreens are better than deciduous trees, because they keep their leaves throughout the year. But it is interesting how effective the sycamore is in reducing noise, because of its heavy leaves. People are even making living tree walls of willows.

Finally, trees provide us with important products. In forestry, trees are managed to produce timber and other wood materials as rapidly and as economically as possible. This means that the trees are felled just as soon as they have reached maturity. In cities this is the time when they begin to make their maximum contribution to our environment. So we keep the trees longer, until they are what the forester would call 'over-mature'. This makes them less good for timber. But even so there remain many possible uses for the material. Perhaps, if we know we can encourage new trees to grow quickly, we shall be more prepared to fell some trees earlier, to obtain better wood products (Chapter 16). Such younger trees are likely to be safer and less likely to blow down.

We will not die without trees in our cities, but many aspects of the unpleasant harshness of city life are softened by them. Planted and cared for correctly, they have an important contribution to make. Unlike buildings, once trees are planted they grow, without any further cost or trouble to us, to their own ultimate size. But as living organisms they will not reward us if we do not recognize their own particular needs and make sure these are provided for.

References

Arboricultural Association (1990) *Amenity Valuation of Tree and Woodlands*, Arboricultural Association, Ampfield, Hampshire.

Bernatsky, A. (1978) *Tree Ecology and Preservation*, Elsevier, Amsterdam.

Land Use Consultants (1993) *Trees in Towns: a survey of trees in 66 towns and villages in England*, HMSO, London.

Other reading

Aldous, T. (1988) *Inner City Regeneration and Good Design*, HMSO, London.

Colvin, B. (1948) *Land and Landscape*, Murray, London.

Dutton, R.A. (1937) *The English Garden*, Batsford, London.

Fairbrother, N. (1970) *New Lives, New Landscapes,* Architectural Press.

Farmer, A. (1984) *Hampstead Heath*, Historical Publications, New Barnet.

Forestry Research Co-ordination Committee (1988) Arboricultural research. *Arboricultural Journal*, **12**, 307–60.

Hibberd, B.G. (1989) *Urban Forestry Practice*, HMSO, London.

Howard, E. (1902) *Garden Cities of Tomorrow,* Swan Sonnersden, London (reprinted 1946, ed. F.J. Osborn, Faber, London).

Joseph, S. (1988) *Urban Wasteland Now*, Civic Trust, London.

Kielbaso, J.J. (1975) Economic value of trees in the urban locale. *Trees,* **Jan–March**, pp. 9–18.

Last, F.T., Good, J.E.G., Watson, R.H. and Greg, D.A. (1976) The city of Edinburgh – its stock of trees: a continuing amenity and timber resource. *Scottish Forestry*, **30**, 112–26.

Laurie, I.C. (ed). (1979) *Nature in Cities*, Wiley, Chichester.

McHarg, I.L. (1969) *Design with Nature*, Natural History Press, New York.

Rasmussen, S.E. (1937) *London: the Unique City*, Jonathan Cape, London.

Scott, D., Greenwood, R.D., Moffatt, J.D. and Tregay, R.J. (1986) Warrington New Town: an ecological approach to landscape design and management, in *Ecology and Design in Landscape* (eds A.D. Bradshaw, D.A. Goode and E. Thorp), Blackwell, Oxford, pp. 143–62.

USDA Forest Service (1976) *Better Trees for Metropolitan Landscapes,* USDA Forest Service General Technical Report **NE-22**, USDA NE Forest Experiment Station, Upper Darby, Philadelphia.

2 *Problems for trees in cities*

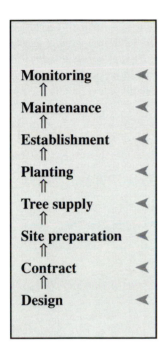

Monitoring ◄
⇑
Maintenance ◄
⇑
Establishment ◄
⇑
Planting ◄
⇑
Tree supply ◄
⇑
Site preparation ◄
⇑
Contract ◄
⇑
Design ◄

- Despite the excellent growth of some individuals, trees in cities have very high death rates; 5–10% of newly planted trees die each year, often more.
- Most but not all of this is visible in the early stages after planting.
- Trees planted as replacements often have even higher failure rates.
- Of those that survive, many grow very slowly.
- These growth and death rates vary from place to place, and city to city.
- This suggests that technique is to blame and that, although urban sites are often difficult, poor performance can often be avoided.
- There is general agreement that water is the most important problem, both drought and water-logging.
- Other problems include soil compaction, stake, tie and mower damage.
- Vandalism is, in reality, considerably less important than many people believe.
- The cost of such failure is the need to replace at £25–£50 per tree, amounting to £10 million each year for the country as a whole.
- Also the loss of the contribution of the tree until its replacement has properly taken its place.

Much to our delight, trees can grow well in urban areas. Yet this is not always the case because of the wide range of stresses to which they are subject. Some of these are almost exclusive to urban environments, others can be found to a greater or lesser degree in more natural habitats. Many, however, have little to do with urban environments, but are the product of bad practice. Too often individual trees, even whole groups, can be found dead or growing badly (Figure 2.1). Where the purpose of planting is environmental enhancement, this failure has a very negative effect. Not only is the contribution of the trees to the landscape delayed or lost, but the cost of the replacements is eventually passed on to the customer.

If this is true, then we need to know how much poor growth and death there is, what are the costs, and what are the causes. If we want to plant trees in our cities and towns, we shall be most successful if we can understand the problems that are faced by urban trees and what we may be doing wrong when handling them.

Figure 2.1
A line of dead newly planted trees, not an uncommon sight in urban areas.

2.1 *Survival of trees*

Most estimates suggest that approximately 10% of newly planted trees die in their first year. In Brussels it was found that a higher percentage die in their first year compared with the annual death rate for street trees of all other ages (Table 2.1). There is, however, good evidence that death rates may actually be high again in the second year after planting, particularly when the trees are leafing out (Figure 2.2) when those already weakened are subjected to further stresses. Trees are normally planted to replace those that die because of contractors' liabilities. But often too few replacements are planted and their success or failure is not monitored accurately. Death rates can be as high in re-plants as in the original plantings (Figure 2.3). Some surveys suggest lower death rates but this is because the observations have been made some years after planting, by which time it may be difficult to trace those that died early on.

In general, trees are more likely to die in the first few years after planting than in later years once they are established. This implies that the majority of resources should be channelled into overcoming the problems facing the newly planted tree. At the same time, however, factors which can cause decline and death in later years should not be ignored. It is estimated that the equivalent of

Table 2.1 *The percentage of street trees in different states over a 4-year period in Belgium (Impens and Delcarte 1979). Newly planted trees are more likely to suffer than older trees*

Year	Healthy		Declining		Dead	
	All	Young	All	Young	All	Young
1974	92.0	90.8	5.2	2.7	2.8	8.5
1975	95.0	85.6	2.4	4.1	2.6	10.3
1976	93.7	75.9	3.0	4.4	3.3	19.7
1977	95.0	77.7	3.1	13.6	1.9	8.7
Mean	93.9	82.5	3.4	6.2	2.7	11.8

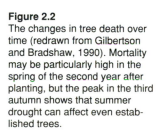

Figure 2.2
The changes in tree death over time (redrawn from Gilbertson and Bradshaw, 1990). Mortality may be particularly high in the spring of the second year after planting, but the peak in the third autumn shows that summer drought can affect even established trees.

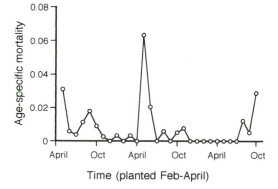

Figure 2.3
Cohort life table for 401 newly planted trees and their replacements (redrawn from Gilbertson and Bradshaw, 1990). The replacement trees planted under contractors' liabilities are often too few and show poor survival themselves.

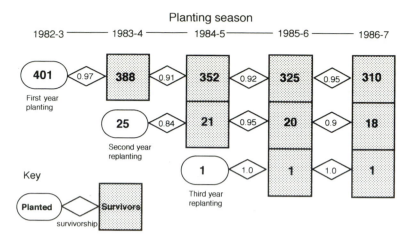

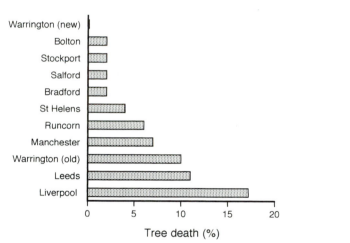

Figure 2.4
Regional variation in tree death in the north of England (redrawn from Gilbertson and Bradshaw, 1985). Levels of mortality can vary widely between towns and cities .

50% of the tree canopy of Washington DC is replaced every 6 years. In another survey, it was found that after 5 years only 54% of 5671 standard trees planted on 30 different sites were still alive.

Most urban trees should be expected to live for a minimum of 50 years if they are to make any substantial impact, especially since many of the trees most admired in our towns and cities, such as the planes of London squares, are a great deal older than this. It is worth remembering the enormous public reaction to the damage caused by the hurricane which swept across southern England in October 1987. In many areas this was a response to the destruction of a relatively small number of trees, but ones which were mature and prominent.

In all the statistics on tree survival, one fact is outstanding. There is considerable variation in the frequency of tree survival between different towns and cities – in some it can be 100%, in others much less (Figure 2.4). There can also be large differences between individual planting schemes; when what survives is compared with what was originally planted survival can range from 100% down to as little as 10% in the same city (Figure 2.5).

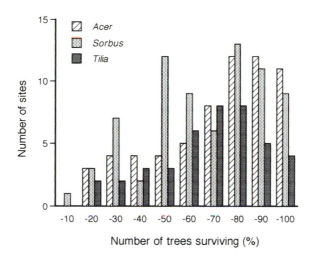

Figure 2.5
Variation in tree survival in different plantings up to 5 years old in a northern city (Capel, 1980, in Bradshaw, 1991). There can be remarkable differences between one site and another.

It is difficult to believe that this variation is all due to inescapable factors, related to the conditions where the trees are planted. It seems clear that technique must also be to blame and that much poor performance could be avoided. When failure occurs, a thorough investigation of all aspects of planting designs and execution should be undertaken, just as it would be in engineering and other situations, firstly to discover why the trees failed, secondly to find out what was different from other more successful schemes, and thirdly to ensure that the failures are not repeated. Unfortunately this is rarely done; otherwise trees replaced the following season would not show the same mortalities as their predecessors.

2.2   *Growth of trees*

Even when trees do not die, they may not grow well. A survey of a 1000 newly planted trees in the north of England shows that a wide range of shoot extensions is possible. Some grew over 1m in a single year, while others showed 1m of die-back (Figure 2.6). For trees which survive the first few years after planting, levels of growth tend to increase, but a considerable range still exists. The crucial point is that trees can grow well from time of planting onwards – at least 20 cm growth each year and much more in some species – yet a large number of trees do not achieve this.

The contribution of a stunted, sickly and mis-shaped tree to the environment is much less than that of one with a healthy, dense canopy. A healthy tree is also less prone to stresses such as drought and disease, and is less likely to be the target of vandals who find it more difficult to snap the stem or branches. It is a common misconception that trees automatically recover from initial set-backs, and that poor growth in the first year of establishment will be superseded by more vigorous growth in the following year, once the tree has established a new root system. Whilst this can happen, it is frequently not the case; growth of both

Figure 2.6
The range of shoot extensions of newly planted trees (redrawn from Gilbertson & Bradshaw, 1985). Whilst some trees show over 1 m of growth, others show the same level of die-back.

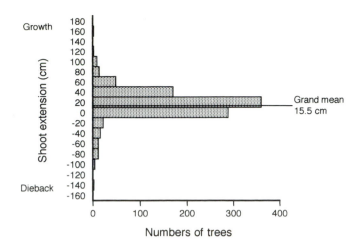

shoots and roots in one season is closely linked to what happened in the previous year. Some trees show poor growth for a number of years before eventually dying. Others do pick up, but only after 4 or 5 years have elapsed.

2.3   *The cost of tree failure*

When trees die or grow badly many of their benefits are lost. It is difficult to assess accurately the cost of all facets of tree failure. For instance, what monetary value can be placed on the failure of a young tree to soften the appearance of a modern building within a few years? From the overall cost of tree planting, the money wasted when trees fail is easy to calculate. A recent estimate of the amount of money spent nationally each year on tree stock and its planting is approximately £50 million. If 20% of these trees die within the first 3 years, this represents a waste of approximately £10 million each year.

Trees do vary in price according to size, species or cultivar, and availability. Unusual species or cultivars and those difficult to produce in the nursery will be expensive. A whip will usually be only approximately 10% of the price of a standard tree. Different tree sizes are not always interchangeable; the purpose of a mass whip planting is often very different from the use of standard or semi-mature trees. It is also clear, however, that costs of tree failure can be more easily absorbed when smaller sizes are planted. If all trees were inexpensive there would be less need to pay any attention to tree death and its causes. Estimates for one major planting scheme in Liverpool show a 13% death rate. This may not seem particularly high until it is realized that all of the trees were expensive root-balled, extra-heavy and semi-mature standards. Thus a sum approaching £100 000 was wasted in tree stock alone over the whole site.

The standard tree remains the backbone of urban plantings. Mass plantings of smaller tree sizes are suitable for many inhospitable sites and for forest production; but larger, extra-heavy and semi-mature trees are also used widely. The

Table 2.2 *The average cost of planting a heavy standard, bare-rooted tree using minimal planting methods (*Spon's Landscape and External Works Price Book 1994*). The price of the tree stock is only part of the wastage if the tree dies*

	Average cost (£)	% of cost
Standard		
Purchase of stock	10	30
Staking and tying	8	24
Excavation of planting pit and planting tree	15	46
Total	33	100
Additional costs		
Replacing entire backfill	10	
Tree guard	15	
Tree grill	250	
Possible total, as much as	310	

standard has been the middle ground of tree planting; its cost in 1994 is about £10. However there is now a great tendency to use a heavy standard, costing about two or three times as much. The cost of tree stock, however, is usually only a relatively small part of the total planting cost (Table 2.2). Thus the money wasted when trees fail is likely to be much higher than the estimates given above. If expensive items such as grills, guards and imported backfill are also included, dead trees which are not successfully replaced represent a considerable waste of resources.

For the rest of this book we shall use the cost of a standard tree as a unit (a **tree unit**) by which to compare the costs of other materials and operations, rather than refer to actual prices which can change with inflation. These costs will mostly be derived from *Spon's Landscape and External Works Price Book, 1994* to which reference can be made.

2.4 *Causes of tree failure*

Urban areas present a complex, variable and often harsh environment for plant growth. Consequently the causes of tree death and poor growth are numerous and can be difficult to ascertain. Many deleterious factors occur only temporarily, and so are no longer visible upon inspection. The waterlogging of a site, for instance, may occur for only a few days, but could have serious consequences for survival and growth. Unfortunately, it is inevitable that investigations of tree health take place well after the event, when such sites may have drained. Below-ground problems can be particularly difficult to assess without detailed and time-consuming measurements. These difficulties are often compounded by the simultaneous action of several different factors. This can lead to erroneous diagnosis.

Table 2.3 *The conclusions of different researchers on the principle causes of poor growth and death in urban trees: they have all highlighted the importance of below-ground problems*

Kozlowski and Davies (1975)	Most deaths caused by drought
Impens and Delcarte (1979)	Water < salt < soil aeration < low nutrients
Patterson *et al.* (1980)	80% of urban problems due to soil conditions
Dery and Rocray (1983)	52–73% of trees affected by abiotic (physical and chemical factors;10–30% of trees affected by biotic (human and other) factors
Gilbertson and Bradshaw (1985)	Water and nutrient stress < vandalism < tree guards < soil compaction < ties

Despite these difficulties, several investigators have attempted to assess the relative importance of different factors determining tree performance (Table 2.3). Problems of water supply, soil conditions and mechanical injury stand out as being considered the most important. Each of these involves a complex set of processes, which are often inter-related.

Many people in cities believe the principle cause of tree death to be vandalism. In answers to a questionnaire sent to local authority officers in England, Wales and Scotland, vandalism was ranked highest in a list of possible causes of poor growth and death of trees (Table 2.4). Available evidence suggests that this does not reflect reality (Chapter 5). The impression that vandalism is so common almost certainly arises because below-ground problems are overlooked, whilst vandalism is highly visible. Perhaps the most interesting feature of this questionnaire was that, even in the opinion of those responsible for tree planting, many of the problems they emphasized are not

Table 2.4 *Ranking of possible causes of poor growth and death of urban trees by 178 local authority officers. Although vandalism was ranked highest, in practice it is not. Notice that many of the suggested causes are due to factors which could be controlled by good practice*

Highest
vandalism
drought
planting technique
soil compaction
stock quality
waterlogging
mower/strimmer damage
tie/stake/guard damage
soil fertility
disease
road salt
other
Lowest

those that are specific to site conditions, but those that are within their own control, for instance poor planting technique. Successful planting and establishment will depend both on improving the urban environment and ensuring good plant handling and site management.

2.5 *The major problems*

At this point it is crucial to outline the many factors which can affect tree growth and put them in perspective in relation to the stage of life of the tree concerned. A small number stand out as being of paramount importance (Table 2.5). It is these that will be dealt with in detail in later chapters. Other factors are either rare, or tend to debilitate the tree rather than kill it.

The structure of the soil of the site has important implications for water supply and aeration and must be considered early on (Chapter 4). Many urban soils are poorly textured, low in organic matter and over-compacted by machinery and traffic. Compaction causes a hard barrier to root penetration, and can combine with poor site drainage to produce waterlogged conditions. In dry weather these same compacted soils can dry out, increasing drought stress.

The nutritional status of urban soils varies greatly, and any one of the major plant requirements can be deficient. Again this must be considered early on, although treatment can also be given later (Chapters 4 and 11). The most common deficiency is of nitrogen, followed by phosphorus. Conversely, some inhospitable sites contain toxic substances. These are very site-specific, and range from methane release from landfill sites to phenols and road salt, often reflecting the history of the site.

There are also a number of above-ground problems (Chapter 5). Temperature extremes can occur, especially where trees are widely spaced and where heat is reflected from hard surfaces. Wind speeds may be high between buildings. Air pollution was a major problem in urban areas in the past, due to sulphur emissions. These have left a legacy of acidified soils. Now there are problems of NO_x and ozone caused by car exhausts, which could cause increasing difficulties in the future.

Before planting, the type and quality of tree stock and the species to be used must be considered. They are crucial to the success of any planting scheme (Chapters 7 and 8). The right choice of stock and species sets the planting on course for success or failure and allows considerable financial savings.

At planting time handling is all important. Trees which are badly handled during lifting at the nursery, during transit, or when planted, do not establish well (Chapter 9). Desiccation of the root system is the most common problem. Bad planting can lead to several problems, especially wind-rock.

Once trees have been planted, water stress is likely to be the single most common cause of death. A truncated root system makes the tree extremely vulnerable to drought (Chapter 10). Unless water input to the planting pit is maintained, and a soil used which possesses an adequate water-holding capacity, trees are likely to suffer.

Table 2.5 *The major factors determining tree growth in the urban environment at different stages in the life of the tree with ratings for their likelihood of occurrence and severity. Final score provides warning of need for attention.*

Stage	Factors	Details	Occurrence	Severity	Score
Occasional factors	Salt	Road salt can cause complete death even to long established individuals	•	••	3
	Air pollution	NO_x and ozone are possible threats	•	•	2
	Exposure	Important in coastal areas and between high buildings	•	••	3
	Pests and diseases	Occasionally cause serious trouble	•	••	3
Site maintenance	Mowing	Bark can be damaged or completely ringed causing reduced growth or death	•••	•••	6
Protection	Vandals	Often over-emphasized, but can lead to serious problems on some sites to badly-placed trees	••	•••	5
	Guards	Can cause serious damage if not maintained	••	••	4
Support	Stakes and ties	Can cause serious stem damage if not maintained	•••	•••	6
Aftercare	Weeds	Compete seriously for water and nutrients and cause reduced growth or death	••••	••••	8
	Waterlogging	Can kill trees if prolonged during period of growth	••	••••	6
	Drought	The most important factor, affecting most newly planted trees	•••••	••••	9
	Nutrients	On poor substrates nitrogen and other deficiencies can cause poor growth	••	••	4
Planting	Root damage	Arises only from poor technique	•	•	2
	Pit qualities	Can restrict root growth	•	••	3
Tree handling	Exposure	Exposure of roots to dry conditions can severely damage trees before planting	•••	••••	7
Tree preparation	Lifting	Can lead to poor truncated root systems	••	••	4
	Growing conditions	Can lead to weak stock incapable of vigorous growth	••	••	4
Site treatment	Cultivation	Important to achieve good physical conditions	••	••••	6
	Drainage	Can be serious problem on some sites if not carried out properly	•	•••	4
Site conditions	Compaction	Impedes root growth and water and air movement	••	•••	6
	Poverty	Lack of nutrients and organic matter can affect long-term growth	•••	••	5
	Toxicity	Methane in landfill sites otherwise uncommon and local	•	•••	4

Human beings place pressures on urban trees. Vandalism can result in the death of vulnerable individuals or groups of trees. Stem damage by mowers and strimmers (Chapter 12) is the result of bad site management, and often poor staff training. Perhaps even more deplorable is damage caused by lack of attention to stakes, ties and guards; this indicates an absence, rather than a poor standard, of site management. Unfortunately its effects are usually worst on those trees which have been growing well.

Surprisingly, another major problem for urban trees is weed growth (Chapter 13). Left unchecked, weeds will compete vigorously for soil water and nutrients. Drought stress can be greatly increased if effective weed control measures are not undertaken.

The factors given in Table 2.5 have been given a rating in importance in terms of their likelihood of occurrence and severity, based on the experience of the authors and published work. The predominance of site factors is plain. The real problem that has to be remembered is that most urban sites are very artificial, and have little or nothing in common with sites where trees grow naturally. Trees growing in natural woodlands and forests form part of a complex ecosystem of soils, flora and fauna. Urban sites, in contrast, usually consist of a raw, poorly structured substrate material, with little or no organic matter. Additionally, the area outside the planting pit may have an artificial, impermeable cover, impeding water infiltration and gas exchange. When these factors are combined with wide spacings, and planting material with a truncated root system which has been handled badly, it is not surprising that trees often perform poorly.

Urban areas encompass a wide range of site types with their associated difficulties (Figure 2.7). Each will require different approaches to make them more hospitable for tree growth. For successful tree planting an awareness of the

Figure 2.7
Many different types of site occur in urban areas, from (left) housing clearance areas to (right) colliery spoil heaps.

Figure 2.8
A successful tree in a difficult site at Charing Cross, London. If the problems are understood trees can be made to grow well.

diversity of sites and substrates, and their histories, is an essential pre-requisite. Some substrates need little or no treatment. Others require some improvement, but are often not as bad as might appear on first inspection. Frequently there are only one or two factors which are limiting plant growth. Of course, there are some sites which are extremely complex, requiring detailed investigation and major treatments prior to planting; but these are the exception rather than the rule.

Only by understanding the problems which urban environments pose for trees, identifying which of these occur at the planting site, and applying appropriate treatments, can good survival and vigorous growth be achieved (Figure 2.8). But this is useless without a basic understanding of the needs of trees, which are dealt with in the next chapter.

References

Bradshaw, A.D. (1991) Arboriculture: the research need, in *Research for Practical Arboriculture,* (ed. S.J. Hodge), Forestry Commission Bulletin **97**, HMSO, London, pp.10–22.

Dery, P. and Rocray, R. (1983) Problems affecting urban trees in Quebec City. *Journal of Arboriculture,* **9**, 167–9.

Gilbertson, P. and Bradshaw, A.D. (1985) Tree survival in cities: the extent and nature of the problem. *Arboricultural Journal,* **9**, 131–42.

Gilbertson, P. and Bradshaw, A.D. (1990) The survival of newly planted trees in inner cities. *Arboricultural Journal,* **14**, 287–309.

Impens, R.A. and Delcarte, E. (1979) Survey of urban trees in Brussels, Belgium. *Journal of Arboriculture,* **5**, 169–76.

Kozlowski, T.T. and Davies, W.J. (1975) Control of water loss in shade trees. *Journal of Arboriculture,* **1**, 81–90.

Patterson, J.C., Murray, J.J and Short, J.R. (1980) The impact of urban soils on vegetation. *Proceedings of the Conference of the Metropolitan Tree Improvement Alliance,* **3**, 33–56.

Other reading

Derek Lovejoy Partnership (eds) (1994) *Spon's Landscape and External Works Price Book,* 13th edn, E & FN Spon, London.

Foster, B.S. & Blaine, J. (1978) Urban tree survival; trees in the sidewalk. *Journal of Arboriculture,* **4**, 4–14.

Gilbertson, P., Kendle, A.D. and Bradshaw, A.D. (1987) Root growth and the problems of trees in urban and industrial areas, in *Advances in Practical Arboriculture* (ed. D. Patch), Forestry Commission Bulletin **65**, HMSO, London, pp. 59–66.

Hodge, S.J. (1991) *Urban Trees – a Survey of Street Trees in England,* Forestry Commission Bulletin **99**, HMSO, London.

Michael, N. (1989) Do you get what you pay for? *Horticultural Week,* **12 May**, 35–7.

Patterson, J.C. (1976) Soil compaction and its effects upon urban vegetation, in *Better Trees for Metropolitan Landscapes,* Forest Service Technical Report **NE-22**, USDA, Washington, pp. 91–102.

Skinner, D.N. (1986) *Planting success rates – standard trees.* Arboricultural Research Note **66:86**, DoE Arboricultural Advisory and Information Service, Farnham, Surrey.

Thoday, P.R. (1983) Tree establishment in amenity sites, in *Tree Establishment* (ed. P.R. Thoday), University of Bath, Bath, pp. 12–23.

3

The biology of trees

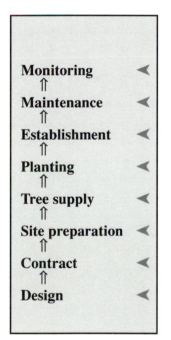

Monitoring ◄
⇑
Maintenance ◄
⇑
Establishment ◄
⇑
Planting ◄
⇑
Tree supply ◄
⇑
Site preparation ◄
⇑
Contract ◄
⇑
Design ◄

- The growth of trees depends on three supply processes:
    1. nutrient and water uptake, in the roots;
    2. photosynthesis, in the leaves;
    3. transport of materials, between the roots, stems and leaves.
- At the same time there is a fourth process, transpiration, the loss of water from the leaves which is inevitably associated with photosynthesis, which means that the tree is losing water continually.
- A fifth process, respiration, dependent on the supply of oxygen- and energy-containing materials, provides the energy needed for the activities of the living tissues.
- If any of the three supply processes is upset, oxygen becomes unavailable or the water losses are not replaced, growth slows down or comes to a complete stop.
- The tree may not die immediately but its future is inevitably prejudiced.
- Since water and nutrient uptake only take place in the very young parts of the root system, root growth must not be upset.
- Since photosynthesis can only occur if the leaves are present and functioning properly, with their stomata open, leaves must not be damaged or subjected to drought.
- Since transport of food materials and nutrients can only occur if the conducting tissue is intact, damage to the bark can have serious consequences.
- Since trees are composed of living tissue, this itself makes demands for the supply of materials and energy just for its maintenance.
- Since new growth in the spring is from reserves accumulated in the previous season, bad treatment in one year can cause poor growth in the next, and even in successive years.
- It is therefore important that trees being planted are not subjected to conditions which will cause them any sort of set-back.

Although trees, like other plants, are complex organisms, their growth, which takes place in all parts of the tree, depends on only three supply processes (Figure 3.1)

1. uptake of nutrients and water from the soil, in the roots;
2. manufacture of food materials by photosynthesis, in the leaves;
3. transport of materials, to and from the sites where these processes occur.

There are however two other important processes:

4. the loss of water from the leaves by transpiration which does not contribute to growth but which occurs when photosynthesis is taking place because the plant cannot prevent it;
5. the supply of energy for cell processes by respiration, the breakdown of food materials which occurs in all living tissues.

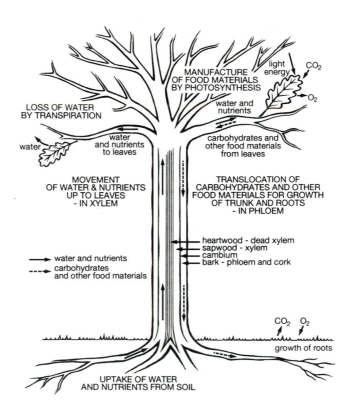

Figure 3.1
Diagram of the growth processes in a tree. Without these functioning in unison, growth is impossible.

If for any reason any of the three supply processes is upset, the whole tree suffers. Growth is reduced, or the tree even dies. To plant trees successfully we must therefore understand these processes and particularly the factors which can upset them.

3.1 *Growth*

Life cannot take place without materials and energy. After an acorn or other seed is sown, a tree appears and increases in size over many years, apparently without anything being provided for it. From this it is easy to fall into the trap of thinking that somehow what is produced (despite the fact that a large mature oak or other tree may weigh 2–3 tonnes) comes from nowhere. In fact, the substantial amount of material which is added to a growing tree each year comes from particular sources by a series of elaborate steps (Figure 3.1).

Growth requires a combination of raw materials and energy. In plants the starting materials are CO_2 and water, and various nutrient elements such as nitrogen, potassium, calcium and phosphorus taken up from the soil, together with energy from sunlight, by the process of **photosynthesis**. From this, carbohydrates and all other more complicated substances are produced, such as the structural materials lignin and cellulose, which are the main constituents of wood, and all the proteins and enzymes which form the machinery of the living cell. The energy for this comes from some of the carbohydrates or their derivatives, which are broken down by **respiration**,which uses oxygen.

For plant growth to begin there must be a starting core of living material. This is the seed. This germinates and grows initially by virtue of the material already stored within it. But this is soon used up, and all subsequent growth depends on the formation of new material by the combination of photosynthesis and the uptake of water and nutrients. Growth accelerates exponentially, by the process of 'compound interest', since as the plant grows so it is able to make more material, and this new material is itself capable of growth. As a result the plant is able to make more material more quickly as time progresses. Because of this, in trees as well as other plants, any checks or set-backs occurring early have a serious effect on subsequent growth.

In temperate regions, because of the changes of the seasons, most trees have a seasonal pattern of growth so that they pass the winter in a resistant phase. Trees which are deciduous lose their leaves, having taken back the labile materials into the woody parts of the tree. In the spring the burst of new growth is mostly produced from materials which have been stored in the tissues of the tree from photosynthesis the previous summer and autumn. Once the new leaves have been produced, further growth is from current photosynthesis. But some trees are evergreen; in these growth is more continuous.

Growth is in all parts of the tree. It is most visible in the leaves and new shoots, but it occurs also within the twigs and stem, which increase in thickness, putting on in the course of a year a ring of new woody tissue 1–3 mm in thickness. Growth also occurs in the roots, which spread out through the soil, extending from their terminal growing points by as much as 3 m in the course of a year and branching at the same time.

What is crucial about all this growth is its interdependence. If the leaves of a tree are damaged and fail to grow properly, photosynthesis is upset. If a newly planted tree suffers from drought, growth is directly stopped by lack of water, but photosynthesis is also again upset. In these situations not only will the twigs not elongate, but also the stem fails to increase in thickness, and new roots will not be produced. Because the roots are below ground their lack of growth will not be visible, but this does not stop it being very important, because the increasing need of the growing tree for water and nutrients depends on sustained root growth.

Because new season's growth is very dependent on materials taken into store the previous year, damage or stress in one year can affect the amount of growth made in the subsequent year. So a tree that grows poorly in one year because of some stress can be expected to grow poorly in the next year. As a result it may take several years for a good root system to be re-established. A tree once badly stressed may take several years to recover (Figure 3.2). It is therefore very important to ensure that, when trees are planted, they are given as little set-back as possible.

Figure 3.2
If a tree is damaged or stressed when it is young, it takes a long time to recover. New growth is dependent on what was laid down in the previous year.

3.2   *Water and nutrient uptake: roots*

3.2.1 WATER

Water is essential for all plants. Over 90% of all living tissue is water; it is the medium which is required for all the processes of life. In plants, water has an extra role in maintaining structure; plant cells and tissues are kept blown up, and therefore rigid, by the pressure of water, known as **turgor pressure**, inside them. Plants have another characteristic which increases their need for water. Photosynthesis, as we shall see, involves the uptake of CO_2 from the air by the leaves through special pores in the leaf surface. While this is going on, most plants cannot avoid losing water from their leaves by evaporation, through the open pores. This loss, due to what is termed **transpiration**, is very considerable, and has to be replaced by water taken up from the soil.

When there is not enough water to balance this loss, the plant gradually loses water so that the pressure within the cells of the stem and leaves falls, the cells become soggy and the plant wilts. At the same time all growth stops, in roots as well as stems and leaves, because new cells cannot expand. When a tree runs short of water, however, the stem does not collapse because it is held up by its woody tissues; only the leaves wilt. A tree therefore may not appear to be so upset as a herbaceous plant, but its growth is being upset just as profoundly.

3.2.2 NUTRIENTS

There are 16 elements required for plant growth, all of which, except carbon and oxygen, come from the soil (Table 3.1). If any one of them is absent or deficient then growth is upset. For this reason they are called **essential** elements. They have individual roles within the tree. Nitrogen is a major component of all proteins, including enzymes, without which plants cannot function. Phosphorus and magnesium have a crucial role in enzyme function, phosphorus being

Figure 3.3
The effects of adding nitrogen to birch growing on a very poor sandy soil. Nitrogen deficiency affects both root and shoot growth (redrawn from Gilbertson *et al.*, 1987).

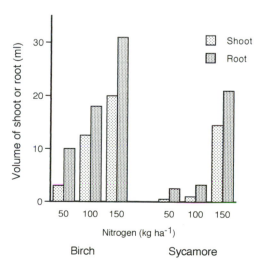

Table 3.1   *Typical concentrations of nutrients in plants, and minimum concentrations required in nutrient culture (Hewitt and Smith, 1975)*

Element	Concentration in plant (ppm)	Concentration in nutrient culture (ppm)
Carbon (C)	450 000	
Oxygen (O)	450 000	
Hydrogen (H)	60 000	
Nitrogen (N)	15 000	210
Potassium (K)	10 000	195
Calcium (Ca)	5 000	200
Magnesium (Mg)	2 000	35
Phosphorus (P)	2 000	30
Sulphur (S)	1 000	50
Chlorine (Cl)	100	3.5
Iron (Fe)	100	5.5
Manganese (Mn)	50	0.5
Boron (B)	20	0.05
Zinc (Zn)	20	0.01
Copper (Cu)	6	0.01
Molybdenum (Mo)	0.1	0.005

concerned with energy transfer. Potassium is involved in the regulation of the cell environment and in the transport of organic materials throughout the tree. Calcium is involved in cell walls and cell membranes. Because of these individual roles it is common for people to believe that they have distinct effects on growth, nitrogen enhancing leaf growth and phosphorus root growth, for instance. Although there may be some truth in this (Chapter 10), it is more useful to realize that all growth, whether above or below ground, will be affected by a deficiency of any nutrient (Figure 3.3).

Not all nutrients are required in the same amount. Relatively large quantities

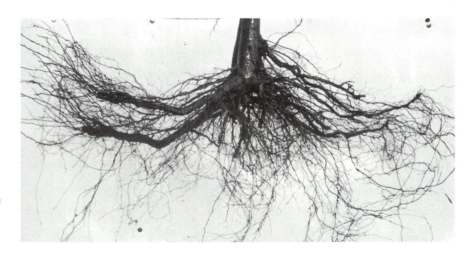

Figure 3.4
The root system of a standard tree one year after planting. The success of establishment has depended on the development of the new root system which is clearly visible and which will continue to grow every year

of nitrogen, potasium, calcium, magnesium and sulphur are required, which are therefore called **macronutrients**. The rest are only required in small amounts and so are called **micronutrients**. Despite the total amounts that are ultimately needed for the full development of a tree, the concentrations that are sufficient at any one time in solution to allow the tree to grow satisfactorily are exceedingly low (Table 3.1).

3.2.3 ROOTS

The roots of the tree are the means by which the tree obtains its essential nutrients and water. They also, of course, provide anchorage. The root system is a complex branching system, in which the individual roots vary from thick woody structures several centimetres in diameter protected by a corky layer, to fine terminal elements not more than a millimetre in diameter ramifying widely through the soil (Figure 3.4).

The fine roots are the only place where significant water and nutrient uptake occurs. The critical part of the fine roots is the outer layer of cells, many of which are elongated out from the root to form root hairs, 2–3 mm long, which have thin walls and grow out between the soil particles. In the centre of roots are strands of cells along the main axis which form the conducting tissue. Root hairs

Figure 3.5
The root plate of a fallen tree. In a mature tree the roots are almost completely confined to the upper layers of the soil where most of the nutrients reside.

live for only a few days or weeks before they are lost and the root ceases to take up water and nutrients from this region. It develops more conducting and support tissue and becomes much stiffer, so that it acts increasingly as an anchorage and conducting organ. The outer region of the root becomes relatively impermeable so that it is able to transport water and nutrients into the plant without loss back into the soil. Meanwhile the root continues to grow forwards into the soil, producing further root hairs.

Although a seedling tree has a main root, known as a tap root, which grows downwards into the soil, this does not usually persist. Later roots spread sideways through the surface layers of the soil to form what is often called a root plate (Figure 3.5). The root plate is in a good position to absorb the water and nutrients that are stored in the surface layers of the soil and are constantly replenished by rain and the decomposition of surface litter.

The root systems of trees are extremely efficient at nutrient uptake. The individual cells of the root, particularly the root hairs, have powerful mechanisms by which nutrients, occurring as ions in low concentration in the soil solution, are taken up and passed into the interior of the root. At the same time, since the root system itself is diffuse and spreading, the tree can obtain its nutrients from a very large volume of soil.

The root hairs provide the pathway for water from the soil into the root. Although water can move through soil, this process is slow as the hydraulic conductivity of soil is low. The diffuse and spreading root system of an established tree is therefore important, since it means that the tree can draw on water from a very large volume of soil. As a result established trees rarely run out of water. However, newly planted trees, with truncated root systems, are completely different (Chapter 10).

Since the cells upon which uptake depends only remain active for a few weeks, new ones have to be produced by continual growth of the roots. This root growth has the added importance of ensuring that the tree is continually foraging into new soil where there are new supplies of nutrients and water. This root growth, however, requires energy and materials. The energy has to come from the breakdown of the products of photosynthesis by respiration using oxygen from the soil. If the supply of materials or oxygen is upset, then root growth suffers and subsequently water and nutrient uptake; if the roots are deprived of oxygen they can die in a few days.

3.3 *Photosynthesis: leaves*

3.3.1. PHOTOSYNTHESIS

The growth of green plants depends on the process of **photosynthesis** which occurs in the leaves. Carbon dioxide, present in very low concentration in the atmosphere, is combined with water in a complex process driven by light energy, to form initially the sugar glucose, which is subsequently converted into other carbohydrates. Photosynthesis takes place within the green cells of the leaf. Oxygen is released as a by-product into the atmosphere, where it plays a crucial role for other living organisms, especially animals. The carbohydrates produced are transported to other parts of the plant to be built up into other compounds and to be used for growth.

3.3.2 LEAVES

In relation to the process of photosynthesis, the structure of the leaf is very elegant (Figure 3.6). There are small pores in the leaf surface, the **stomata**, through which CO_2 enters and the oxygen by-product is released. The size of the stomatal pore is controlled by **guard cells**, which close at night and also when the plant experiences a water shortage. The CO_2 is absorbed by the cells of the leaf, especially the loose **spongy mesophyll cells** in the lower part. Photosynthesis takes place within the microscopic bodies, called **chloroplasts**, containing the green pigment chlorophyll. These occur particularly in the columnar **palisade cells**, in the upper part of the leaf where light intensities are highest.

Leaves are flat to ensure maximum capture of light. They are covered on both surfaces by single layers of cells, the **epidermis**, which have an impermeable waxy layer on the outside. This layer prevents loss of water. But when the stomata are open, as CO_2 diffuses in through the stomata, water diffuses out, with the surplus oxygen, and is therefore lost from the leaf. If the leaf is unable to replenish its water loss then the stomata close, usually before the plant wilts. This protects the plant from destructive desiccation, but at the same time brings photosynthesis to a halt, since CO_2 uptake is prevented.

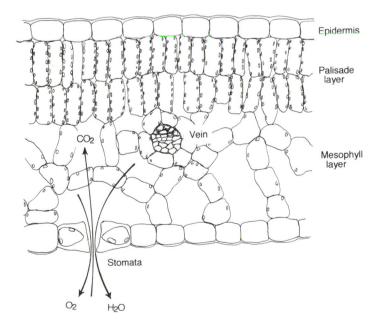

Figure 3.6
The microscopic structure of a leaf. Photosynthesis depends on the passage of CO_2 in, and oxygen out, through the fine pores (stomata), but unfortunately water is lost at the same time. This is partially controlled by the closure of the stomata at night and under conditions of drought stress.

3.4   *Transport of materials: stems*

3.4.1 TRANSPORT

The products of photosynthesis have to be carried to other parts of the plant where growth is taking place. This may be anywhere within the plant, even to the ends of the finest roots. At the same time nutrients and water have to be transported from the roots to wherever they are needed, i.e. where growth is taking place. Finally, large quantities of water have to be conducted from the roots up to the leaves to make up for the water which is being lost by transpiration. The patterns of transport are therefore very complicated, with different materials going in different directions at the same time.

The flow of water is a passive process driven by the negative pressures developed by the water lost from the leaves. It occurs in hollow tubes composed of chains of specialized dead, **xylem**, cells. The movements of photosynthates and nutrients are, by contrast, active processes requiring the expenditure of energy, termed **translocation**, occurring within special columns of living, **phloem**, cells.

3.4.2 STEMS

The leaf has a network of veins, containing both xylem and phloem, which connects through to conducting tissues in the twigs and main stem or trunk. In these the living phloem cells, which conduct nutrients and photosynthates, are towards the outside, protected by corky tissue which forms the characteristic

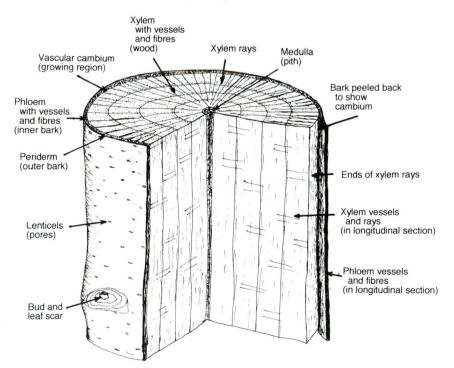

Figure 3.7
The structure of a woody stem (a four year old plane). Water is transported from the roots to the leaves in the woody tissue (xylem). Nutrients and photosynthates are transported in the bark (phloem); the bark is critical to the functioning of the tree and can easily be damaged.

surface of the tree trunk. The dead xylem cells, in combination with tough fibrous cells, form the wood which composes the whole of the inner part of the tree trunk (Figure 3.7).

In many ways it is curious that a very important part of the tree, the phloem, is situated in a very vulnerable position on the outside of the tree. It is equally curious that when the trunk of the tree grows, it does so by means of a special layer of cells, the **cambium**, between the phloem and the xylem. As a result, despite the fact that most trees develop a thick protective corky layer outside the phloem, it is very easy for the phloem to be damaged or removed. If a split occurs at the cambium, all the material outside it, the phloem and the corky layer, the bark, comes off.

If the bark is completely removed from around the stem, which can so easily happen when a strimmer is used round a young tree, the conducting pathway for nutrients and photosynthates is destroyed. The tree does not die immediately because water can still flow up the xylem, and there will be stores of nutrients and photosynthates in different parts of the tree. But ultimately the roots will cease growing because they are starved of photosynthates, and the upper parts of the tree will cease growing as they become starved of nutrients. The tree is doomed, and after about a year it will die (Figure 3.8).

If only a patch of bark has been damaged, the tree does not die, because some

Figure 3.8
A tree dead because its bark has been removed by a strimmer. It did not die immediately because water could still pass up through the xylem, but the tree was doomed because nutrients and photosynthates could no longer circulate.

conducting tissue remains. Healing, however, is slow because the cambium and the new bark can only spread in from the edges of the wound. A large patch can take several years to heal. If damage is restricted to one side of the stem, although the tree does not die, a substantial weak point is formed from which the tree may take many years to recover.

3.5 *Maintenance*

Finally it must be remembered that because the tree is made of living tissue, important processes have to go on by which this living material is maintained, just as in animals. The main requirement for maintenance is energy. This comes from the energy-containing carbohydrates produced by photosynthesis. So despite the fact that much of the inner part of the tree trunk is made of dead tissues, the large amount of living tissue in the tree as a whole means that there is a considerable and continuing requirement for carbohydrates even when the tree is not apparently growing. If these are not provided by photosynthesis the tree will soon run out of steam.

This brings us back to the first point of this chapter. It is easy to take trees for granted, and forget that their growth and maintenance depend on a series of important processes. The tree has some reserves, but if these processes are upset for more than a short period of time the future of the tree is placed in jeopardy.

References

Gilbertson, P., Kendle, A.D. and Bradshaw, A.D. (1987) Root growth and the problems of trees in urban and industrial areas, in *Research for Practical Arboriculture* (ed. D. Patch), Forestry Commission Bulletin **65**, HMSO, London, pp. 59–66.

Hewitt, E.J. and Smith, T.A. (1975) *Plant Mineral Nutrition,* English Universities Press, London.

Other reading

Bernatsky, A. (1978) *Tree Ecology and Preservation,* Elsevier, Amsterdam.

Harris, R.W. (1992) *Arboriculture*, 2nd edn, Prentice, New Jersey.

Kozlowski, T.T. (1979) *Tree Growth and Environmental Stress,* University of Washington Press, Seattle.

Kramer, P.J. and Kozlowski, T.T. (1979) *Physiology of Woody Plants,* Academic Press, New York.

Money, P.R. (1973) *How Trees Grow,* Arnold, London.

Raven, P.H., Evert, R.F. and Curtis, H. (1976) *Biology of Plants,* Worth, New York.

4 Intrinsic site problems

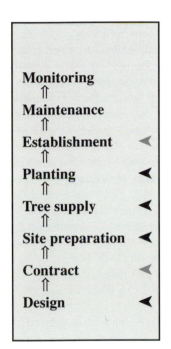

Monitoring
⇑
Maintenance
⇑
Establishment ◄
⇑
Planting ◄
⇑
Tree supply ◄
⇑
Site preparation ◄
⇑
Contract ◄
⇑
Design ◄

- Urban sites may have general problems intrinsic to them which require whole site treatments in advance of planting.
- These relate to the nature of the starting material which is usually very different from ordinary soil.
- Texture may range from very coarse sandy substrates, to very fine heavy clays.
- Organic matter is frequently absent or very low, as there may have been little or no previous plant growth.
- Consequently normal soil structure, including water- and air-filled pore space, may be absent.
- Poor soil structure can lead to both drought and waterlogging at different times.
- The soil may be too compacted and hard for root penetration.
- Certain nutrients may be deficient; this is particularly true of nitrogen, which is stored in the organic fraction of the soil.
- There may also be elevated levels of toxic substances due to past industrial activity.
- Landfill gas may be a problem where trees are established on old refuse disposal sites.

The basic requirements of trees were described in the previous chapter. Above ground, trees need air and light for photosynthesis and respiration. Below ground, roots require water to satisfy demand from the canopy, oxygen for respiration, an adequate supply of nutrients, and good cohesion with the soil to give secure anchorage for the tree. An ideal planting site will satisfy all of these requirements, and impose no additional stresses upon the tree.

In most natural woodlands an extremely complex system, involving interactions between plants, soil and climate has developed, termed an **ecosystem**. Trees are the dominant component of the vegetation, but their growth is closely linked to a variety of factors such as drainage and topography, understorey vegetation, rainfall, soil conditions, and woodland fauna. Nutrient supply involves the fall of leaves and woody material from tree canopies, input from ambient rainfall, weathering of minerals in the soil, organic matter decomposition by soil flora and fauna, incorporation of humus into the soil matrix, and leaching of nutrients before uptake by plant roots can take place. The nutrient cycling system is well buffered and nutrient problems are uncommon.

Most urban sites, however, are very different from this. Trees are planted far apart, often with impervious materials covering substrates which bear little resemblance to natural soils. Leaf litter is usually removed before it can be incorporated into the soil, and there is often a deficiency of both large and small soil organisms to break down organic matter. Tree growth rarely has the opportunity to adapt to the extremes of urban hydrological and temperature patterns. These conditions are imposed on transplanted trees that can be of varying size, root development, species and cultivar.

Considering all these difficulties, it may seem inevitable that trees will perform badly in urban areas, but it need not be so. Many characteristics of the urban environment are more than adequate. What is necessary is to ameliorate those other aspects which might cause trouble. This can be achieved by operations carried out at four principle stages in the tree planting process: design, preparation, planting and establishment. This chapter identifies the below-ground, intrinsic, site problems. These require treatment over the whole of a site before planting takes place. The techniques used to overcome them are given in Chapter 6.

Substrate conditions are central to many of the difficulties encountered in urban planting schemes. They can only be identified and treated economically if the basic properties of soils, how soil problems can affect tree growth, and what substrates occur on different types of site, are understood. With this knowledge the most appropriate site treatments can then be applied.

4.1 *Soil composition and properties*

Natural soils develop over centuries as a result of physical, chemical and biological processes. This usually begins with the weathering of parent rocks to give a mixture of coarse and fine particles which form the mineral component of a soil. Weathering releases mineral elements, which may be taken up immediately by plants or precipitated as secondary minerals in the soil. Over time, organic matter, largely derived from the growth and decay of plant material by soil micro-organisms, is accumulated and becomes combined with the mineral fraction, forming an important store and source of nutrients. All these processes interconnect to make a complete cycle (Figure 4.1). At the same time, the action of soil organisms and movement of dissolved and suspended substances contained in percolating water can lead to the creation of distinct soil horizons.

Many urban substrates, in contrast, have been formed recently, by the activities of human beings. Their major constituents are often unweathered materials such as bricks and concrete. Sometimes substrates are merely the by-products of an industrial process, or the abandonment of a site which is no longer useful. Often there has never been any plant growth, and therefore no development of organic matter. Sometimes poor materials are imported, such as unweathered sub-soil or low grade, badly handled topsoil.

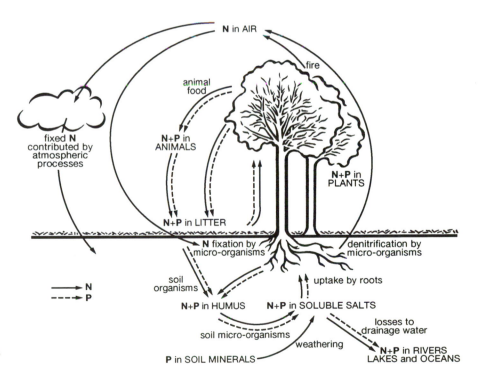

Figure 4.1
Nutrient cycling in a natural ecosystem: a complex set of processes involving plants, micro-organisms, animals, water, and the constituents of the soil.

4.1.1 TEXTURE

The simplest division of soil constituents is into mineral and organic fractions. It is the mineral fraction which determines the texture, or 'feel' of soil. Soils are placed in different textural classes, based on the particle-size distribution of the mineral fraction, excluding stones (Figure 4.2). Fine textured soils have relatively high proportions of the smallest particles, the clay minerals. Coarse textured soils contain relatively large amounts of the largest particles, sands. Silty materials are intermediate.

Texture has important implications for the properties of soils. Fine textured soils, containing more than 30% clay, such as clays and clay loams, are said to be 'heavy'; they are difficult to break up when dry, but sticky and prone to waterlogging when wet. This is because clay minerals have a very large surface area, and can absorb a large amount of water which is tightly held, resulting in slow drainage. At the same time saturation makes clays highly plastic.

Coarse and medium textured soils behave very differently. Sandy, 'light', soils have a much lower surface area than clays, and water is held more loosely. Consequently soils with a high sand content tend to drain relatively quickly, and, because of their lack of cohesive strength, are easier to work when wet.

Good estimates of the textural composition of soils can be made by experienced operators using simple observations. Sand grains can be felt when a moist soil sample is rubbed between the fingers. Silty soils give a 'soapy' feel, in contrast with clays which generally give a 'platy' sensation. The plasticity of clays can be easily demonstrated. If a wet lump of a clay soil is rolled between the hands, a doughnut-like ring can be formed; this cannot be achieved with

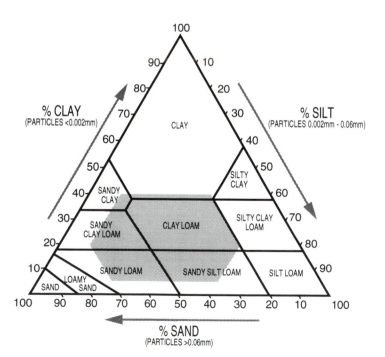

Figure 4.2
Particle size classification of soils. Textural properties are largely determined by the relative proportions of sand, silt and clay. Soils within the shaded area are normally considered to give rise to productive conditions (Voelker and Dinsdale, 1989).

soils with a low clay content, which tend to fall apart when moulded in this fashion. When dry, however, clays lose their plasticity and become very hard. These observations will allow the timing and mode of soil handling operations to be chosen carefully.

Productive soils in agriculture have a balance between clay, silt and sand which allows adequate drainage, but retains sufficient water for plant uptake (the shaded area in Figure 4.2). Whether soil texture requires amendment will depend on other factors such as organic matter content, soil structure and overall site drainage, but it should be remembered that these other factors are usually easier to manipulate than soil texture. Store content, however, does not matter for trees because they can root around stones, and even bricks, easily.

4.1.2 ORGANIC MATTER

Soil organic matter is formed as the result of biological activity, the combination of plant growth and decay. In some soils plant litter remains only partially decomposed, lying on the soil surface as a distinct horizon. In good soils, litter, if not removed, is broken down into finely divided particles to form what is known as humus, intimately mixed with the mineral fraction.

Organic matter is crucial both in the development of a good soil structure, and as a source of plant nutrients. Soils with textures which make them difficult to work can be improved by organic matter addition; the water retention of free-draining soils can be raised similarly. At the same time organic matter can be a source of essential plant nutrients which are not released in sufficient quantities by mineral weathering. Most importantly, it is the only place where nitrogen is stored in the soil. The soil organic matter content in typical lowland soils in Britain ranges from 2 to 15% by weight. In undisturbed woodland soils the values are often at the higher end of the range; in long cultivated arable soils the values are usually at the bottom end.

4.1.3 STRUCTURE

The structure of a soil reflects the aggregation of mineral and organic particles into lumps of different size and shape, known as 'peds'. It is these which form the familiar crumbs of a good soil. Whilst soil texture is relatively easy to define and is a constant feature of natural soils, structure is more difficult to describe, since it depends on variable factors such as soil management.

When a soil is examined, the peds can usually be distinguished. They may be angular or flat, with gaps between them when dry, but swelling to give little or no pore space when wet. This kind of structure occurs frequently in soils with a high clay content. Alternatively, the peds may be crumb-like collections of granular material, with a wide range of void sizes within and between them, as in many loams. Ped formation is a very complex process, dependent on many different factors, but essentially mineral and organic fractions are held together by inorganic cements such as aluminium hydroxide, and organic compounds produced by microbiological activity. The process is affected by soil texture, the humus present, cultural practices, and soil flora and fauna.

4.1.4 PORE SPACE

Texture and structure together determine the amount and distribution of soil voids, which are a crucial part of good soils. Pore space comprises between 30 and 60% of soil volume. Values for clay soils are often higher than for sandy soils, but this is misleading since much of the pore space in clays is made up of water-filled micropores, which contribute little to drainage or the supply of water to roots. Despite sometimes having lower total pore space, sandy soils possess better drainage and aeration characteristics, as the large macropores, which contain air as well as water, predominate. But sometimes a soil can be too free-draining, and little water will be available for plant uptake, e.g. pure sand. Whatever the textural properties of a soil, the development of an open structure with a wide range of pore sizes can be aided by the presence of decomposed humus which encourages crumb formation. Even then, the soil must be managed correctly so as not to destroy this structure.

4.2   *Urban soils*

Urban substrates are made up of a wide range of materials, from agricultural soils to brick waste. Any one of a range of physical and chemical factors can limit plant growth. In particular, the water retention, drainage, aeration and nutrient status of urban soils are often poor, and problems of toxicity can occur.

An indication of the problems to be expected in urban soils is given in Table 4.1. From this it is clear that some types of site, for instance street sides and mine wastes, are consistently difficult for tree growth. It is also clear that some types of site, such as industrial wastes and neglected land, can vary greatly in the problems they pose. Each site must be taken on its merits.

4.2.1 WATER SUPPLY

Plants rely on soils to maintain a ready supply of water between rainfalls, and will suffer from drought stress if this water store becomes exhausted. Special emphasis has to be given to ensure an adequate water supply when a tree is planted (Chapter 10). Although trees may become more robust after the initial transplanting phase, vigorous growth will be maintained only if roots can continue to take up sufficient water to satisfy transpirational demand throughout the life of the tree.

After heavy rainfall or irrigation, water drains from the macropores, which become at least partly filled with air. The total amount of water a soil can hold against gravity is known as the **field capacity**. Roots exert suction pressure on the soil to extract this water, but not all of it is available. The soil holds on to some of the water, exerting a negative pressure. When this reaches about -10 bars (-1 MPa), plants can no longer extract enough water to maintain turgor, and begin to wilt. At approximately -15 bars (-1.5 MPa) any water still held by the soil is completely unavailable to plants. The water available to plants, the **avail-**

bars (-1 MPa), plants can no longer extract enough water to maintain turgor, and begin to wilt. At approximately -15 bars (-1.5 MPa) any water still held by the soil is completely unavailable to plants. The water available to plants, the **available water capacity**, is, therefore, the amount of water held by the soil between field capacity and -15 bars.

The plant-available water capacity of a soil is determined by texture, organic matter content and structure. Fine textured soils with poor crumb structures and little organic matter will hold large amounts of water, although relatively little of this is available to plants. Coarse, sandy soils drain quickly, retaining only small quantities of water, though most of this will be available to plants. In between these extremes are soils with textures and structures which have a combination of both properties. Organic matter can absorb large quantities of

Table 4.1 *The problems to be expected in different types of urban planting site: conditions vary greatly but some site types such as mine wastes and factory clearance areas are consistently difficult*

	Physical					Nutrient			Toxicity				Total*
	Stability	Structure	Compaction	Drainage	Drought	Nitrogen	Other macro	Micro	Metals	Organic	pH	Other	
Housing clearance	2	0	1	1	0	2	0	0	0	0	0	0	6
Factory clearance	0–2	0	2	2	0–1	2	0–2	0	0–2	0–2	0	0–2	6–17
Transport disuse	0–2	0–2	1	0–1	0–2	2	0–2	0	0	0	0	0	3–12
Quarry/ borrow pit	0–2	0–2	2	0–2	0–2	2	0–2	0	0	0	0	0	4–14
Mine waste	0–2	2	1	2	2	2	0–2	0	0–2	2	0–2	0–2	11–21
Industrial waste	0–2	2	0–2	0	0	0–2	0–2	0	0–2	0–2	0–2	0–2	2–18
Gas works	0	0	2	2	0	0–2	0	0	0–2	2	0	0	6–10
Refuse disposal	1	0–2	1–2	0–2	0	0–1	0	0	0–2	0	0	2	4–12
Neglected land	0	0	0	0–1	0–1	0	0	0	0–2	0–2	0	0–2	0–8
Old parkland	0	0	0	0–2	0	0–1	0–1	0	0	0	2	0	2–6
Farm land	0	0	0–1	0	0	0	0–1	0	0	0	0	0	0–2
Roadsides	0–2	0	0–2	2	0–2	0–2	0–1	0	0	0	0	0–2	2–13
Street sides	0–2	0	2	2	0–2	2	0–1	0	0	0	0	2	8–13

0, rarely a problem; 1, moderate; 2, severe problem.
* <6, few problems to be expected; >12, problems likely.
Differences between figures indicates potential variation.

Table 4.2   *The available water capacity (%) of some typical urban site materials (Kopinga, 1985). The water holding capacity can vary considerably depending on the substrate*

Humus-poor dune sand	7
Fine sand	15
Humus-rich sand	19
Humus-rich sand (loamy)	24
Very humus-rich sand (loamy)	26
Sandy clay	22
Light clay	16
Heavy clay	14
Peat	50
Street sand (coarse, no humus)	6.5
Tree pit soil (2% organic matter)	*ca* 10
Tree pit soil (5% organic matter)	*ca* 15

Because of a combination of coarse texture and lack of organic matter, many urban substrates are prone to drought. The water-holding properties of some typical urban soils are given in Table 4.2. Problems are most likely to occur outside the planting pit area, especially in coarse materials such as brick wastes on housing clearance sites, old railway lines, and in the sandy materials often found under paving stones. Planting on steep slopes may also reduce infiltration into the soil. The effects of drought are serious because they result in reduced leaf area and shoot extension, giving trees a stunted appearance and low canopy density. In extreme cases, trees wilt, leaves brown and fall early, and eventually the trees die.

4.2.2 COMPACTION

Figure 4.3
The effects of compaction on soil structure. Compaction not only reduces total pore space but also increases the proportion of water-filled micropores at the expense of air-filled macropores.

Soils in urban areas frequently become compacted by heavy machinery, foot and road traffic, and by overworking when wet, all of which destroy soil structure. The results are twofold. Firstly, there is an increase in soil strength, and hence greater resistance to root penetration. At the same time the total pore space within the soil is reduced, with an increase in the number of water-filled

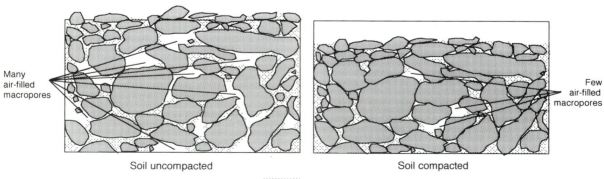

Many air-filled macropores   Few air-filled macropores

Soil uncompacted   Soil compacted

Water filled pores

Figure 4.4
The bulk densities of soils in and outside the planting pit, of 192 urban trees; values above 1.6 g cm^{-3} are not uncommon.

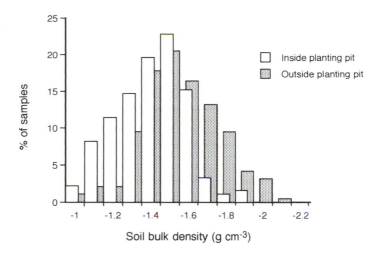

micropores at the expense of the air-filled macropores (Figure 4.3). As a consequence, soil aeration is likely to be impeded during periods of wet weather. Conversely, during dry spells soils will be hard, and greater root-suction will be required to extract water from the micropores, exacerbating drought stress. Clay soils are particularly prone to compaction if worked when wet, but any soil type subjected to heavy loads, impacts or vibration will have its structure destroyed.

In good agricultural soils the bulk density (i.e. including both solids and voids) is approximately 1.2–1.4 g cm^{-3}. Evidence suggests that root, and consequently shoot, growth are likely to be suppressed above 1.6 g cm^{-3}. The bulk densities of urban materials cover a wide range, but can be as high as 2.0 g cm^{-3} (Figure 4.4). The effects of compaction on the growth of trees can be seen in Figure 4.5. Increasing the area of compaction around a tree reduces growth by approximately 50%. Roots growing in compacted soil tend to be shorter and thicker than those growing in uncompacted soil.

The effects in urban planting sites are complex. Compaction is unlikely to actually kill trees, at least not quickly, but its effects over a number of years may

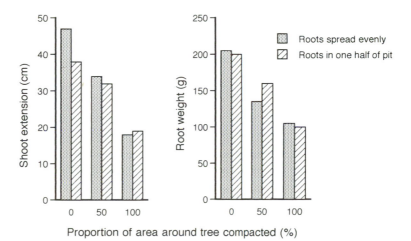

Figure 4.5
The effects, 2 years after planting, of increasing the area of soil compaction around the base of rowan whips (redrawn from Hunt *et al.*, 1991); compaction can reduce growth by up to 50%.

Figure 4.6
Compaction on one side of a tree can lead to a distorted root system and hence instability. This tree blown over in south London in the gale of October 1987 had no roots penetrating the soil under the kerb or the road.

be serious. Where soils have been placed by heavy machinery the whole of a site may be compacted. In other instances compaction will be limited to an area close to the tree, such as a well-frequented footpath or a road. With large trees, this can lead to instability (Figure 4.6). Compacted layers may occur but become covered up and therefore remain as a hidden problem under an uncompacted surface. In grassy areas the root systems of the grass can help to produce an open structure in the upper layer of a soil which is heavily compacted below. Figure 4.6 shows how, where there is compaction, roots may only grow in a shallow layer of uncompacted sand below paving stones.

4.2.3 DRAINAGE

Poor drainage can lead to soils becoming deficient in oxygen, which severely limits root activity. This can result in a reduction in nutrient and water uptake, a distorted rooting pattern, and consequently poor growth and stability of trees. It comes about because gaseous exchange between the soil atmosphere and the air above is prevented. Gas exchange to and from the soil pores is usually rapid, and in the uppermost layers of the soil there is little difference in gas composition between the soil atmosphere and the air above. Lower in the soil profile, the oxygen content tends to decrease and the CO_2 content to increase.

When waterlogging occurs, the macropores will become filled with water rather than air, so that oxygen levels become depleted. As a result roots start to respire anaerobically. The by-products of this anaerobic respiration are toxic to most trees, and so the situation can only be maintained for short periods before the roots are damaged or killed.

Waterlogging is particularly harmful during the growing season, and is surprisingly common (Figure 4.7). It can occur in prestigious planting schemes.

Figure 4.7
Newly planted trees which established well and then died. Large numbers of trees are killed by waterlogging due to bad drainage of the planting pit.

Figure 4.8
The effects of waterlogging at different times during the growing season on the growth of maple (redrawn from Hunt *et al.*, 1991). The effects are greatest when trees are in full growth.

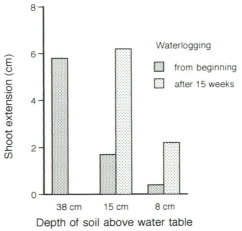

The time and depth at which anaerobism occurs are important. Trees are most vulnerable in the spring and early summer, when only a few days of waterlogging may kill a tree. Increasing depth of anaerobism has a drastic effect on tree growth, but this is reduced if it occurs only late in the season (Figure 4.8).

Figure 4.9
Waterlogging can occur even if
the surface is well structured. A
hard layer below the surface can
lead to the planting pit filling with
water like a bowl.

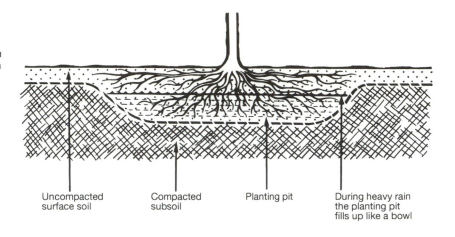

Figure 4.10
The minimum depth of fully
aerated soil recorded in the
planting pits of 192 urban trees,
using the steel rod method
(Carnell and Anderson, 1986).
One in five trees experienced
waterlogging to within 15 cm of
the soil surface over a 2-month
period during the year.

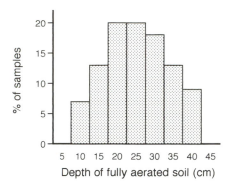

Figure 4.11
The root plate of a tree growing
in a poorly drained site blown
over in the gale of October 1987.
The shallow and stunted roots
indicative of waterlogging can be
seen.

There is a close link between compaction and drainage. In a survey of soils and trees 3–5 years after planting, soil bulk density and aeration were found to be major determinants of tree growth. Compacted soil horizons can impede drainage, as water percolates downwards extremely slowly in the absence of macropores and fissures. Rainwater runoff from hard surfaces such as paving is sometimes channelled into tree pits. If sub-surface compaction exists, the pit can fill up like a bowl, and waterlogging will occur even if the soil used to fill the pit is well structured (Figure 4.9). A depth of only 15 cm of aerated soil is not uncommon in tree pits (Figure 4.10), sometimes lasting for several months.

It has long been the experience of foresters that thorough site drainage is necessary to maintain high levels of growth and to develop root systems which will ensure that the tree is stable. Poorly drained soils tend to lead to the development of a shallow root plate. This could clearly be seen in many of the trees blown over in the great storm of October 1987 (Figure 4.11).

4.2.4 NUTRIENTS

Plants require a supply of nutrients to sustain growth. They take up most of their nutrients from below ground, although small amounts can be absorbed by the leaves from aerial input. In addition, therefore, to providing favourable gaseous exchange and water supply, soils must also maintain a supply of the essential plant nutrients in a form suitable for root uptake. The nutrient status of urban soils can vary widely, but it is possible to make certain generalizations. Many substrates are not as infertile as might appear on first inspection, and the addition of only one of the major plant nutrients can often remedy nutrient deficiency (Table 4.3).

Potassium is rarely deficient in natural soils. It is released in soluble form from the weathering of rock-forming minerals, and is present in large concentrations in clays, including those contained in materials such as bricks. Typical

Table 4.3 *Nutrient levels in urban site materials compared to natural topsoil (Dutton and Bradshaw, 1982). Urban materials frequently lack one major plant nutrient, usually nitrogen*

Site	Phosphorus	Potassium	Magnesium	Nitrogen Total	Mineralizable* NH$_4$	NO$_3$	Total
Topsoil	30	83	66	1027	120	-1	119
Clearance sites							
Site 1	12	81	72	480	3	1	4
Site 2	22	173	145	480	-9	14	5
Site 3	5	77	323	405	-6	8	2
Site 4	65	94	393	870	-4	10	6

* Released after 14 days incubation at 30°C.
All values in parts per million (mg kg^{-1}).

urban soils contain at least 80 ppm potassium, more than sufficient for plant growth. Although potassium is easily leached by percolating rainfall, there is usually a plentiful supply in the soil minerals to replenish that which is lost to drainage water.

Phosphorus occurs in soils in organic and inorganic forms. Phosphates are present as complex ions, which are relatively insoluble, and so are only slowly lost by leaching. However, this can also result in low levels of phosphorus available for plant growth. The content of inorganic phosphorus in soils is closely linked to texture, clay minerals providing most of the sites where ions are exchanged. Most urban substrates have relatively high concentrations of phosphorus, e.g. a typical brickwaste contains approximately 20 ppm of available phosphorus. Deficiencies requiring remedial action, however, can occur, for example where phosphate ions have been immobilized by high pH, due to high lime content.

Nitrogen is the nutrient which most commonly limits plant growth. It is totally absent from all rock-forming minerals, and has to be obtained from rainfall, the atmosphere, or the decomposition of organic matter. The most plentiful source of nitrogen in the environment is the atmosphere. Unfortunately, higher plants cannot use atmospheric nitrogen directly, and must obtain most of their nitrogen from below ground in an inorganic form. Certain micro-organisms can fix nitrogen by taking gaseous nitrogen from the atmosphere and converting it into inorganic compounds. These micro-organisms occur particularly in association with certain species of higher plants, providing them with a nitrogen supply when the soil is otherwise impoverished. This is why leguminous species are able to colonize many infertile substrates. Most species, however, have to rely for their nitrogen on the breakdown of organic matter, and the conversion of organic nitrogen compounds into ammonium and nitrate ions by soil bacteria and fungi. A store of organic matter is clearly essential if nitrogen supply is to be maintained.

In raw substrates, which have had no previous connection with plant growth, the level of humus has to be built up before an adequate nitrogen supply can be maintained without fertilizer addition. The level of total nitrogen in urban soils can range from 0 to 2000 ppm; a typical material will contain only about 500 ppm, one fifth of that in ordinary soils. Even where organic matter is plentiful, nitrogen may not be made available for uptake. High levels of acidity, low soil oxygen and low temperatures all inhibit the micro-organisms involved in the breakdown of organic matter. Where soils become waterlogged, some micro-organisms use nitrates as a source of oxygen in organic matter decomposition, and so available nitrogen levels may actually fall. Where organic matter has a high carbon:nitrogen ratio, the micro-organisms responsible for its decomposition require more nitrogen than is released by their activities, so that there is a net loss of available nitrogen. Carbon:nitrogen ratios in excess of 30:1 will not provide sufficient available nitrogen.

Some soils, for instance in older parks, have been so acidified in the past by air pollution that decomposition is greatly reduced. As a result, although they contain large amounts of organic matter, little nitrogen is available. More recently, however, SO_2 pollution has declined whilst NO_x from car exhausts has increased. In some areas this results in between 20 and 50 kg ha^{-1} of extra nitrogen input to the soil each year, a significant boost to depleted soil.

Available evidence is mixed as to the importance of soil nutrient levels in limiting tree growth on urban sites. Table 4.1 shows the urban substrates which are likely to be seriously deficient in nutrients. Trees growing in these soils can benefit greatly from nutrient addition (Chapter 11). In general, however, most reasonable soils contain sufficient nutrients for tree growth.

4.2.5 TOXICITY

There are several substances which can occur in toxic concentrations in urban substrates. But although toxicity is often considered important, it is limited to particular sites.

Heavy metals may seem an obvious problem. Toxic levels are uncommon, however, being restricted to sites associated with industrial or mining activity (Table 4.1).

A sporadic problem is methane damage. The damage is not caused by the direct action of the gas, but by the anaerobic conditions which can result from its occurrence in the soil. Where methane gas is released in the soil, oxygen is driven out and CO_2 levels rise. Methane itself is not toxic to plant roots. Gas release can result from broken gas mains near to tree pits, especially where the seals on old pipes have dried out due to the low water content of natural gas compared with coal gas which was used previously. This is, however, relatively rare.

More common is damage to trees growing on landfill sites, where the decomposition of putrescible refuse by micro-organisms results in large amounts of methane being released. If this gas escapes through the surface of the tip, for instance through cracks or porous areas in an otherwise impermeable capping material, vegetation close to the gas escape will suffer anaerobic conditions and die. Soil CO_2 and methane levels may be elevated even in a well-constructed site. This does not mean, however, that trees cannot be planted on landfill sites, as shown in Chapter 6.

Occasionally toxicity is caused by miscellaneous chemical compounds, such as phenols, but this is most uncommon, limited to former industrial processing works, gas works and similar sites.

References

Carnell, R. and Anderson, M.A. (1986) A technique for extensive measurement of soil anaerobism by rusting of steel rods. *Forestry,* **59**, 129–40.

Dutton, R.A. and Bradshaw, A.D. (1982) *Land Reclamation in Cities,* HMSO, London.

Hunt, B., Bradshaw, A.D. and Walmsley, T.J. (1991) The importance of soil physical conditions for urban tree growth, in *Research for Practical Arboriculture* (ed. S.J. Hodge), Forestry Commission Bulletin **97**, HMSO, London, pp.51–62.

Kopinga, J. (1985) Research on street tree planting practices in the Netherlands. *Proceedings of the Conference of the Metropolitan Tree Improvement Alliance*, **4**, 72–84.

Voelker, R. and Dinsdale, M. (1989) A guide for specifying topsoil, Parts I & II. *Landscape Design,* **179**, 15–16; **180**, 47–8.

Other reading

Colderick, S.M. and Hodge, S.J. (1991) A study of urban trees, in *Research for Practical Arboriculture* (ed. S.J. Hodge), Forestry Commission Bulletin **97**, HMSO, London, pp.63–73.

Dobson, M.C. and Moffat, A.J. (1993) *The Potential for Woodland Establishment on Landfill Sites,* Department of the Environment, HMSO, London.

Gill, C.J. (1970) The flooding tolerance of woody species – a review. *Forestry Abstracts*, **31**, 671–88.

Gilman, E.F., Leone, I.A. and Flower, F.B. (1989) Growth and stomatal responses of sugar maple in irrigated and non-irrigated landfill soil cover. *Landscape and Urban Planning,* **17**, 215-20.

Graecen, E.L. and Sands, R. (1980) Compaction and forest soils: a review. *Australian Journal of Soil Research*, **18**, 163–89.

Hodge, S.J. (1993) *Using steel rods to assess aeration in urban soils,* Arboriculture Research Note **115 : 93**, Arboricultural Advisory and Information Service, Farnham.

Norton, C.R. (1991) Analysis of performance of semi-mature trees in relation to a high water-table, in *Research for Practical Arboriculture* (ed. S.J. Hodge), Forestry Commission Bulletin **97**, HMSO, London, pp.45–7.

Patterson, J.C. (1976) Soil compaction and its effects upon urban vegetation, in *Better Trees for Metropolitan Landscapes,* USDA Forest Service General Technical Report, **NE-22,** USDA, Washington, pp. 91–102.

Ruark, G.A., Mader, D.L. and Tattar, T.A. (1982) The influence of soil compaction and aeration on the root growth and vigour of trees – a literature review. *Arboricultural Journal,* **6**, 251–65.

Scott Russell, R. (1977) *Plant Root Systems: their function and interaction with the soil,* Academic Press, Maidenhead.

5 *Extrinsic site factors*

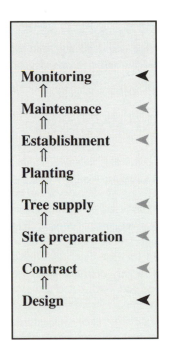

Monitoring ◄
⇑
Maintenance ◄
⇑
Establishment ◄
⇑
Planting
⇑
Tree supply ◄
⇑
Site preparation ◄
⇑
Contract ◄
⇑
Design ◄

- There are a number of factors which have an impact on tree growth that originate outside the site; their potentially serious effects must be taken into account.

- Vandalism is usually perceived to be the most important, but surveys show that it is not; it is usually the result of careless play, and affects only the most exposed trees.

- Serious damage can be caused where vehicles are allowed close to unprotected trees.

- Salt has become a very serious problem for all trees close to roadsides; it can partly or completely kill both young and well-established trees.

- Wind can cause damage to trees; it can be as severe between high buildings as on raised exposed ground.

- In the past SO_2 has been a serious air pollutant restricting the growth of trees in city centres.

- Its effects have now almost completely disappeared, but have left a legacy of acidified soils.

- NO_x and ozone are increasing in seriousness although so far only ozone seems to have reached concentrations which may cause trouble.

In addition to the intrinsic problems of urban sites, the urban environment can impose external factors which will limit plant growth. Often these are more difficult to treat directly and so must be dealt with by careful design of tree planting schemes, allowing for site difficulties so that damage to trees is avoided. Remedial action can sometimes be taken, but is often expensive and ineffective (Chapter 12). A third course of action is to use tree species which will tolerate extrinsic site problems (Chapter 8). The most important extrinsic site problems in urban areas are vandalism, salt damage, wind damage and air pollution, but people-pressures such as damage caused by vehicles can also be important.

5.1   *Vandalism*

The importance of vandalism is often overstated as a cause of poor growth and death of urban trees. It is true that in some cases the effects of vandalism can be severe. Urban woodlands, for instance, may be badly damaged by fire. In terms of the proportion of newly planted trees which die, however, it has become clear that vandalism is in fact less significant than other factors (Figure 5.1). A more detailed analysis has shown that vandalism accounted for less than 1% of tree deaths during the first 3 years after planting, and was largely confined to minor canopy damage. After this period vandalism is most commonly directed towards the stem. Surveys of stem damage show that vandalism is far less important than the combined effects of bad maintenance, e.g. damage due to stakes, ties, guards and mowing (Figure 5.2). These unfortunate effects of bad maintenance will be discussed in detail in Chapter 12.

Despite this, vandalism is often blamed for tree deaths, serving as a scapegoat for poor practice, and obscuring the underlying problems of tree establishment

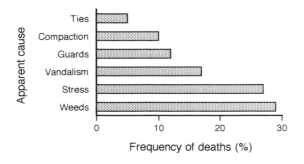

Figure 5.1
The causes of death of newly planted trees in northern cities (redrawn from Gilbertson and Bradshaw, 1985). Vandalism is less significant than other factors.

Figure 5.2
Causes of damage to the stems of trees 3–5 years after planting. Vandalism is much less important than the combined effects of bad maintenance, e.g. damage due to ties, stakes, guards and mowing (damage assessed by circumference affected: 0, no damage; 1, 1–25% ; 2, 25–50%, 3, >50%).

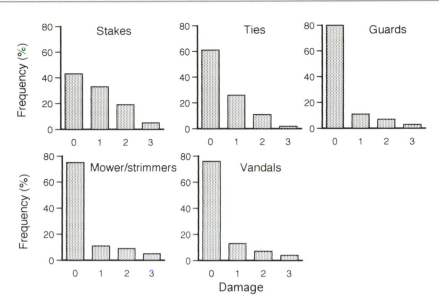

Figure 5.3
Vandals may strip the bark from trees, snap branches or even the main stem, but it is usually incidental to play.

and maintenance. This is because where vandalism does occur it has a high visual impact.

Damage by vandals can occur on any part of the tree. Branches may be pulled off, bark stripped from the trunk, and the stem snapped off (Figure 5.3). In some cases this will be partial, in others the tree may have to regrow from the base. Where the latter is unacceptable, the tree will have to be replaced. Obviously, small trees such as transplants and whips can be uprooted entirely, and are unsuitable for planting in isolated, street-side situations where vandalism is more likely. Intermediate-sized trees, such as standards, may be snapped off at the stem, so consequently large trees such as extra-heavy and semi-mature standards are often planted in an attempt to prevent large-scale losses through vandalism. Although this is likely to prevent total destruction due to people swinging on the trunk, it will not stop the removal of branches from the canopy, or bark-stripping. Large trees are also more likely to encourage children to climb into the canopy. The advantages gained by planting very large trees may be outweighed by the difficulties of establishment and the high cost of purchase and adequate maintenance. It is certainly true, however, that vandalism becomes less important as the tree gets older.

Trees planted in paving and grass suffer the most damage, and those planted amongst shrubs the least (Figure 5.4). Where trees are planted close to a thoroughfare, damage is particularly likely (Figure 5.5). Vandals will usually target the most easily accessible tree, and so closely spaced groups situated away from concentrations of people are more likely to survive unscathed.

It is important to remember that a certain amount of vandalism is inevitable in urban areas. Most vandalism is not directed and wilful, but is incidental to childrens' play; they will pull branches from a tree to play with, not necessary with the intention of damaging the tree. They will carve their initials in the bark of a tree in the same way they will carve them on a seat or a desk; the tree is not the specific object of damage, it is just something convenient to use.

Figure 5.4
The incidence of damage in relation to planting position in a survey of 3600 trees (redrawn from Hodge, 1991). Trees that are readily accessible are most likely to be damaged.

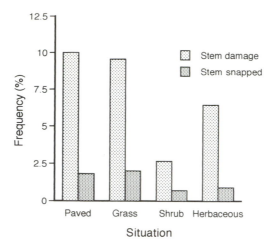

Figure 5.5
Trees in or close to thorough-fares are likely to be vandalized. Only seven out of the original 15 trees planted in this busy walkway between blocks of flats are still alive.

Trees can rarely be totally isolated from people; and nor should they be, except where timber production is the sole purpose of a planting. The sensible use of intelligent planting designs, different tree sizes, and limited protection measures which are adequately maintained, can reduce the effects of vandalism to a minimum (Chapter 12).

5.2   *Vehicle damage*

Occasionally cars and other vehicles can be agents of stem damage. Trees of all sizes can be badly damaged if left unprotected in vulnerable situations such as car parks (Figure 5.6). Sometimes vehicle damage is indirect, such as the heaping up of road-salt-laden snow and slush around the bases of roadside trees. This does not occur where sensible design has allowed the trees to be separated from the vehicles. Guards, however, can have an important role (Chapter 12).

5.3 *Salt*

Figure 5.6
Trees can easily be damaged by vehicles if they are not adequately protected. Out of 24 trees originally planted in this car park, only two remain.

Road salt is used widely in urban areas on roads and pavements to prevent vehicle and pedestrian accidents. Large amounts can be used each year. While the recommended amount to be applied in a single salting is 10 g m^{-2}, this is often exceeded. The cumulative amount used on roads in a typical winter is as high as 3000 g m^{-2}. But in a severe winter this can rise to as much as 5000 g m^{-2}. The amounts being used have increased enormously in the last three decades, and tree die-back can be related to years of high use (Figure 5.7).

It is now well understood that the effects of road salt on urban vegetation can be devastating. Certain species may be particularly vulnerable, for instance the sugar maples of North America. The maritime climate in Britain suggests that less road salt would be used here. In mild winters this is true, but salt use in Britain is generally more than equal to that of other European countries experiencing far colder winters. This is because of the lack of experience in this country of driving on frosty roads and of applying salt efficiently. Even when used lightly it can become concentrated to toxic levels in certain situations.

The principal components of road salt are sodium and chlorine, or Na$^+$ and Cl$^-$ ions in solution. Salt can affect trees either by being sprayed on to leaves by fast-moving traffic, or by entering the roots through the soil. In high concentrations chloride ions are toxic to plant cells, interfering with metabolism. Salt water sprayed on to leaves can enter the leaf relatively quickly, causing chloride toxicity as well as creating a high osmotic potential across the cell wall, which can lead to cell dehydration. The result is leaf scorch.

However, salt spray is uncommon after leafing out. What is more important is the salt water that enters the soil. Not only are the roots which experience the

Figure 5.7
The amount of salt purchased annually for use on roads in Britain in relation to crown die-back in plane trees (redrawn from Dobson, 1991). Severe die-back corresponds to high salt use.

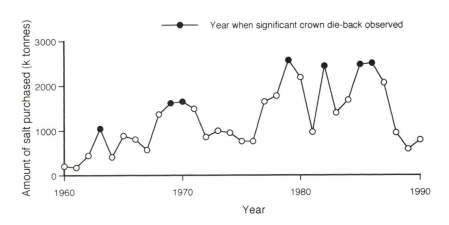

Figure 5.8
One-sided death of the trunk of
a well-established plane tree,
typical of the increased use of
salt on roads.

salt often killed, but the chloride ions move up the tree and the whole of the part of the tree affected can die. Unexplained slow expansion of leaves in spring, and death of one side of a roadside tree, is nearly always due to salt (Figure 5.8). The tree may show marginal browning or whole leaf necrosis, die-back after the first flush of leaves, and premature senescence, as well as death of the bark on the affected side. Small trees are usually killed completely (Figure 5.9).

In addition to this, sodium ions replace many other cations on the exchange sites in the soil, leading to deflocculation, and a collapse of the soil crumb structure. This increases the likelihood of soil compaction. Chloride ions are readily leached from soil.

Figure 5.10 shows the results of an experiment set up to show the effects of road salt added to the planting pits of newly planted trees. The amounts of salt added equate to doses of 250 and 750 g m^{-2}, respectively. As already mentioned, rates of application amounting to 3000 g m^{-2} per year are not uncommon. This can be exacerbated by the melting of ice and frozen snow which have accumulated many doses of road salt, the piling up of snow and slush close to the tree base, and the channelling of salt-laden runoff into tree pits. In isolated cases salt dumps are actually placed close to trees. Hence the reduction in tree growth due to salt addition shown in Figure 5.10 by no means represents an extreme situation.

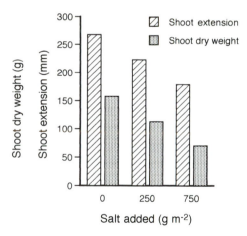

Figure 5.10
The effects on growth of adding salt to the planting pits of newly planted trees. The amounts
added are equivalent to what is commonly used on roads.

Figure 5.9
Complete death of a well-established young tree in Trafalgar
Square. Unless salt applications
can be stopped the tree is in the
wrong place.

5.4   *Wind damage*

Despite the fact that most urban areas are located in lowland Britain, wind damage to trees can limit growth, sometimes severely so. Wind damage occurs only in a minority of sites, and may even be restricted to individual trees in a planting.

Trees which experience high winds suffer scorched leaves and shoots, which leads to a stunted canopy, especially on the windward side. The result is a tree which is one-sided, accentuated if the wind has caused the tree to lean (Figure 5.11). Newly planted trees will transpire more rapidly in windy situations, which can lead to the death of any tree that is already severely drought stressed. Unfortunately these phenomena are difficult to assess quantitatively, and so there has been little research to examine how important wind damage is in relation to other stresses imposed on urban trees. Trees can also suffer from wind rock if not planted well or given support. This can loosen the roots of the trees completely.

Where is wind damage most likely to occur? Individual trees planted adjacent to gaps between buildings may suffer from the high winds which are funnelled between them. This can lead to the situation where a line of healthy trees is punctuated by poor specimens. These individuals can, of course, be removed

Figure 5.11
Wind scorching will produce a one-sided canopy, as shown by these trees planted 3 years previously on an extremely exposed hill.

later when the trees are thinned, but it would have been cheaper and more effective to have recognized the site conditions at an early stage and adapted the planting design accordingly.

More widespread damage can occur when trees are planted in very exposed spots, such as the crests of slopes in elevated sites. Reclaimed spoil or refuse tips often suffer from high wind speeds. Dense plantings tend to suffer less, and species which are naturally resistant to exposure (Chapter 8).

In coastal areas wind-scorch is exacerbated by the damaging effects of salt spray. The importance of this should not be underestimated; salt spray has, in some cases, been found to travel up to 25 miles inland. If trees can be established in such sites, stunted tree plants can, however, produce an aesthetically pleasing vegetation. Such growth forms are, after all, characteristic of natural seaside areas. The importance of carefully chosen design criteria cannot be overstated. Planting tall standard trees of unsuitable species, with large canopies, represents the worst of options.

5.5   *Air pollution*

The presence of air-borne pollutants in the atmosphere has been a characteristic feature of the urban environment since the beginning of the industrial revolution. Air pollution can occur in a variety of forms, but the principle ones are dust, SO_2 and NO_x. Each of these has its own particular distribution, related to its origin, and its own effects.

5.5.1 DUST

During dry weather large amounts of dust can be produced by road traffic, as well as by operations such as quarrying and waste disposal. This dust may be deposited on the leaves of trees. The principle effect of this is a reduction in photosynthetic efficiency of the leaves. In one study, the leaves of roadside lime trees showed that photosynthesis occurred at a rate 20% below that of parkland trees. This reduction in photosynthesis will affect the whole tree, reducing root growth and therefore limiting water and nutrient uptake. There is no evidence that species behave differently in this respect, and there is no method for protecting trees from dust. These problems either have to be accepted, or avoided by not planting in dust-prone areas. However in normal urban areas dust is not a serious problem.

5.5.2 SULPHUR DIOXIDE

Emissions of sulphur dioxide by industry and domestic coal burning in the past led to winter concentrations of over 700 mg SO_2 m^{-3}, and summer concentrations of over 250 mg SO_2 m^{-3}, in the centres of conurbations, causing severe difficulties for plant growth. The range of species which could be established in urban areas was formerly very restricted. One of the reasons for the domination of the London plane in the tree composition of many cities is its reputation for tolerating air pollution. Because of the Clean Air Acts, changes in industry, and widespread use of electricity and gas for domestic heating, SO_2 levels in the atmosphere have fallen dramatically in the last 50 years, and are likely to continue to fall, winter levels of >100 mg m^{-3} are now unusual. Today sulphur dioxide, either as SO_2 or as acid rain, appears to represent no major problem, despite public belief. This is borne out by careful surveys.

However, it has left a legacy of acidified soils in some cities. In many urban parks on sandy soils the pH is now extremely low, with a thick surface layer of undecomposed and unincorporated organic matter. This leads to a low carbon:nitrogen ratio, little available nitrogen and an absence of microbial and earthworm activity, as described in Chapter 4. Unless these soils have been limed, this situation can persist to this day.

5.5.3 NITROGEN OXIDES AND OZONE

Whilst SO_2 emissions have declined in recent times, the production of NO_x and ozone has increased, particularly by the emissions from car exhausts. The direct effects of NO_x on urban tree growth are unclear. It can have a negative effect at high concentrations, above 0.5 ppm, but these are only found very close to main roads. Soils may, however, benefit from nitrogen deposition, acting as a substantial fertilizer, as described in Chapter 4.

Ozone is produced photochemically, in relation to bright sunshine, and is therefore present in high concentrations for only relatively short periods of the day, but occurring in wide areas in and downwind of cities influenced by emissions of NO_x and hydrocarbons. Natural levels are only approximately 0.02 ppm, but this rises to 0.1 ppm in London and 0.9 ppm in Los Angeles. Of the two urban figures quoted, the former is unlikely to cause any damage to trees, but the latter, which occurs for only a few hours each day, almost certainly will. Levels of 5 ppm can cause damage; these have not yet been reached in the UK, and are unlikely to be in the near future. However, in cities such as Mexico substantial damage is now occurring in long-established trees due to the build-up of motor traffic and little air circulation.

References

Dobson, M.C. (1991) *De-icing Salt Damage to Trees and Shrubs,* Forestry Commission Bulletin **101,** HMSO, London.

Gilbertson, P. and Bradshaw, A.D. (1985) Tree survival in cities: the extent and nature of the problem. *Arboricultural Journal,* **9,** 131–42.

Hodge, S.J. (1991) *Urban Trees – A Survey of Street Trees in England,* Forestry Commission Bulletin **99**, HMSO, London.

Other reading

Good, J.E.G. (1991) Air pollution and tree health in relation to arboriculture, in *Research for Practical Arboriculture* (ed. S.J. Hodge), Forestry Commission Bulletin **97**, HMSO, London, pp. 107–19.

Innes, J.L. (1991) Acid rain: tree health surveys, in *Research for Practical Arboriculture* (ed. S.J. Hodge), Forestry Commission Bulletin **97**, HMSO, London, pp. 120–8.

Shaw, J.L. and Hodson, M.J. (1981) The effect of salt dumping on roadside trees. *Arboricultural Journal,* **5**, 283–9.

Thompson, J.R. and Rutter, A.J. (1986) The salinity of motorway soils. IV. Effects of sodium chloride on some native British shrub species, and the possibility of establishing shrubs on the central reserves of motorways. *Journal of Applied Ecology,* **23**, 299–315.

6

Site treatments

Monitoring
⇑
Maintenance
⇑
Establishment
⇑
Planting
⇑
Tree supply
⇑
Site preparation ◄
⇑
Contract ◄
⇑
Design ◄

- Even sites that look difficult, such as recently tipped subsoils and brick wastes, may in fact be able to grow trees with little treatment.
- Some sites, however, have problems that can only be effectively dealt with by treatments applied over the whole site before planting.
- To prevent waterlogging, sites should be properly drained by creating appropriate slopes and installing under-drainage.
- Compacted soils should be broken up by ripping across the slope and cultivation, and by the incorporation of organic matter.
- Creating a good soil structure will improve water-holding capacity and drainage.
- Soil acidity can be overcome by liming.
- Metal toxicity is unlikely but can be treated by dilution or by covering with an inert material; otherwise the only solution is removal.
- Methane emissions from landfill should not be a problem if there is a properly constructed cap covered with 1 m or more of rooting medium.
- Often existing site substrates can be improved cheaply by locally available organic waste materials, removing the need for expensive imported topsoil.
- If topsoil is used, its quality must be confirmed and it must be handled correctly.

Many of the problems inherent in urban planting sites, detailed in the previous chapters, can be dealt with by good planting design, careful choice of species, and the use of the correct planting techniques. Some problems, however, are best dealt with by preparing the site as a whole before planting, to create an overall environment suitable for tree growth. Indeed, problems such as soil compaction are extremely difficult to treat once trees have been planted.

Such site preparations should concentrate on developing suitable soil conditions, since they can yield benefits in two ways. Firstly, problems such as water-logging, which can kill trees in a short space of time, are removed. Secondly, longer-term benefits such as increased soil-available water capacity and fertility are accrued. Although in the short term these can be dealt with at planting time, in later years tree roots will grow well outside the planting pit. In addition, the amelioration of one site deficiency can lead to an improvement in others. Creating a good soil structure, for instance, can simultaneously help to relieve drought, improve drainage, and reduce soil compaction.

The major problems which can be dealt with prior to planting are: poor drainage, compaction, drought and nutrient deficiencies. The site must first be constructed by creating the correct landforms to drain excess surface water, installing an under-drainage system where necessary, and relieving excess compaction. Attention can then focus on the creation of a well-balanced soil. This is a soil which will retain sufficient water for plant growth as well as permitting adequate drainage of excess water, whilst at the same time maintaining gaseous exchange with the atmosphere and a supply of available nutrients.

This can be achieved by the direct amelioration of the materials already present, or by the importation of material from elsewhere. But imported material must be well chosen. Otherwise the characteristics of the site may be degraded rather than improved.

Specific treatments are now considered and their costs are given, so that the reader can obtain a perspective of the implications of different solutions.

6.1 *Surface drainage*

On the urban fringe there can be large sites suitable for tree planting (Chapter 16). These can suffer if surface drainage is inadequate. The simplest solution is to create slopes which will shed excess rainfall as surface runoff. In some types of site slopes are present already. Colliery spoil heaps and refuse landfills, for instance, often have relatively steep sides on which trees are planted. Very steep

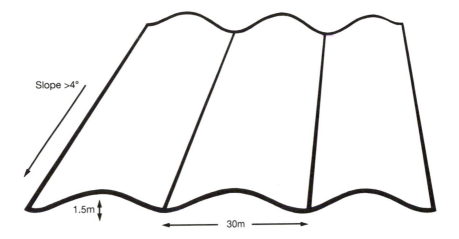

Figure 6.1
On large flat sites a landform of ridges and furrows can be constructed to enhance surface drainage (redrawn from Moffat and Roberts, 1989).

Slope >4°

1.5m

30m

slopes should be avoided, as the working of machinery on slopes in excess of 1 in 3 can become hazardous, and such slopes are often prone to erosion. The latter is also true of very long unbroken slopes, in excess of 25 m. Surface runoff in these cases should be intercepted by drains or ridges to slow the movement of water down the slope. As we shall see later, this can also have implications for the treatment of drought.

In general, slopes of at least 1 in 14 should be created to remove excess water from the planting area. On flatter sites this can be achieved by creating broad ridges and furrows, approximately 30 m across and 1.5 m high, planting right across these ridges. But this will incur substantial earthmoving costs. Where necessary the ridges and furrows themselves can be gently sloped to further improve drainage (Figure 6.1) although this means extra earthmoving costs.

In smaller sites within urban areas surface drainage can also be a problem, even when paving and drains are provided. In all situations what must be avoided is the concentration of surface runoff into the planting pit. In wet weather, in summer or winter, this can quickly lead to waterlogging if downward drainage is impeded. Trees surrounded by impervious surfaces such as paving stones are particularly vulnerable. A balance between water supply and drainage must be found.

The simplest method of assessing waterlogging is to insert a mild steel rod into the soil. When removed after 1–3 months, the pattern of rusting will indicate the severity of waterlogging over that period. In those parts of the soil profile which have been waterlogged, the rod will remain without rust. This technique was used in collecting the data for Figure 4.10.

6.2   *Soil compaction*

Even when the correct landform has been created, soil physical problems can be severe, in small as well as large sites. As was discussed in Chapter 4, compacted soils present a barrier to root penetration and can easily become anaerobic. To

Figure 6.2
Soil compaction can be avoided by the use of machinery to deposit and spread the material which avoids having to drive over it.

allow adequate root growth an open soil structure must be maintained. This can be achieved in a variety of ways.

Compaction can most easily be avoided by reducing the traffic of heavy machinery over the substrate present on the site. In soil-placing operations, wherever possible, large-wheeled scrapers should not be used. Tracked vehicles, which spread the load over a wider area, are better. If possible, soils should be loose-tipped from back-acting trucks, or long-armed excavators (Figure 6.2). Even more critical is the water content of the soil when handling takes place. Considerable loss of structure occurs when soils are worked in wet conditions; this should never be allowed. This is particularly important for soils with a high clay content.

Even when soils are handled in a dry state, compaction can occur. Most compaction occurs during the first passage of large vehicles, so it is better to restrict the routes of soil-placing vehicles to lines which have already been traversed. In this way compaction is confined to a more limited area, on which subsequent treatments can be focused. This can be particularly important when layers of material, for instance separate subsoils and topsoils, are placed in succession.

The simplest techniques used to relieve compaction involve breaking up the whole soil mass by ripping or cultivation to create fissures and macropores deep into the substrate. This will allow downward and lateral drainage of water, as well as reducing resistance to root penetration. It should be stressed that this is not a substitute for good soil handling, and will do little for crumb structure as disturbing the whole soil mass has little effect on the formation of individual soil aggregates. In some instances the beneficial effects of ripping and cultivation can be quickly reversed by a heavy downpour of rain or vehicle traffic soon

after the soil loosening has been performed. This is because the aggregate stability of worked soils is low.

Where only a surface crust of compacted soil is present, this can be relieved by shallow discing or ploughing (costing 10–20 tree units ha^{-1} depending on the site and the depth required). Compaction of deeper horizons will require ripping by either straight or winged tines (costing about a further 90 tree units ha^{-1}) (Figure 6.3). Winged tines are more effective but more prone to damage by rocks, etc. In coarse, sandy substrates the entire profile can be broken up by ripping after the full depth of soil has been placed. Machinery is now available which can pull equipment capable of penetrating down to 1 m. In most soils, however, this will only be effective when the soil is in a dry state. When wet, the soil will not be broken up into smaller units by ripping, but will deform around the tines. Clay soils, which are highly plastic when wet, and have lower horizons that are often slow to dry out, will be difficult to break up. When a series of layers are being imported, it will often be better to rip each layer in turn, as it is placed. It is essential that careful site supervision ensures the use of the technique most appropriate for the site and its moisture conditions.

To ensure that ripping is effective, it is generally accepted that the spacing should be no more than 1.5 times the depth, and ideally should be carried out in two passes. The planting strip should then be rotavated along one of the rip lines (about 0.02 tree units m^{-2}) (Figure 6.4). Equipment is now available which can both break up and mix soils to a depth of 75 cm (Figure 6.5). This is particularly useful when incorporating soil ameliorants on a large scale.

Ripping will only be effective if combined with the formation of a suitable topography and drainage system. Low-lying areas, where drainage is poor, are

Figure 6.4
The recommended procedure for ripping prior to planting on large sites. Ripped lines are rotavated and further ripping takes place between the rows.

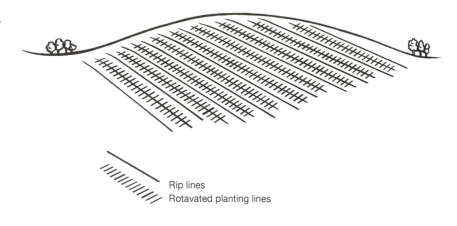

/////////// Rip lines
//////// Rotavated planting lines

unlikely to be significantly improved by breaking up the whole soil mass in this way without additional site drainage.

Another technique used to alleviate compaction is blasting air into the subsoil, 'inflating' the substrate. This can be combined with an injection of polystyrene beads to maintain the open structure thus created. The benefits of such treatments for tree growth remain, however, unproven, and they are expensive to apply over large areas. They may be of benefit to individual, highly

Figure 6.5
Large-scale equipment is available which can cultivate to a depth of 75 cm, incorporating ameliorants where appropriate.

Figure 6.6
(a)The results of an experiment in which standards of lime were grown in a variety of compacted soils for 2 years (redrawn from Hunt *et al.*, 1991). The negative effects of compaction are partially relieved by incorporation of organic matter. (b) Root growth of the trees in the experiment shown in (a): (i) uncompacted, (ii) compacted. Compaction can cause serious reduction in root growth even in the establishment stage.

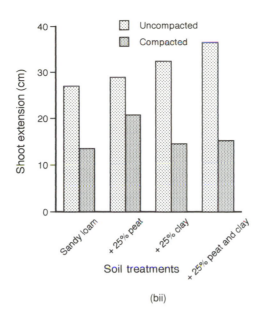

(a)

(bi)   (bii)

valued trees. The insertion of perforated pipes into compacted soils close to the tree is also unlikely to significantly benefit tree growth.

Where vehicle traffic and overworking of soils cannot be avoided, their effects may be reduced by incorporating organic matter into the soil beforehand. Bulk density and soil strength are reduced, and structure is improved. Figure 6.6 shows the effects of adding peat to soils in which trees were grown for 2 years. Organic matter makes the soil more resilient, and so is ideal for street trees where vehicle and foot traffic will continue indefinitely. Bulky organic materials, such as bark mulches, are particularly good for surface application (Figure 6.7).

However, organic matter eventually decomposes and is therefore not a solution for areas, such as in car parks or close to roads, where the soil is going to be subject to continued compaction. In these cases it is essential to install a soil that has a texture that is permanently resistant to compaction. From work in the Netherlands, and on football pitches in this country, such soils must have a

Figure 6.7
Bark mulch can be used around street trees to reduce the effects of soil compaction from foot traffic.

high percentage of sand and very little clay (Figure 6.8), although soils of type A will be rather susceptible to drought. Specially prepared tree soils are now available of this texture, made from selected sandy subsoil to which has been added organic matter to help compaction resistance and water retention as well as long-term fertility. This approach is recognized by the modifications that have been made to the British Standard for topsoil and topsoil substitute, BS 3882, which recognizes grades which can be of synthesized material. It can be surmised that a suitable tree planting soil could be prepared on site from suitable materials such as sandy subsoils and brick wastes.

6.3   *Under drainage*

Even where a good soil structure has been encouraged and slopes created to remove excess water, there can still be problems. Relief of compaction in soils which have been worked or imported is never wholly successful, and such soils will often deteriorate if an additional drainage system is not installed. These can

Figure 6.8
The textural composition of soils resistant to compaction in sports areas (Baker 1990): A will maintain aeration and drainage whatever compaction is applied, B will do the same when compaction is not excessive, C will maintain good conditions only when compaction is light. For trees, soils similar to A and B should be used when compaction is expected.

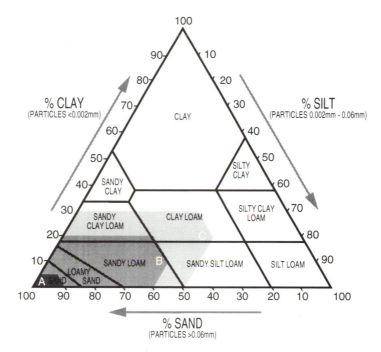

be channels dug into the substrate, back-filled with a coarse material such as hard-core or rubble, leading to a more substantial ditch, sewer or water-course. This can be supplemented by the installation of perforated pipes or french drains (total cost about 1 tree unit per linear metre). The aim should be to create a network of drains, moving water downslope across the contours of a site.

The density of drains will depend on the specific conditions at the site, so it is difficult to make generalizations, but they should usually be no more than 10 m apart. Where substrates are suitable, an alternative system of soakaway trenches can be installed. These have to be designed with a capacity sufficient to hold all the runoff from the slope above, so that this can then infiltrate down to the water-table below. It should be borne in mind that artificial or replaced soils generally have a smaller capacity for retaining water whilst at the same time maintaining adequate gas exchange than do natural soils. The capacity of a drainage system to deal with heavy rainfall on such sites should therefore be greater than most agricultural drainage systems.

For street trees, drainage is just as important, yet is often disregarded. A simple drainage system can be installed which runs the length of an avenue of trees. Installed below the planting pit, and linking with any pit-drainage installed at planting time, a single pipe can provide adequate drainage for several trees. The essential feature is that the horizons above the drainage channel must have a good enough structure to allow downward percolation of water (see also Chapter 9).

6.4   *Drought*

As with soil compaction, droughting of soils is best dealt with by improving structure. There is, however, something of a contradiction with site drainage. Whilst it is imperative to avoid waterlogging, which rapidly kills trees, local circumstances must be observed, so that sufficient water enters the soil profile to supply the trees' needs. Coarse textured soils on steep slopes often need no extra drainage; in fact unless some water can be encouraged to enter the rooting zone and remain there, drought will rapidly occur in dry spells. Small terraces can be created, not to pond water, but to slow its passage downslope. This, in fact, is what is achieved by the ripping and rotavation treatments described earlier. Local rainfall levels must, however, be taken into account. The ridge and furrow drainage system mentioned previously, for instance, is not recommended for the eastern part of Britain, where rainfall is often only 60% of that found in the west.

An alternative approach is to increase water-holding capacity, for instance by introducing organic matter. This will improve both coarse and fine-textured soils (at a cost of about 0.3 tree units m^{-2}). Combined with careful tillage to create macropores, which release water readily to plant roots, the plant-available water content of soils can be greatly enhanced. It is also evident from the discussion on compaction that this will have other beneficial effects. The types of material that can be used are discussed later.

Introducing organic matter outside the planting pit is sometimes difficult to achieve, especially in situations such as paved areas. An alternative is to irrigate trees during dry weather. Sprinklers and trickle irrigation systems are available, and are used extensively in the production of nursery stock. As a whole site treatment, however, these are likely to be prohibitively expensive to install, maintain and operate (the capital cost would be about 0.6 tree units m^{-2}). Irrigation should concentrate on watering the planting pit during establishment, and on maintaining a water supply in the longer term to larger, expensive trees, and highly valued specimens. There is further discussion of this important topic in Chapter 10.

6.5   *Nutrient deficiencies*

Most normal soils contain sufficient nutrients for tree growth in the first years after planting. Some substrates, however, are very low in nutrients, and a supply of nutrients must be maintained by creating a more balanced soil. In addition, tree roots spread over a wide area, and whilst the planting pit may contain a fertile soil, the surrounding material can be quite different in nature.

The key to solving this problem is to conduct a thorough substrate analysis prior to planting. Material can be taken from the site and chemically analysed; many laboratories offer this service (costing about 2 tree units per sample but dependent on the number of elements requiring analysis). Provided with the

Table 6.1 *Soil indices for phosphorus, potassium and magnesium (MAFF, 1979). Urban materials with indices above 2 will not require any nutrient addition*

Index	Phosphorus (ppm)	Potassium (ppm)	Magnesium (ppm)
0	0–9	0–60	0–25
1	10–15	61–120	26–50
2	16–25	121–240	51–100
3	26–45	245–400	101–175
4	46–70	405–600	176–250
5	71–100	605–900	255–350
6	101–140	905–1500	355–600
7	141–200	1510–2400	610–1000
8	205–280	2410–3600	1010–1500
9	> 280	> 3600	> 1500

analysis will be an index for each nutrient assessed, as a relative measure of the level of that nutrient. Alternatively a bioassay can be carried out using the growth of plants on the substrate, with different amounts of each nutrient added to see which are deficient. Although this is more time consuming, it has the advantages of being less affected by site conditions at the time of sampling, and of removing the difficulties of relating chemical analysis to plant growth.

There still remains the problem of how chemical analysis or bioassays of herbaceous vegetation relate to the needs of trees. For long-term growth of trees current knowledge is unclear, but research indicates that the high fertilities required for agriculture are not essential. In general, for tree growth an index of 3 will provide sufficient nutrients without the addition of fertilizer (Table 6.1). Nitrogen is not on an index, but there should be >0.2% total N.

When a nutrient deficiency has been identified, a decision has to be made concerning the form in which the nutrient should be added. Simple inorganic fertilizers are readily taken up by plants but are also easily leached, and repeat doses will have to be added in successive years until the ecosystem has built up its own nutrient pool. Slow release fertilizers are available, but are extremely expensive to use over large areas. As highlighted in Chapter 4, many urban substrates contain adequate supplies of potassium, and frequently of phosphorus. Nitrogen is the most commonly deficient soil nutrient, and is most efficiently supplied by incorporating organic matter into the soil. Luckily, this may already have been done in order to improve soil structure and resistance to compaction. Together with the introduction of organic matter, the increased soil aeration produced by ripping will also encourage soil microflora and microfauna which are essential components of nutrient cycling. The addition of nutrients is discussed in more detail in Chapter 11.

6.6   *Toxicity*

Problems of toxicity in planting sites fall into three main groups: pH, heavy metals and other pollutants, and methane. Some urban planting sites have low pH values. Plant growth begins to be affected when the pH is below 4.5, because certain constituents of soil minerals become mobilized to toxic concentrations, particularly aluminium and manganese ions. Most urban materials, however, have relatively high pH values, in the range 5.5–8.0. Where there is acidity, the substrate should be limed heavily, the amount required being assessed by chemical analysis. Liming has the added benefit of encouraging biological activity and nutrient release. It is not easy to give repeat doses in situations where weathering causes continuous release of acid, for instance in colliery spoils with a high pyrite content. The total amount of lime necessary to neutralize the potential as well as the actual acidity should therefore be applied at the outset.

Heavy metals and other pollutants such as toxic organic compounds are only rarely found in high concentrations in urban soils. Safety guidelines for the permitted levels of heavy metals in soils (Table 6.2) point out that the levels for soils in public open spaces can be higher than those for soils used for food production. It must be remembered, however, that these levels are designed to protect human beings, and are far lower than the thresholds for tree growth.

If problems do occur, it may be possible to disperse the toxic material and lower its concentration in the soil by mixing it with imported material. Alternatively the toxic material can be covered with inert material to a depth at which it is no longer harmful to tree growth. At least 1 m will be necessary to ensure adequate root room, but the cover material can be brick waste, subsoil or

Table 6.2   *Threshold levels for metal contaminants, below which no action need be taken (ICRCL, 1987). These levels are designed to protect human beings, trees will be able to cope with much higher levels*

	Threshold level (mg kg^{-1})
Primary hazard is to health	
Arsenic	40
Cadmium	15
Chromium	1000
Lead	2000
Mercury	20
Selenium	6
Primary hazard is to plants	
Boron	3
Copper	130
Nickel	70
Zinc	300

Figure 6.9
Widnes golf course with vigorous healthy trees. This is built over toxic waste which has been isolated with 1 m of subsoil.

any other innocuous material suitable for tree growth. These may often be available at no cost because a contractor is looking for tipping space. Only rarely is it sensible, where trees are to be planted, to excavate the offending material and dispose of it in a controlled waste disposal facility, replacing it with a suitable growing medium. The application of a surface covering with trees provides excellent isolation for toxic materials, especially since disturbance of the covering is unlikely once the trees have been established (Figure 6.9).

Methane emission from landfill sites should not be in such concentrations as to harm tree growth if a properly constructed impermeable cap has been placed over the refuse. This is further avoided by the installation of a gas venting system. Where uncontrolled gas escapes do occur and harm plant growth, the effects are usually a local death of vegetation. In an informal planting such death can be acceptable. Otherwise it will be necessary to excavate and repair the cap. But if sustained tree growth is to be achieved there must be a layer of inert material over the cap, at least 1.5 m deep over mineral caps (such as clay) and at least 1.0 m over synthetic caps, into which the trees can root. Again it can be brick waste or some other innocuous material if suitable soil is not available. Planting schemes need to be designed to leave gaps or rides for access to leachate and gas monitoring pipe runs.

6.7   *Topsoil*

Topsoil is often treated as an essential requirement for all planting sites. This is due to a mistaken belief that topsoil is always of a quality which is superior to other alternative soil-making materials. For a variety of reasons this is often not the case. Good quality topsoil is a valuable resource, but not readily obtainable, and its quality is only conserved if it is handled and managed correctly.

Where topsoil is not present at a planting site, it should not be imported until the current site conditions have been appraised, for several reasons. Firstly, good topsoil is very expensive, both because of its intrinsic value and because it may have to be transported to the planting site (about 0.4 tree units m^{-2} or 2500 tree units ha^{-1} for a 150 mm layer). Secondly, other materials on site may be adapted to form a substrate which will support good tree growth by the addition of the correct ameliorants. Many urban substrates can be improved inexpensively by utilizing what would otherwise be waste products, themselves presenting disposal problems. Thirdly, much of the material sold as topsoil is in fact a low grade substrate originating from the less well-developed layers below topsoil, i.e. subsoils. These soils can be very useful in the construction of planting sites, but may require amendments to improve their properties, and should obviously not command the premium of good topsoil.

If the decision to use topsoil at a planting site has been made, a number of procedures should be followed to ensure that its quality is assessed and maintained. Good topsoil is taken from the upper 25–30 cm of a soil profile, and possesses a high organic matter content, a well-developed crumb structure, and a balanced texture. This leads to good water-holding, nutrient and gas-exchange properties as described in Chapter 4. Not all natural soils possess these qualities. Using topsoil in most cases will involve it being stripped from its site of origin. This is often where the most damage to soil occurs. Topsoil stripped when wet will lose its structure, especially if heavy machinery is used, so operating when weather or site conditions are wet must be avoided.

Similar principles apply to soil placement on site. Ideally topsoil should be single-handled, i.e. stripped from its point of origin and placed on the new planting site immediately, in one operation. Where this is not possible, topsoil should be stored carefully in shallow mounds, not more than 2 m in height. Storage in very large mounds will quickly lead to much of the soil becoming

Table 6.3   *The properties of a good topsoil*

Sand (%)	Silt (%)	Clay (%)	Nitrogen (total, %)	Phosphorus (extrble) (ppm)	Potassium (extrble) (ppm)	Organic matter (%)	Stone content (%)
>20 <70	>10 <60	>5 <40	>0.2	>45*	>240*	>4	<35

*Or Ca, P, K and Mg index of >2.

anaerobic, with the consequent deterioration in structure, nutrients, and beneficial soil micro-organisms. Large storage mounds are often compacted during their construction, exacerbating these problems. Some of the effects of soil anaerobism can be reduced by seeding storage mounds with an appropriate grass/clover seed mix, which reduces erosion and leaching, and keeps the structure open through root growth and associated biotic activity. Whether single- or double-handling is employed, the placing of topsoil should involve the minimum of traffic possible, as described earlier.

Even when great care is taken to monitor the stripping, storage, quality and placement of topsoil, it can still present problems in tree planting areas. Many topsoils contain large quantities of weeds, both as seeds and as vegetative fragments. This is not a problem in grassed areas, where weed control around trees is to be expected. It may be a problem, however, when topsoil is used in non-grassed areas such as open areas in pavements. Species such as horsetail and couch-grass emerge, which can be difficult to control. In these instances it would be better to use subsoil, for instance, which is relatively weed-free, and ameliorate any deficiencies.

In some instances, however, topsoil represents a viable and useful way of ensuring good results. The characteristics it should possess to achieve these are summarized in Table 6.3. Its capacity to contribute nutrients is discussed in Chapter 11.

6.8   *Ameliorants and alternative materials*

A number of materials commonly found in urban areas can be greatly improved using ameliorants and alternative materials. Brickwaste, for instance, contains adequate supplies of calcium, phosphorus and potassium, and has a free-draining structure. What is needed in this case is to increase the available water capacity of the substrate, and to provide a sustained source of nitrogen for tree growth, readily achieved by incorporating organic matter into the soil matrix. This organic matter can be derived from a number of wastes. Opportunistic use of these materials as and when they arise can cheaply and effectively ameliorate conditions over a whole site without the need to import expensive and scarce topsoil or peat.

Sewage sludge, which is presenting a disposal problem for water companies, is increasingly used as an ameliorant on planting sites. Sludge is produced in either raw, digested liquid, or digested 'cake' form. Digested material should be used. It is innocuous and contains high levels of available nitrogen, phosphorus and potassium as well as organic matter (Table 6.4). Its treatment will have removed any pathogenic organisms. Its main disadvantages are that it may still smell slightly, transport to the planting site may not be free (although it is usually free within 10 miles), and there may be contamination, principally by heavy metals from industrial processes. Whilst this may prohibit its use in some urban planting sites, these problems can be overcome.

Table 6.4   *The major constituents of two common types of sewage (Byrom and Bradshaw 1989). An application of 200 t ha⁻¹ will provide the most raw substrate with a store of nutrients which will equal topsoil*

Average contents	Digested liquid	Digested cake
Dry solids (ds) (%)	2–8	20–50
Organic matter (% ds)	50–60	50–70
Total N (% ds)	0.9–6.8	1.5–2.5
Total P (% ds)	0.5–3.0	0.5–1.8
Total K (% ds)	0.1–0.5	0.1–0.3
Total Ca (% ds)	1.5–7.6	1.6–2.5
Total Mg (% ds)	0.3–1.6	0.1–0.5

Effect of 200 t ha⁻¹	Dry solids		Total nitrogen		Total phosphorus	
	%	t ha⁻¹	% ds	kg ha⁻¹	% ds	kg ha⁻¹
Digested liquid	4	8	5	400	1.7	140
Digested cake	25	50	3	1500	1.5	785

Sewage sludge can vary in composition, but Table 6.4 shows the contribution of a typical dose of 200 t ha⁻¹, in terms of total nitrogen and phosphorus content. What is most important to recognize is that much of the nutrient content is released over an extended period of time. Nitrogen, in particular, is made available to plants as the organic matter fraction decomposes, with relatively little being lost through leaching, as long as a healthy vegetation cover is maintained. This compares favourably with the addition of inorganic fertilizers, where much of a single dose can be lost through leaching, and repeated doses are required since no store of nutrients is maintained. By means of a single application of sludge a nitrogen capital of 1000 kg N ha⁻¹ can be built up, sufficient for a self-sustaining ecosystem.

Sewage sludge is now frequently used on mine and quarry waste heaps, in particular in tree planting areas where soil cover is thin or not available. It can equally be applied to any nutrient-poor substrate. Other benefits accrue, principally the physical improvements due to its organic matter content (Table 6.4), especially bulk density, resistance to compaction and slumping, and water retention. For the improvements due to sludge addition to be effective, it must be fully incorporated into the substrate by ripping or rotavation.

The most significant problem associated with sewage sludge is its contamination by heavy metals. Careful monitoring will be required to ensure that the particular batch of sludge to be used does not contain excessive concentrations of toxic metals; this will usually be carried out by the company supplying the sludge. It should be pointed out, however, that by applying a single dose of sludge rather than several applications over an extended period of time, the build up of these metals in the soil and their release to water courses in toxic conditions is highly unlikely.

Figure 6.10
The effect on the growth of willow of a waste material, pulverized refuse fines, compared with more conventional materials, incorporated into urban brickwaste (redrawn from Chu *et al.*, 1991). The waste material can yield growth rates as good as more conventional material.

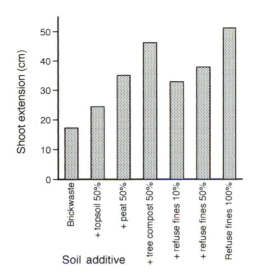

Another material high in organic matter and nutrients, which can be used to assist the formulation of a good soil for tree growth, is **pulverized refuse fines** (PRF). It is clear both that difficult substrates can be improved by this material, and that it is also a satisfactory growing medium in its own right (Figure 6.10). Other materials have specific applications. **Crushed concrete**, from tower-block demolition for instance, and **sugar-beet washings** are both lime-rich wastes which can be used to raise soil pH, thereby removing possible toxicity and improving soil nutrient release and biotic activity. **Peat** is too scarce a non-renewable commodity to be used on a whole-site basis.

What limits the use of all these materials are problems of transport and supply. A ready and constant supply, particularly if other outlets are competing for the materials, is not always possible, and advance planning is often required to secure this. The materials may sometimes be available free. But there is always the cost of transport to the site. Careful consideration needs to be given to balancing the cost of importation against the benefits accrued. The production of PRF and sugar-beet washings are highly localized operations. Sewage sludge has the advantage of being produced at a large number of more widely dispersed sites.

6.9 *Ground surfaces*

In many urban sites, the soil surface is covered after planting, or the tree is placed into a planting pit dug out of an existing covering material. Unfortunately such sites are often constructed without the needs of trees being considered.

Individual sites can vary in their properties, particularly in the degree to which their soil characteristics mollify the deleterious effects of any surface covering. Nevertheless it is possible to establish a series of surfaces of increasing disadvantage to trees :

bare ground > gravel > grass > paving > tarmac > asphalt.

Figure 6.11
Since asphalt has been spread around these long-established planes in the interests of tidiness, the trees have gradually gone into decline.

Bare ground is best because there is no competition for water or nutrients, and there is maximum aeration so long as the soil is not compacted by walking or vehicular traffic. Where there are pedestrians then **gravel** helps to prevent surface compaction and is permeable to air and water. **Grass** is usually seen as the natural ground cover. This it is, once the tree has become well established. But in the early stages serious competition from grass for water and nutrients can occur (Chapter 13). **Porous paving stones**, **setts**, and **open-grain tarmac** have few negative effects; they allow the penetration of air and water and protect the surface from compaction. This may appear to contradict their low position in the above ranking. The point is that they are usually part of engineered features, installed without the needs of the tree in mind. In paved areas, for instance, it is usually the compacted soil below the sand on which the paving stones are laid which causes the problems (Chapter 4). **Close-grain tarmac** and **asphalt** are totally different, because they are usually impermeable to the water and oxygen required by both the tree roots and the soil for proper functioning (Figure 6.11).

Special grids to surround individual trees, usually made of cast iron, are often used in conjunction with the latter surfaces (Chapter 9). They will help during the early years of the growth of the tree. But it seems very unlikely that they will work in the long term if the surrounding areas are left highly compacted and impermeably covered, because of the distance that tree roots spread.

6.10   *Assessment*

Pre-planting site investigation is the key to the correct use of site treatments. Table 6.5 gives a guide to the likely problems, and their identification and treatment options. When viewed in conjunction with Table 4.1, the areas for investigation at different types of planting site can be focused.

Table 6.5   *Identification and treatment of problems that may be found over the whole or part of tree planting sites. Treatments given in order of complexity and permanence*

Problem	Identification	Treatment
Compaction	Penetrometer; direct examination by soil pit	Rotovate or disc; rip; incorporate organic matter
Waterlogging	Lack of rusting on inserted steel rods; direct examination by soil pit	Improve surface drainage by creating ridge and furrow landform; create slopes >1 in 4; avoid drainage from hard surfaces into tree pit; install sub-surface drainage system
Drought	Direct examination by soil pit	Incorporate organic matter; irrigate for first three years after planting; install irrigation system
Nutrient deficiency	Chemical analysis; bioassay	Nitrogen: inorganic fertilizer; incorporate high N organic matter; apply topsoil Other: inorganic fertilizer; apply topsoil
Alkalinity or acidity	pH meter with electrode	Too high: incorporate organic matter Too low: incorporate lime
Heavy metal toxicity	Chemical analysis; bioassay	Incorporate organic matter; create new rooting zone by >1 m covering layer of imported material; excavate toxic material and remove from site
Landfill gas	Lack of rusting on inserted steel rods; examination by soil pit (soil blackening and smell)	Create adequate depth (>1 m) of uncompacted soil material; install gas drainage system; construct impermeable capping layer overlain with >1 m soil layer
Salinity	Chemical analysis	Prevent saline drainage entering site; provide good drainage and allow soil to weather

References

Baker, S.W. (1990) Criteria in topsoil selection for sports turf. *Agricultural Engineer,* **Autumn 1990**, 87–8

Byrom, K.L. and Bradshaw, A.D. (1989) The potential use of sewage sludge in land reclamation, in *Alternative Uses for Sewage Sludge* (ed. J.E. Hall), Pergamon, Oxford, pp. 1–21.

Chu, L.M., Gilbertson, P. and Bradshaw, A.D. (1991) The effect of pulverised refuse fines (PRF) in arboriculture. II. Tree planting on an urban demolition site. *Arboricultural Journal*, **15**, 345–53.

Hunt, B., Walmsley, T.J. and Bradshaw, A.D. (1991) The importance of soil physical factors for urban tree growth, in *Research for Practical Arboriculture* (ed. S.J. Hodge), Forestry Commission Bulletin **97**, HMSO, London, pp. 51–62.

ICRCL (1987) *Guidance on the Assessment and Redevelopment of Contaminated Land*, 2nd edn, Department of the Environment, London.

MAFF (1979) *Fertilisers Recommendations,* 2nd edn, HMSO, London.

Moffat, A.J. and Roberts, C.J. (1989) The use of large scale ridge and furrow landforms in reclamation of mineral workings. *Forestry,* **62**, 233–48.

Other reading

Bacon, A.R. and Humphries, R.N. (1988) Loose soil profiles using scrapers and deep ripping. *Mine, Quarry and Environment,* **2**, 13–17.

Bradshaw, A.D. (1989) The quality of topsoil. *Soil Use and Management,* **5**, 101–8.

British Standards Institute (1994) *Specification for topsoil, BS 3882: 1994.* British Standards Institute, London.

Dobson, M.C. and Moffat, A.J. (1993) *The Potential for Woodland Establishment on Landfill Sites*, HMSO, London.

Hodge, S.J. (1993) *Using steel rods to assess aeration in urban soils,* Arboriculture Research Note **115 : 93**, Arboricultural Advisory and Information Service, Farnham.

Stewart, V.I. and Scullion, J. (1989) Principles of managing man-made soils. *Soil Use and Management,* **5**, 109–16.

Voelker, R. and Dinsdale, M. (1983) A guide to specifying topsoil. *Landscape Design* **179**, 15–16; **180**, 47–8.

7

Tree stock

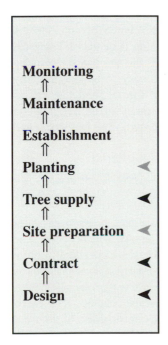

Monitoring
⇑
Maintenance
⇑
Establishment
⇑
Planting ◄
⇑
Tree supply ◄
⇑
Site preparation ◄
⇑
Contract ◄
⇑
Design ◄

- A wide variety of different sizes of nursery stock is available, with different characteristics and costs.

- In urban plantings, standards are commonly used for instant effect and presumed tolerance to urban stress.

- In many situations however smaller stock has great advantages in cost and better performance.

- Extra heavy material should only be used in prestige situations, and where it can be maintained properly.

- Stock quality can vary considerably, leading to high failure rates and negative growth after establishment.

- Much of this can be related to poor growing conditions and to poor treatment after lifting, especially in exposure of root systems.

- In bare root material most of this damage can be avoided if the trees are kept in a waterproof bag from the moment of lifting until planting.

- Great care should therefore be taken in purchasing and handling stock before planting

The starting point for any tree planting scheme, once the problems of the site have been assessed and treated properly, is the tree stock that is to be planted. Usually this will be bought in from a nursery which specializes in raising nursery stock, although in a big local authority, for instance, it may be produced in-house. Whatever the origin, there is a wide variety of material to choose from, quite apart from the problem of choice of species or cultivar, which is discussed in the next chapter. There is also a wide choice of suppliers. A successful scheme which grows well from the beginning depends on using the right stock. This is firstly the type of stock which suits the site and the planting scheme, and secondly stock of the best quality. It is easy to believe that any stock will be acceptable, providing it is of the right species, and that choice should be based on price. But this is far from true; many of the failures and disappointments in planting schemes arise from inappropriate or bad stock, and are not due to poor work later.

7.1   *Types of stock*

Trees can be bought as small seedlings only one year old, or as large semi-mature trees which may be 10–15 years old, or at any size in between. The commonly recognized sizes are given in Table 7.1. They are specified in more detail in BS 3936. It may seem best always to buy the largest trees that can be afforded. But this is not necessarily sensible. Each size has its own advantages and disadvantages, and its own particular use in landscape schemes. The variation in costs are large, not only because of differences in the costs of the trees themselves, but also because of the great differences in the trouble involved in planting them. The sizes are discussed, for convenience, in order of their normal use in urban situations.

7.1.1 STANDARDS

In most urban plantings standards are normally used. There are several reasons for this. Firstly, the standard tree can have a definite landscape impact in its first year (Figure 7.1). Secondly, in situations where people have access, it is believed that standards are unlikely to be trampled on or damaged accidently, particularly if they have been provided with support. Thirdly, it is believed that larger trees will not suffer from the effects of weed competition as would smaller trees. Finally, there is an assumption that a big tree will be more able to withstand transplanting stress; if trees are given a 'good start in life' they will surely grow better.

Table 7.1 *The sizes of tree stock commonly available (BS 3969, 1992) (costs expressed in tree units = the average cost of supplying but not planting a standard tree; 1994 tree unit = £10 approximately)*

Type	Size	Cost of tree	Planting cost	Characteristics
Seedling, transplant, undercut	0.2–0.9 m (can be up to 1.25 m)	0.02–0.09	0.02	Very cheap. Easy to plant, readily stands stress of transplanting, but essential to provide weed control from beginning. Vulnerable to damage, must be protected or isolated from damage for 5–10 years. Only sensible way to achieve large-scale plantings, although may take several years to create impact.
Whip	1.0–1.75 m (can be up to 2.0 m)	0.08–0.2	0.03	No side shoots. Cheap. Quite easy to plant, quickly recovers from stress of transplanting, but still requires good weed control. Requires protection or isolation from damage for at least 5 years. A quicker way to achieve an impact than transplants.
Feather	1.25–2.5 m (can be up to 3.0 m)	0.08–0.3	0.04	Side shoots. Fairly cheap, easy to plant and recovers fairly quickly. But can suffer stress in establishment phase because more branches and usually larger. Must be well planted or can loosen in wind.
Standard extra light light standard selected half	2.0–3.5 m (girth 4–6 cm) (girth 6–8 cm) (girth 8–10 cm) (girth10–12 cm) (branching from 1.25 m)	1 (0.8–1.5) (difficult species more expensive)	1.5–2	Normally specified by girth (circumference in cm at 1 m). Expensive. Not all species can recover from stress of transplanting. Careful handling and aftercare important, weed control still essential for 3–5 years. Less susceptible to damage than smaller stock, but some protection or isolation still required. Normal method of achieving an immediate effect.
Heavy and extra-heavy standard	above 3.5 m (girth 12–14, 14–16 cm)	2–4	3–5	More expensive. Stock must be specially prepared to resist transplanting stress, aftercare for at least 3 years essential. Even less susceptible to damage. Appears to be a good way of achieving an immediate effect, but may fail completely because of inadequate aftercare.
Semi–mature	usually +5 m	10–20	5–10	Extremely expensive. Stock has to be prepared for several years in advance, special equipment has to be used for lifting and planting, elaborate steps have to be taken to ensure survival and recovery. Often contemplated for prestige schemes, but rarely succeeds because of inadequate appreciation of site preparation and aftercare liabilities.
Cutting	25–30 cm	0.01	0.015	Applicable only to species that root easily from cuttings (see Table 7.3). But for these it is very economical and reliable.
Seed	10–20 cm in first year	0.015	0.01	A developing technique, simple to use in some situations for native species in informal plantings. Weed control essential from outset. Gives well-rooted plants.

The first reason is difficult to refute. However, it is an argument that only applies where immediate results are required. If landscaping schemes can be established in good time, 2 or 3 years before people have access, then the argument does not hold. In the development of New Towns it has been found possible to carry out advanced planting as the normal routine and, for instance

Figure 7.1
Standards in the car park of a new supermarket. The impact is immediate.

at Warrington, dispense with the use of standards almost entirely.

The second reason seems equally difficult to refute. However, as will be discussed in Chapter 12, protection must be given to all trees no matter what their size. Standard trees are themselves liable to damage if planted in situations where they are exposed to people. The answer is to design more carefully. Then large trees may not be necessary.

The third reason is both right and wrong. It is obvious that a transplant, or even a whip, can be swamped by vigorous weed growth. If weed growth control cannot be relied upon, then there is no point in even contemplating the use of small trees. But the major effects of weeds are below ground, by root competition, so that even standards can suffer astonishingly, and even be killed, by weeds (Chapter 13). So weed control is essential whatever size of stock is being used, and large size is therefore hardly an advantage.

This then raises the last reason. If it pays to give trees a good start, then surely whether the other reasons are right or wrong is irrelevant. Here the answer is very interesting. It is simply that large size is not an insurance for good growth but the reverse; Justice realized this in 1759. The larger is the tree when it is transplanted, the greater is the likelihood that it will suffer stress during and after transplanting. This is particularly connected to the damage inevitably caused to the tree's root system during the transplanting process. Even with careful preparation, half or more of the root system is lost. The amount lost is greatest in large trees, because of the practical difficulties in excavation and transport. As a result the growth of the tree is bound to suffer considerably, unless great care is taken (discussed in Chapters 9 and 10). In practice most standard trees grow very little in the year of transplanting, and may take several years to recover.

There are a variety of different sizes of standard, specified by girth and height, suitable for different situations (Table 7.1). The half-standard, where branching is allowed lower down the stem, from about 1.25 m, is an interesting variant on these, and is useful where a more natural growth habit is required.

7.1.2 TRANSPLANTS, WHIPS AND FEATHERS

Smaller trees, whose root systems suffer relatively little damage, are likely to be set-back very little by transplanting (Figure 7.2). As a result, after 5–10 years,

Figure 7.2
A comparison of the growth of whip and standard birch planted in an industrial situation (Kendle, 1988). Small stock is likely to grow much faster in the first few years than larger stock.

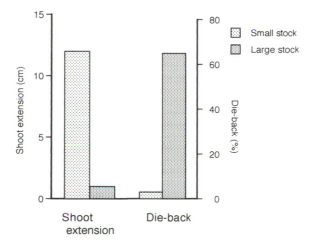

Figure 7.3
An informal planting on brick-waste in Liverpool after six years. Mass planting of whips can be the most successful and economical technique of establishment, particularly on difficult sites.

Table 7.2 *Species which must be planted as transplants or whips unless specially prepared material is available*

Cockspur thorn *(Crataegus crus–galli)*
Hawthorn *(Crataegus monogyna)*
Holly *(Ilex aquifolium)*
Blackthorn *(Prunus spinosa)*
Turkey oak *(Quercus cerris)*
Holm oak *(Quercus ilex)*
Red oak *(Quercus rubra)*
Common oak *(Quercus robur)*
Sessile oak *(Quercus petraea)*
Yew *(Taxus baccata)*
Gorse *(Ulex europaeus)*
All conifers

trees only 1–1.5 m high when planted can catch up the height of standards planted at the same time. The smaller tree also has the possibility of establishing a more natural, and less distorted, root system. The cost of planting is very small because little excavation is required and there is no need for any sort of support.

This provides strong arguments for planting small stock wherever possible (Figure 7.3). Large organizations such as the Forestry Commission, planting thousands of trees at a time, never use standards. In the urban situation the use of small planting stock does, however, require careful planning, and attention to protection, especially weed control. Developments such as the protective tree planting tubes have an important part to play, but a well-considered layout is even more important (Chapter 12). There will, however, always be many situations where a larger tree is essential.

Overriding all this is the fact that there are a number of species that are extremely difficult to transplant except as small stock These are species which do not possess either an extensive fibrous root system or do not readily produce new roots from cut root ends. This includes in particular the common oak, which as a result is being omitted from almost all new planting schemes because designers think it is too difficult to establish. Yet it is obvious from the richness of our hedgerows in planted oaks that, in the past, this was not a problem, probably because young stock was used. Similarly, nearly all conifers have to be planted as very young stock; the norm is what are known as 1+1 transplants, plants which have spent one year in a seed bed and then one year lined out. Attempts to transplant conifers of a larger size usually fail. The species which must be planted young are given in Table 7.2.

The smallest stock are seedlings, either 1 or 2 years old, coming straight from the seed bed, although sometimes now cell-grown in tubular containers. These have their original root system. Transplants are usually 2 years old, having been transplanted at the end of their first year. This gives them a more branching root system, better adapted to transplanting. The same effect can be achieved without transplanting, by undercutting in the seed bed. Whips and feathers are 2- or 3-year-old transplants, usually of faster-growing species. Whips have not been allowed to branch whereas feathers have. Feathers are most useful where low bushy growth is wanted. Larger feathers with a small stake are a cheap way of achieving an immediate effect. In urban situations whips and feathers are the most widely used small material.

7.1.3 EXTRA-HEAVY STANDARDS AND SEMI-MATURE TREES

These are so expensive that they should only be used in prestige situations where a special effect is required. It is essential that the trees have been specially prepared, by undercutting in the nursery, so that their root system has been forced to proliferate within a small volume. They will then have to be transplanted with care, to ensure that this root system is retained without damage. Finally they need extremely good aftercare, in particular to ensure that they do not run out of water and nutrients (discussed in Chapter 9). Unless this special care is given, the use of such large trees is a waste of time and money.

7.1.4 CUTTINGS

Some species can be planted not as plants at all, but as cuttings or setts. This might seem to be an unreliable method, only suited for propagation of material in nurseries, but for certain species (Table 7.3) it is a very effective and cheap technique in both cost of material and planting. Indeed, for willows it is better than other methods. A section of new stem, about 300 mm long and 20 mm diameter, taken from the growth of the immediately preceding season, is all that is needed. The cuttings can be stored for several weeks in cool conditions in a plastic bag before planting.

Table 7.3 *Species which can be readily established from cuttings (hybrids involving these species usually have a similar behaviour)*

White poplar *(Populus alba)*
Grey poplar *(Populus canescens)*
Aspen *(Populus tremula)*
White willow *(Salix alba)*
Sallow *(Salix cinerea)*
Violet willow *(Salix daphnoides)*
Crack willow *(Salix fragilis)*
Osier *(Salix viminalis)*
Hybrid black poplar *(Populus* x *euramericana)*
Black poplar *(Populus nigra)*

7.1.5 SEED

It is possible to establish trees, in the situations where they are to grow finally, by seed. It is however not a completely reliable method. Seeds may be eaten by predators before they germinate. Germination and establishment may be upset by drought. It is of course not possible to ensure a regular spacing; the seedlings will come up at random. It is most appropriate for informal naturalistic schemes where a random mixture of species is wanted, for instance on a roadside. A mixture of native species which includes colonist trees, such as birch, and colonist shrubs, such as gorse, as well as structural species, is likely to be the most effective.

7.2   *Root treatment*

For simplicity and economy most material is supplied **bare-root**. This applies to material as large as standards as well as to normal transplants. It makes handling easier and allows a large root system to be provided, if done properly. However it leaves the roots exposed and vulnerable to desiccation. The considerable problems this can cause are discussed in the next section.

An alternative is that the stock is supplied **root-balled**. This method is applied particularly to standards, but it can equally well be used on whips. The tree is lifted in the nursery with a substantial mass of soil remaining on the roots. The roots and the soil mass are immediately wrapped up carefully, usually using hessian, to form a substantial ball. For a standard the ball is about 1 m in diameter; with a heavy standard it may be as much as 2 m, with the ball now in the shape of a flattened hemisphere.

This technique is expensive (the price of equivalent material is likely to be doubled) but it gives much better protection of the roots. It is almost universally used in the USA because of the aridity of the climate, which is likely to cause root damage while trees are being moved. Carried out with care, and with good preparation of the tree beforehand, it allows trees to be moved even in leaf (Figure 7.4). It can cut down transplanting losses from 25% to less than 5% for species like oaks which are difficult to transplant as standards. It is particularly valuable for evergreen conifers, which continue to transpire water even in winter and therefore require the maintenance of a functioning root system through the planting operation. It does not, however, increase the total rooting volume and therefore the water immediately available to the tree (Chapter 10). It is crucial therefore that such stock is given normal watering during and after planting.

The final alternative is that the stock is **container-grown** or **cell-grown**. Seedlings and transplants can be grown in small tubes or paper pots. Larger plants can be grown in correspondingly larger-sized containers. It is unlikely that larger material will have spent all its life in the container; it has probably spent only the last 1 or 2 years. At first sight, apart from the extra expense (about 2 times, but small cell-grown material only 1.5 times) and greater problems of handling, it would appear to be a valuable technique. It has certainly revolutionized the garden centre business, because it allows plants to be sold at any time during the year.

However, experience indicates that it should not be preferred for normal planting. Although the container protects the roots, it constrains them, and may

Figure 7.4
Tree planting in Chicago, USA.
Root–balling gives greater
protection to root systems in dry
spells of weather and allows
trees to be moved in leaf.

cause them to become pot bound and permanently distorted; they can even form a complete circle. The result is that the plant does not develop as good a root system as bare-rooted material. In the field it will not be in contact with any greater volume of soil than a bare-root plant. Planting trials have shown no advantage, but it does allow special plantings to take place late in the season or even in summer. This material will, however, require careful watering, just as if it was standing out in its container.

Cell-grown material is rather different, because the plants are always very small and the roots have not been allowed to become distorted. Experience suggests that this material can perform better than bare-root seedlings or transplants because the roots are better protected during transplanting.

7.3   *Quality of stock*

As with all other materials, the quality can vary enormously. It is obviously important to purchase stock which has a satisfactory shape. With standards there is a tendency for growers to raise stock in the nursery at too close spacings. This leads to elongated spindly material quite unsuitable for planting out.

Such material can easily be recognized. The unfortunate fact, however, is that because trees are living, tree stock can be upset and degraded not only much

Figure 7.5
Typical symptoms of poor stock
quality in newly planted
sycamores. When trees grow
badly despite being well planted
the quality of the stock should be
suspected.

more easily than inanimate material, but also in ways that may not be at all apparent at the time of purchase. Tree stock can vary from being completely alive and capable of vigorous growth, to being nearly dead (Figure 7.5). This was first made clear by work in the 1970s by the Forestry Commission, which showed that a common cause of poor performance was the way material was treated between the time of lifting in the nursery and its being planted on site. This aroused a great deal of interest; but unfortunately it appears from a survey published 8 years later (Figure 7.6) that little has changed in the quality of material that may be delivered. It is possible to receive material that is completely dead, or nearly so. It is well known that birch is rather sensitive to transplanting, but it is significant that some nurseries in this survey were able to deliver material showing excellent survival. It is equally interesting that, although on the whole the survival of beech was good, one nursery delivered material which showed over 40% mortality.

The die-back and subsequent growth of the material in this trial were similarly very variable, but were not closely related to mortality. The contribution of intrinsic factors to the performance of stock is therefore very complicated. The clear fact remains that stock quality can vary between very wide limits, and that sound planting schemes can be ruined by bad stock.

Part of these differences in performance may be due to the conditions under

Figure 7.6
A comparison of the first year's growth of birch and beech whips supplied by 12 different nurseries (50 trees in each sample) (redrawn from Kendle *et al.*, 1988). The possibility of receiving poor stock is quite high.

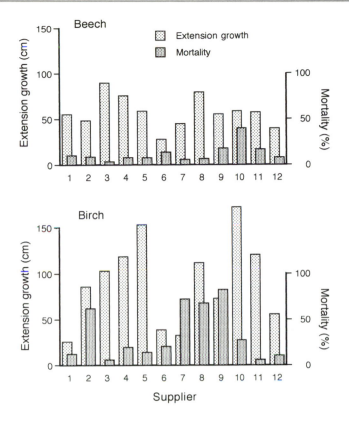

which the stock was raised rather than to subsequent handling. Stock raised under poor conditions, without fertilizer, watering or weed control, can show very poor recovery after transplanting, measured in terms of survival and extension growth, compared with otherwise similar material raised in good conditions (Figure 7.7).

At the same time there is good evidence, for example that given in Figure 7.8, to suggest that a very important factor is the exposure of the tree root system to

Figure 7.7
The effects of good and bad nursery conditions (water, fertilizer, weed control) on the performance of otherwise similar stock in the year after transplanting (Dutton, 1991). The conditions under which stock is raised in the nursery are important.

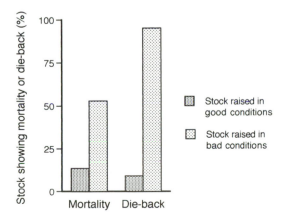

Figure 7.8
The relationship between moisture content at planting and the survival of seedlings of three different species (redrawn from Insley, 1980). Differences in survival of nursery stock can be due to their having been allowed to dry up.

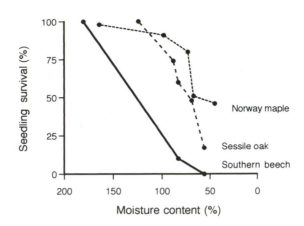

desiccation. This can occur during lifting, storage or planting, and will be affected by the particular way in which the tree is treated. Experience suggests that a short period of rapid desiccation is not as troublesome as a longer period of more gentle desiccation during which time the whole tree loses moisture. A standard storage shed or cold store can therefore be extremely debilitating, unless steps are taken to prevent water loss. Enclosure in a plastic bag, because it prevents water loss (Figure 7.9), can overcome the problem completely (Figure 7.10). These results also show that different species are markedly different in their sensitivity. Birch and rowan are fairly typical of the extremes to be expected. The sensitivity of birch is probably related to its high proportion of fine roots which can dry out rapidly.

The material should obviously remain in its bag during transport. But it should also remain there until the moment of planting out. To prevent over-heating, plastic bags which are white on the outside are now available commercially.

Figure 7.9
Changes in moisture content over time in birch seedlings subject to different amounts of protection (redrawn from Insley, 1979). Moisture loss in nursery stock can be greatly reduced by enclosure of the stock in a plastic bag.

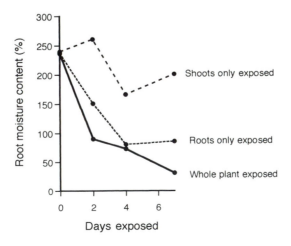

Figure 7.10
The survival of birch and rowan subjected to different storage treatments before planting (redrawn from Dutton and Bradshaw, 1982) 0, Lifted and immediately replanted; 1, lifted and kept in store for 1 day before replanting; 7, lifted and kept in store for 7 days before replanting; 7P, lifted and kept in store with roots in polythene bag for 7 days before replanting. Survival after planting is very dependent on careful handling, especially in sensitive species such as birch.

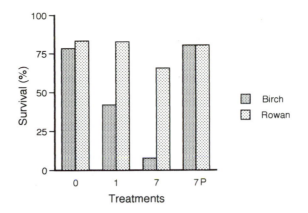

Hessian and many other traditional wrapping materials are very permeable to water. Trees wrapped in these materials, although they appear protected, may suffer almost as much desiccation as those which are not covered at all.

Are there many ways in which good stock can be recognized, bearing in mind that stock may be delivered thoroughly wrapped, but have been through the hands of a previous supplier who was not so careful? Although experiments show that percentage water content is a guide to the likely survival of stock, it makes no allowances for the possibility that, in practice, re-wetting may have occurred after a debilitating period of desiccation. Other investigations have been carried out to see if there is any correlation with measurable morphological characters. Amongst a single batch of the same origin there can be a correlation between size and success. It is not unexpected that the small, weedy, plants in a sample are likely to do worst. But from this it must not be extrapolated that the bigger the plant the better – bigger plants are more likely to suffer post-planting stress.

There is some indication that performance may also be related to higher root:shoot ratios, but this effect is not clear within a set of rather similar material. However, from what is discussed in Chapter 10, it seems that stock with an extensive root system, so long as it has not been damaged, is likely to survive post-planting stresses and establish better. There is evidence from fruit trees (which are close relatives of several popular amenity trees) that a tree that has been well grown in the nursery, with a good store of carbohydrates and mineral nutrients, is more likely to grow better after planting. Such trees are likely to be able to re-establish their root systems more quickly. But little is known about this for most amenity trees. Although a very poorly grown and stunted tree may appear to some people to have been 'well hardened', it is much more likely just to be weak, and capable of only limited new growth.

Since the root system is so important, it is important to preserve as much of it as possible in transplanting. Material which has been allow to root undisturbed for several years in the nursery will be difficult to lift without substantial loss of the absorbtive part of the root system. Some species, such as *Malus* and *Sorbus*, can regenerate their root system without great difficulty. But for most species the loss is serious. It is normal practice for the tree to be moved in the nursery,

which encourages the development of a short branching root system Transplants get their name from this practice. A typical transplant is a 2 year-old which was moved at the end of its first year, referred to as a 1+1. If stock is not moved, careful steps have to be taken to undercut the tree, both at the side and underneath, once or twice while it is in the nursery. The last time should be a year before lifting. This can be of value even for large transplants and whips.

The end-product should be a stumpy root system with an abundance of short roots (Figure 7.11). The larger the tree being prepared, the more important is this process. Done well, it allows heavy standards to be prepared which will establish with little trouble. The root system may be sufficiently large and coherent for the tree to be supported only with underground moorings (Chapter 11). Certain firms specialize in the preparation of such trees.

Trees have not usually lost their leaves before the beginning of November. This restricts the opportunity for suppliers to provide trees before bad winter weather sets in. In order to overcome this it is now common practice to use a defoliant such as potassium iodide. This technique is acceptable, providing it is not over-exploited. If spraying is carried out too early, physiological damage in the form of bud death and shoot die-back, and serious inhibition of root growth, can occur.

There are, therefore, many causes of poor stock quality. Unfortunately, there is no good guide available to the quality of stock except its physical appearance and its actual performance. Some sort of rapid non-destructive biological test is still awaited. This suggests that for a large scheme, a sample of trees should be planted out under optimal conditions in a nursery as a quality control. They need not be wasted; they can be used in subsequent years.

Another solution is to buy from a supplier with a good reputation, inspect the material while it is growing in the nursery, discuss with the supplier how it has been treated, how and when the material will be lifted, how it will be stored, and

Table 7.4 *Points to be checked to ensure planting stock is of high quality*

1. Original site where trees were raised should be known.
2. Growing conditions at this site should be good.
3. If trees have been bought in and replanted, or grown on to reach a larger size, growing conditions must again be good, and trees should have had time to re-establish vigorous growth.
4. If trees have remained in same nursery for some time, they should have been transplanted or undercut to ensure good root system on lifting.
5. Trees should be lifted as late as possible before delivery, so that storage time is minimized.
6. If bare-root trees have to be stored at any time after lifting, conditions should be cool and non-drying, and the whole tree or at least its roots should be enclosed in plastic bag.
7. Root-balled trees must be watered regularly to ensure that the root-ball is always damp.
8. Trees, or at least their root systems, must be kept in bags, which must be tightly sealed, during transport to customer.
9. If bare-root trees have to be held after delivery for more than 10 days before planting, they should be carefully heeled in, with bundles undone and roots completely covered with moist soil. Root-balled material must be kept moist.
10. Trees must be transferred to planting site in plastic bags, and kept in them until moment of planting.

how it will be transported. All this can be included in the specification for supply and delivery. The recommended HTA (1992) *Standard Form* of *Tender for the Supply and Delivery of Plants* is excellent and should be used, but it cannot cover all the detail that a careful purchaser may wish for. In any large scheme at least one visit to the supplier at the time of lifting is crucial and commonsense. If material provided by a supplier has been bought in, it is imperative to know how it was handled by the original producer. The points to look out for in handling, which are most likely to give stock with a good and reliable performance, are given in Table 7.4.

References

Dutton, R.A. (1991) An analysis of the critical stages in tree establishment, PhD thesis, University of Liverpool.

Dutton, R.A. and Bradshaw, A.D. (1982) *Land Reclamation in Cities*, HMSO, London.

Horticultural Trades Association (1992) *Standard Form of Tender for the Supply and Delivery of Plants*, 7th edn, HTA, 19 High Street, Theale, Reading.

Insley, H. (1979) Damage to broad-leaved trees by desiccation. Arboriculture Research Note **8:79**, Arboricultural Advisory and Information Service, Farnham, Surrey.

Insley, H. (1980) Wasting trees? – the effects of handling and post-planting maintenance on the survival and growth of amenity trees. *Arboricultural Journal*, **4**, 65–73

Kendle, A.D. (1988) The optimisation of tree growth on china clay waste, PhD thesis, University of Liverpool.

Kendle, A.D., Gilbertson, P. and Bradshaw, A.D. (1988) The influence of stock source on transplant performance. *Arboricultural Journal,* **12**, 257–72.

Other reading

Atkinson, D. and Asamoah, T.E.O. (1987) The growth of the nursery tree root system and its influence on tree performance after transplanting, in *Advances in Practical Arboriculture* (ed. D. Patch), Forestry Commission Bulletin **65**, HMSO, London, pp. 32–7.

British Standards Institution (1984) *British Standard 3936 Nursery Stock Pt 4 – Forest Trees,* British Standards Institution, London.

British Standards Institution (1992) *British Standard 3936 Nursery Stock Pt 1 – Trees and Shrubs,* British Standards Institution, London.

Committee on Plant Supply and Establishment (1985) *Plant Handling,* Horticultural Trades Association, London.

Das, A. (1992) Containerised versus bare-rooted oak seedlings. *Arboricultural Journal,* **16,** 343–8.

Putwain, P.D., Evans, B.E. and Kerry, S. (1987) Creation of woodland by direct seeding with herbicide management. *1987 British Crop Protection Conference – Weeds*, pp. 639–46.

White, J.E.J. and Patch, D. (1990) *Propagation of lowland willows by winter cuttings.* Arboriculture Research Note **85:90**, Arboricultural Advisory and Information Service, Farnham, Surrey.

8 *Choice of species*

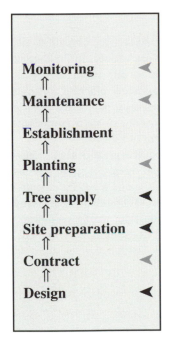

Monitoring ◄
⇑
Maintenance ◄
⇑
Establishment
⇑
Planting ◄
⇑
Tree supply ◄
⇑
Site preparation ◄
⇑
Contract ◄
⇑
Design ◄

- There is a wide choice of species available; the problem is to make best use of it.
- It is imperative to choose species which will grow with reliability.
- The first step is to decide whether to choose native or alien species.
- In general native species are more reliable, fit best into the landscape and support existing wild populations, but there are valuable aliens.
- From the point of view of design and use, species can be divided into four functional groups, distinguished by their contribution to the landscape, rapidity of growth and longevity:
    1. structural species,
    2. filler species,
    3. edge species,
    4. pioneer species.
- Pioneer species have an important role in providing rapid growth in initially difficult conditions.
- Varieties and clones provide an important extra range of variation, in important characteristics such as growth habit and disease resistance.
- The ecological adaptation of individual species to particular environmental conditions should be realized and made use of.
- When groups and large blocks are being planted, species can be used on their own, but it is normally better if they are combined into ecological associations to provide mutual support and maximum effect.
- To make best use of the range of material available, although there are good descriptions, there is ultimately no effective substitute for personal observation and experience.

One of the most remarkable feature of trees in urban areas is the wide choice of species available. Leading nurseries list as many as 1000 species and distinct cultivars. By comparison, forestry in Britain utilizes about 20 species. This richness has been brought about by the patient efforts of countless plant collectors who have scoured the climatically appropriate parts of the world over the last 200 years for suitable species, and nurserymen who have found variants and made new hybrids.

The result is an almost daunting choice – size, growth rate, overall shape, branching pattern, leaf shape, colour, ecology, in endless variety. In the face of this, what is anyone planning a planting programme to do? From surveys it appears that, usually, people are rather unadventurous; many planting schemes rely on very few species (Figure 8.1), although when surveys include the trees in private gardens the range is better. This could be wisdom or narrow-mindedness. We need to find a path through this embarrassment of riches.

All through this book the need for success is stressed. If a great deal of money is spent on a scheme, and it then fails, not only is the money wasted, but the scheme, while it is still alive but half dead, can actually make a negative contribution to the landscape and to the urban environment. Techniques of planting and aftercare are the major contribution to success. But if the wrong species are chosen at the outset, then failure is built in, even if it does not appear immediately. A number of criteria are therefore necessary, which can be used to maximize success and minimize failure.

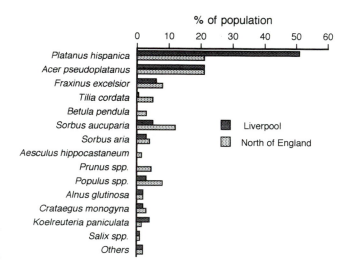

Figure 8.1
The species planted over a 5-year period in the north of England and in Liverpool: reliance is often placed on rather few species (redrawn from Gilbertson and Bradshaw, 1985).

8.1 *General vigour*

Over the years the nursery trade has worked over the material available, and given up material which is obviously unsuitable to our conditions. But its catalogues, to satisfy the demands of gardeners, contain many species which have been chosen for their particular beauty, even though they may be difficult to grow. So the first step is to choose those species that can be relied upon to grow without trouble. The species that are listed in this chapter are therefore those known to possess the general vigour and reliability which make them good candidates for urban planting schemes (Figure 8.2). This is a criterion that should always be uppermost when choices of species are being made.

Figure 8.2
Common white willow (*Salix alba*) is a good example of a reliable, fast-growing tree for urban areas, but it must be backed up by longer lasting species.

8.2   *Deciduous or evergreen?*

Most trees in our landscape are deciduous: they shed their leaves every winter, leaving behind their bare twigs. This has the advantage that it allows more light to penetrate in darker winter days. It also provides a complete change of scenery. In contrast evergreens provide protection and screening all the year round, but at the expense of winter light, and giving a somewhat monotonous uniformity. However they can make splendid specimens (Figure 8.3).

In situations where protection is important, especially from wind, but also from noise, evergreens are valuable. They are valuable as a visual screen, but because of the vigour of many of the species chosen, many people have come to regret evergreens such as Lawson's and Leyland's cypresses, which early on may have seemed such a good idea. Controlling the growth of these species can become an almost impossible task.

Because evergreens retain their leaves over the winter they can provide valuable control of winter air pollutants such as SO_2. But it is just this character which makes them particularly sensitive to air pollutants. In the past when air pollution levels were high, above 500 µg SO_2 m^{-3}, evergreens were unable to grow in the centres of towns. With lower levels of pollution, now down to less than 50 µg SO_2 m^{-3}, they can be used more widely. But there is another character which is a problem – they are very susceptible to vandalism – not only because they are attractive as Christmas trees, but also because they are poor at recovering from physical damage.

Figure 8.3
Conifers can make splendid specimen trees, but often their dense shade and vulnerability to damage make them unsuitable for housing areas.

8.3   *Native or alien?*

The easiest way of ensuring that a species is likely to do well in a planting scheme is for it to be a species native to Britain. This is a sensible approach since such species have certainly proved their adaptedness by their long presence here. It also meets the concern of many people that we should be helping to maintain our native woodland species, which are suffering a continuous process of attrition in the face of modern developments in our landscape. A strong argument can also be made from the point of design. Native species belong to and harmonize with our existing landscapes, whereas aliens do not.

Because of historical accident, however, particularly because the great ice sheets of the recent Ice Ages removed almost all species, our native flora is very restricted by comparison with similar areas elsewhere, even with the rest of Europe. If we go back in geological history all sorts of species once grew in Britain which do not grow here now, and do not grow anywhere in Europe. So if we restrict our choice to native species, we will miss species which could be very valuable to us. At the same time, some of our native species are adapted to such specialized natural conditions that they are unsuitable for towns.

8.4   *Major types of native species*

Nevertheless, native species are a very good starting point. There are over 30 of them which can and should be used in urban planting schemes (Table 8.1). In nature they do not occur at random but have particular ecological preferences, especially in relation to soil and shade tolerance. Excellent descriptions of their individual characteristics are available. The major feature which differentiates many of them, however, is the ultimate size to which they will grow. In nature this determines to a great extent whether or not they will end up as **dominant** trees in mixed woodland associations. Good examples of dominants are oak and beech. These are the species that provide the main framework of the landscape. In landscaping schemes they are the **structural** species, which are by far the most important species in any design, a fact well understood by the great landscape architects of the past.

The other species that occur in woodlands are usually called **secondary** species. They can occur with the dominants in natural woodlands, often forming an understorey, being shade-tolerant. Good examples are cherry and hazel. In landscaping they are often loosely termed **filler** species. In a natural woodland whether a species is dominant or secondary may vary from one site to another so that the categories are not absolute.

A different group are the **marginal** species. These are not shade-tolerant, and are usually to be found on the margins of woodlands or in gaps. Good examples are rowan and hawthorn. In landscaping these are often called **edge** species. Most of these species are relatively small and have attractive foliage and flowers. From a landscape point of view the filler and edge species have an

Table 8.1 *Native tree species suitable for urban areas, divided into major landscape ecological groups*

Structural species (dominants in natural woodland)

Silver birch *(Betula pendula)*: graceful, tall, light penetrates well through canopy; must be transplanted with care; grows well on poor soils, but not very long-lived.

Beech *(Fagus sylvatica):* ultimately tall and very spreading, casting a deep shade, smooth grey trunk; only easy to transplant when young, but grows fast; tolerant of wide range of soils, long-lived, but must have room for surface roots; several ornamental cultivars.

Ash *(Fraxinus excelsior)*: tall, with very open canopy so casts only light shade; easy to transplant, grows fast; tolerant of wide range of conditions, especially dry.

Scots pine *(Pinus sylvestris)*: evergreen, vulnerable to damage, ultimately develops picturesque habit and red trunk; only easy to transplant as a young transplant; best on acid soils and in groups.

Common oak *(Quercus robur)*: majestic, tall, spreading in open conditions; can only be transplanted as transplant or whip; best on good soils, very long-lived.

Sessile oak *(Quercus petraea)*: tall, not very spreading; must be transplanted when very young; particularly adapted to acid soils, very long-lived.

Large-leaved lime *(Tilia platyphyllos)*: tall with spreading branches; easy to transplant; tolerant of a wide range of conditions although best in fertile soils, long-lived.

Filler species (secondary in natural woodland)

Field maple *(Acer campestre)*: small to medium tree, pretty leaves and bushy growth; very easy to establish; tolerant of wide range of soils, excellent in mixtures.

Hornbeam *(Carpinus betulus)*: picturesque medium-sized spreading tree unless pruned, fluted grey trunk; very easy to transplant; tolerant of wide range of soils and shade.

Hazel *(Corylus avellana):* large spreading bush; easy to transplant; prefers fertile soil, but excellent in shade and in mixtures with other species.

Holly *(Ilex aquifolium)*: evergreen shrub or small tree, spiny leaves; transplant when small; very tolerant of shade and poor soils; many cultivars.

Wild cherry *(Prunus avium)*: tall, very open, spreading canopy, beautiful hanging white flowers in spring, good autumn colouring; easy to transplant, fast growing; tolerant of woodland conditions but requires fertile soils.

Bird-cherry *(Prunus padus)*: small tree or shrub, white flowers in spikes; easy to establish; tolerant, but prefers fertile soils.

Whitebeam *(Sorbus aria)*: small rounded tree, white flowers and large red fruits; very easy to establish, but can blow over later if badly planted; reliable on wide range of soils, especially calcareous; wind-resistant; many cultivars.

Small-leaved lime *(Tilia cordata)*: medium-sized, rounded canopy, leaves pale green beneath; easy to transplant; tolerant of shade, prefers fertile alkaline soils.

Guelder rose *(Viburnum opulus)*: large bush, leaves orange or red in autumn, clusters of red fruit; easy to transplant; tolerant of shade and wet, preferably calcareous, soils.

Edge species (margins and clearings in natural woodland)

Hawthorn *(Crataegus monogyna)*: very tough spiny shrub or small ornamental tree, profusion of white flowers in spring and red berries in autumn; best transplanted when small or may be unstable later; excellent as protective matrix; several cultivars.

Crab apple *(Malus sylvestris)*: decorative small tree bearing small apples in autumn; transplants with ease; good in mixtures; parent of many cultivars.

Blackthorn *(Prunus spinosa)*: very tough spiny shrub, white flowers in spring and purple fruits in autumn; transplant when small; excellent protective matrix for structural species.

Mountain ash *(Sorbus aucuparia)*: decorative small erect tree, pretty foliage, white flowers and clusters of red fruit; very easy to transplant, but will blow over later if not well planted; tolerant of extreme and poor soils, good alone or in mixtures; many cultivars.

Yew *(Taxus baccata)*: evergreen bush or small spreading tree; transplant when small; very long-lived, usually associated with churchyards, but valuable as a feature; erect cultivar.

Gorse *(Ulex europaeus)*: evergreen spiny shrub; transplant when small; N-fixer, excellent on very poor soil and to form short-lived matrix into which other species can be planted.

Wayfaring tree *(Viburnum lantana)*: small rounded tree, with round soft leaves and masses of white flowers giving red-black fruits; easy to transplant; tolerant of dry calcareous soils.

Pioneer species

Alder *(Alnus glutinosa)*: large, spreading tree with dark green leaves; transplants easily and has fast early growth; N-fixer, so excellent on poor soils, but prefers damp situations.

Alder buckthorn *(Hippophae rhamnoides)*: grey spiny bush with bright orange berries in autumn; establishes best when young, vigorous; N-fixer, very successful on dry sandy soils in maritime conditions.

Grey poplar *(Populus canescens)*: medium to large tree, with attractive grey trunk, tends to sucker; easy to establish, vigorous; tolerant of wide range of soils and of maritime conditions.

Black poplar *(Populus nigra)*: large, heavily branched tree; very easy to transplant, very vigorous; tolerant of wide range of urban conditions; several cultivars, of which the columnar Lombardy poplar is the the best known.

Aspen *(Populus tremula)*: medium tree with trembling leaves, suckers freely to form thickets; easy to establish, fast-growing; tolerant of wide range of soils.

White willow *(Salix alba)*: elegant, tall tree with attractive grey leaves; very easy to establish, very fast-growing; tolerant of very wide range of conditions, but best with adequate moisture; several cultivars and hybrids.

Crack willow *(Salix fragilis)*: tall spreading tree, which tends to shed twigs; very easy to establish, fast-growing; best in wet places, especially sides of ponds and rivers.

Goat willow *(Salix caprea)*: large shrub or small tree; easy to establish; tolerant of a wide range of poor soils and extreme conditions.

Sallow *(Salix cinerea)*: large shrub or small tree; very easy to establish, grows rapidly; tolerant of wide range of soils especially poor ones.

Osier *(Salix viminalis)*: large shrub consisting of many shoots without a main stem; extremely easy to establish, grows rapidly; prefers fertile damp soils but very tolerant; many hybrid cultivars.

Elder *(Sambucus nigra)*: large tree-like shrub, attractive flowers and berries; very easy to transplant; a natural colonist of poor soils and waste places.

important role as **decorative** species, to be fitted in with the structural species to form the whole design. But some of them may be chosen to act as structural species in situations where the normal structural species would be too large.

A further distinctive group is those species which can grow very large, but in nature are not dominants because they are relatively short-lived. Good examples are willow and poplar. They tend to be species that act as **pioneers**, early colonists, in natural successions, subsequently replaced by longer-lasting species. Some of these species, such as sallow and osier, do not attain a large size, but do grow rapidly. All these pioneers are immensely valuable in landscape schemes because they can create major effects quickly. They can act as short-term structural species, but they will have to be removed after 20 years

Figure 8.4
Common alder is a valuable species for planting on nitrogen-deficient soils. These trees planted on a poor soil are only 4 years old.

or so, leaving long-term structural species, which should have been planted with them, to take over.

Finally there is the special group of species, discussed further in Chapter 11, which are **nitrogen-fixers**, because they possess bacteria or other micro-organisms in nodules on their roots able to convert nitrogen from the air into nitrogen-containing compounds that the plant can use. These species have a special role in urban planting, because of their ability to grow independently of soil nitrogen supply and to contribute nitrogen to other trees growing with them. Some are shrubs, such as gorse and sea buckthorn, but some are large trees, such as alder (Figure 8.4). Although nitrogen-fixing tree species native to Britain are uncommon, on a world scale there are many. They are very important because of their ability to grow on poor, degraded soils.

8.5   *Alien species*

There has been an almost continuous process of introduction of species into Britain. Some species have proved to be unreliable. However, over 70 have proved their worth and almost half of these were introduced before 1600. A good example is the sycamore, *Acer pseudoplatanus,* a fast grower and an excellent species for exposed sites. Alien species suitable for urban conditions in Britain can be divided into major groups in the same way as native species, except that it is more difficult to separate secondary from edge species. These two groups have, therefore, been lumped together as decorative species (Table 8.2). Alien species come from a very wide range of geographical regions of the world. While the ability of the species listed to grow successfully in Britain has

Table 8.2   *Alien species suitable for urban areas divided into major landscape groups*

Structural species

Sycamore *(Acer pseudoplatanus)*: ugly when young but matures into a stately spreading tree; very vigorous, easy to transplant; extremely tolerant of wind exposure, tolerant of wide range of soils especially calcareous (long established so nearly a native).

Red maple *(Acer rubrum)*: tall tree with leaves turning red in autumn; transplants easily; wide tolerance but prefers moist soils.

Silver maple *(Acer saccharinum)*: large erect tree, leaves turning red in autumn; transplants easily, fast-growing; wide tolerance, excellent in streets.

Norway maple *(Acer platanoides)*: medium-sized spreading tree, attractive yellowish flowers in spring; easy to transplant, vigorous; wide tolerance; several cultivars.

Horse chestnut *(Aesculus hippocastaneum)*: ultimately a tall tree, renowned for its spikes of white flowers and conker fruits; transplants easily, vigorous; wide tolerance.

Tree of heaven *(Ailanthus altissima)*: large tree similar to ash, casting only light shade; easy to transplant, fast-growing; wide tolerance especially of urban pollution.

Sweet chestnut *(Castanea sativa)*: large handsome tree with edible fruit; easy to transplant; best on acid soils.

Lawson's cypress *(Chamaecyparis lawsoniana)*: very tall, fast-growing conifer; transplant when small; excellent on poor soils and where exposure to wind.

Leyland's cypress *(x Cupressocyparis leylandii)*: tall, fast-growing conifer; transplant when small; excellent on wide range of soils and where exposure to wind.

American ash *(Fraxinus americana)*: tall tree with open canopy; easy to transplant, rapid growth; wide soil tolerance.

Maiden hair tree *(Ginkgo biloba)*: stiff medium-sized ancient conifer with fan-shaped leaves; transplant with care; tolerant of wide range of urban conditions especially air pollution, long-lived.

Walnut *(Juglans regia)*: eventually a grand broad-crowned large tree bearing nuts; transplant with care; best on good soils, where long-lived.

European larch *(Larix decidua)*: one of the few deciduous conifers, tall, delicate foliage; transplant as young transplant, very vigorous; tolerant of poor, especially acid, but not wet, soils, best in groups.

Norway spruce *(Picea abies)*: elegant conifer best known as Christmas tree; transplant when young; tolerant of poor soils.

Serbian spruce *(Picea omorika)*: tall elegant slender conifer; transplant as young transplant, vigorous; tolerant of wide range of drier soils and of exposure.

Austrian pine *(Pinus nigra)*: dense-headed medium-sized conifer; transplant as young transplant, vigorous; tolerant of maritime exposure, best in groups.

London plane *(Platanus x acerifolia)*: well-known, often very large, urban tree with flaking bark; very easy to transplant, very vigorous; very tolerant of urban conditions but best on fertile soils, long-lived.

Turkey oak *(Quercus cerris)*: large broad-headed tree; transplant only when small, fast-growing; tolerant of wide range of soils especially calcareous, and of maritime exposure, long-lived.

Scarlet oak *(Quercus coccinea)*: large decorative tree with scarlet leaves in autumn; best transplanted when young; prefers better soils, long-lived.

Holm oak *(Quercus ilex)*: magnificent, large evergreen tree with round head; transplant when small, vigorous when established; tolerates maritime exposure and wide range of soils so long as well drained, very long-lived.

Red oak *(Quercus rubra)*: very large tree, splendid autumn coloration; transplant only when young, but very vigorous; excellent on neutral and acid soils, long-lived.

Wellingtonia *(Sequoiadendron giganteum)*: majestic very tall conifer, very large tapering trunk; transplant when young, vigorous; tolerant of poor acid soils and exposure, best as single tree.

Table 8.2 cont.

Common lime *(Tilia X vulgaris)*: tall, majestic when mature, tends to shoot from base; vigorous, easy to transplant; tolerant of wide range of conditions, especially urban, but best on fertile soils, long-lived, frequently infested with aphids causing honeydew (may be native natural hybrid).

White cedar *(Thuja occidentalis)*: medium-sized columnar evergreen conifer; transplant only when young; makes a good screen, but can be planted singly; many cultivars.

Western red cedar *(Thuja plicata)*: large ornamental conifer with spreading branches; transplant only when young, vigorous; tolerant of wide range of conditions; many cultivars.

Western hemlock *(Tsuga heterophylla)*: elegant tall conifer; transplant when young; tolerant of shade and wide range of soils but best where moisture, single or groups.

Decorative species

Red horse chestnut *(Aesculus X carnea)*: medium-sized round-headed tree with red flowers and no conkers; easy to transplant; wide tolerance but best on fertile soil, good in streets.

Himalayan silver birch *(Betula jacquemontii)*: small tree with dazzling white bark; transplant with care; wide tolerance.

Paper birch *(Betula papyrifera)*: medium-sized tree with peeling bark; transplant with care; wide tolerance.

Cockspur thorn *(Crataegus crus-galli)*: spiny shrub or small tree with abundant flowers and red fruit; transplant when young or may be unstable later; wide tolerance to soils and exposure; several useful cultivars and hybrids.

Griselinia *(Griselinia littoralis)*: large evergreen shrub, with leathery leaves; transplants easily; extremely tolerant of maritime exposure.

Crab apple *(Malus* species and hybrids*)*: a complex of different decorative small trees; very easy to transplant; tolerant of wide range of environments; many cultivars.

Flowering cherry *(Prunus* species and hybrids*)*: a wide range of ornamental trees; easy to transplant, quite vigorous; most are unhappy on infertile, wet or dry soils, not long-lived; very many cultivars.

Hupeh rowan *(Sorbus hupehensis)*: small decorative tree with pale pink fruits persisting through winter; very easy to transplant, robust; tolerant of wide range of soils.

Swedish whitebeam *(Sorbus intermedia)*: medium-sized round-headed decorative tree, reddish-brown fruits; transplants very easily; very tolerant of urban conditions and exposure.

Pioneer species

Grey alder *(Alnus incana)*: small tree, leaves grey underneath; easy to transplant, fast-growing when young; N-fixer, excellent on poor soils.

Italian alder *(Alnus cordata)*: small tree; easy to transplant; N-fixer, excellent on poor soils, but requires warm climate.

Buddleja *(Buddleja davidii)*: large shrub with purple flowers in conspicuous spikes; very easy to transplant, vigorous; especially tolerant of poor alkaline soils and wastes.

White poplar *(Populus alba)*: medium to large tree with pretty leaves white beneath, suckers freely and can form dense thickets; very easy to establish, fast-growing; tolerant of wide range of soils especially calcareous, excellent in exposed maritime conditions.

Hybrid black poplar *(Populus X euamericana)*: a complex of vegetatively propagated hybrids forming tall trees; very easy to transplant, very rapid growers; tolerate wide range of soils but best in damp fertile conditions, good wind breaks; different cultivars have own special characteristics.

False acacia *(Robinia pseudoacacia)*: medium-sized tree with delicate foliage; easy to transplant, vigorous; N-fixer so tolerant of very poor soils especially acid, not good in cold climates.

Violet willow *(Salix daphnoides)*: small tree with thin purple shoots; very easy to transplant, very-fast growing; especially tolerant of poor badly drained soils, excellent for rapid effects, wind-resistant.

been well established, it is never easy to be so certain of their long-term health under all British conditions, particularly in the colder and wetter parts of the country. There are also special problems such as the magnetic attraction of chestnut conkers which makes the species unsuitable on housing estates. Care should therefore be taken to establish the suitability of alien species for the particular area where they are to be planted.

8.6   *Varieties and clones*

There is a great deal of natural variation within species. This can take the form of differences between populations coming from different areas, or provenances, and is the result of natural selection. They are commonly described as **ecological races**. This type of material will usually be reproduced as seed.

However, useful variation also exists as differences between individuals: the natural variation which is present in all populations. This material has to be propagated vegetatively, by cuttings or by grafting on to more ordinary material, in order to maintain its characteristics. Such material will be genetically uniform and constitutes a **clone**. Despite their different origins and characteristics, both sorts are commonly referred to as **varieties**.

Some important planting material has been produced by hybridization between species. Two examples are the London plane, a hybrid between the Oriental plane and the American sycamore, and the common lime, a hybrid between the small-leaved and the broad-leaved lime. This sort of material will not breed true from seed and so has to be propagated vegetatively.

Lists of planting stock describe enormous numbers of different varieties for almost every species. Without detailed information it is difficult to know how valuable these different varieties are in particular species. Some represent important differences in growth qualities, others just trivial differences in flowers and fruit or other ornamental characteristics. An experienced supplier will be able to provide advice. There are also good catalogues. However, it is essential that the purchaser knows and is satisfied with the nature of the material chosen, because many specially named varieties are not as good in urban situations as the normal species.

One of the most important aspects of varietal variation is that conferring disease resistance. The origin may be naturally occurring variation, but it is more likely in the present day to be the result of careful work by the plant breeder. Since the advent of Dutch elm disease a great deal of work has been carried out to produce resistant material. The most successful are clones such as *Sapporo Autumn Gold* and *Regal,* produced by hybridization of sensitive species with the resistant Siberian elm, *Ulmus pumila,* and clones such as *Lobel, Dodoens* and *Plantijn* produced by hybridization of the common elm, *U. glabra,* with the Himalayan elm, *U. wallichiana.* With any such new material, developed for whatever purpose, it is most important to obtain up-to-date information about its performance. Earlier material may soon be outclassed by new. Some earlier clones of elm bred for resistance to elm disease proved eventually not to be resistant.

Figure 8.5
Good (left) and bad (right) clones of London plane. The poor clone has a very unattractive trunk but is easy to propagate.

Some commonly used hybrid material, particularly of London plane, which is propagated from cuttings, may come from a number of genetically different original individuals. There is nothing wrong with this except that the individual clones of London plane which are most easy to propagate are the least satisfactory as mature trees (Figure 8.5). At the same time the different clones differ considerably in their resistance to the disease anthracnose (Table 8.3). For any scheme where more than a few individuals of a species are being planted it is important to know not only the suitability of the species and the variety, but also the quality of the particular stock being provided.

A final problem for varietal material, especially if it is a clone propagated

Figure 8.6
A Swedish whitebeam (*Sorbus intermedia*) grafted on to a rowan (*Sorbus aucuparia*) which is producing innumerable shoots. This can be a serious problem when grafted material is used.

Table 8.3   *Crown die-back scores of different clones of London plane, caused by anthracnose. Important differences can occur between different individuals which become propagated widely by vegetative means (Burdekin, 1980)*

Location	Year	Clone type	
		3-lobed	5-lobed
The Mall	1970	1.1	0.7
	1979	0.8	0.4
Ladbroke Grove	1970	1.9	0.7
	1979	0.7	0.4
Victoria Embankment	1979	0.7	0.4
Overall mean		1.0	0.5

vegetatively, is that for simplicity of production the tree may be produced by grafting the special material onto a common seedling stock. Sometimes this works well. But sometimes the stock is more vigorous than the scion material above it, and produces a large number of vigorous but alien shoots that have to be removed constantly (Figure 8.6). Sometimes the graft is a source of weakness; sometimes it forms an ugly change in the characteristics of the trunk. It is necessary to buy varietal material that may be grafted with caution.

8.7   *Tolerance to special ecological conditions*

The species and varieties listed so far in this chapter are known to be satisfactory in urban conditions generally. There are, however, particular environmental conditions to which only certain species are well adapted. Some of these have already been discussed. The species suitable for the special urban environments most likely to be encountered are listed in Table 8.4. But there are also species with useful tolerances to other specific site conditions which cannot necessarily be removed by site modification. The use of the most tolerant species may prevent total failure occurring. Further details are readily available in any good flora or plant list and many special articles.

Table 8.4   *Tree species adapted to particular special environments found in urban areas. Long-term success in difficult conditions depends on choosing ecologically adapted species (* most tolerant)*

Extreme urban environments

Acer platanoides	*Populus nigra* *
Acer pseudoplatanus *	*Robinia pseudoacacia*
Aesculus x carnea	*Salix alba* *
Ailanthus altissima *	*Salix daphnoides*
Buddleja davidii *	*Salix viminalis* *
Crataegus monogyna *	*Sambucus nigra*
Fraxinus excelsior	*Sorbus aria*
Ginkgo biloba	*Sorbus aucuparia* *
Malus spp. and hybrids	*Sorbus hupehensis*
Platanus x acerifolia	*Sorbus intermedia*
Populus x euamericana	*Tilia x vulgaris* *

Maritime and exposed areas

Acer pseudoplatanus *	*Populus tremula*
Chamaecyparis lawsoniana	*Prunus spinosa* *
Crataegus monogyna	*Quercus cerris* *
*Cupressocyparis leylandii**	*Quercus ilex*
Griselinia littoralis *	*Quercus robur*
Hippophae rhamnoides *	*Salix* (most species)
Pinus nigra *	*Sorbus aria* *
Populus alba *	*Sorbus aucuparia*
Populus canescens *	

Table 8.4 cont.

Dry calcareous soils

Acer campestre   *Malus sylvestris*
Acer platanoides   *Malus* spp. and hybrids
Acer pseudoplatanus *   *Pinus nigra*
Buddleja davidii *   *Populus alba* *
Carpinus betulus   *Quercus cerris*
Crataegus monogyna *   *Sorbus aria* *
Fagus sylvatica *   *Sorbus intermedia* *
Fraxinus excelsior *

Acid soils

Alnus incana   *Populus canescens*
Betula pendula *   *Quercus petraea* *
*Betula pubescens**   *Quercus rubra*
Betula jacquemontii   *Robinia pseudoacacia* *
Betula papyrifera   *Salix caprea* *
Castanea sativa *   *Salix cinerea* *
Fagus sylvatica   *Sequoiadendron giganteum* *
Ilex aquifolium *   *Sorbus aucuparia* *
Larix decidua   *Sorbus hupehensis*
Picea abies   *Thuja plicata*
Pinus sylvestris *   *Tsuga heterophylla*
Populus alba   *Ulex europaeus* *

Salt-affected soils (Dobson, 1991)

(tolerant)   (moderately tolerant)
Gingko biloba   *Fraxinus angustifolia*
Populus alba   *Gleditsia triacanthos*
Populus canescens   *Quercus robur*
Pinus nigra   *Quercus rubra*
Quercus petraea   *Ailanthus altissima*
Robinia pseudoacacia   *Prunus avium*
Salix alba
Salix fragilis
Tilia tomentosa

Flooded soils (Bradshaw and Gill, 1990) **and anaerobic soils on landfill sites** (DoE, 1986)

Alnus glutinosa *   *Salix alba* *
Alnus incana *   *Salix caprea*
Betula pendula   *Salix cinerea* *
Betula pubescens   *Salix daphnoides*
Populus nigra   *Salix fragilis*
Populus x euamericana *   *Salix viminalis* *
Populus tremula

8.8   *Associations of species*

In nature different tree species commonly occur together, in recognizable associations. As a result there is a school of thought among landscape designers that such ecological associations should be created when new plantings are being planned, often called **naturalistic plantings** (Figure 8.7). In formal situations such mixtures may be difficult, but in modern less formal landscapes they are both possible and sensible. There are several good reasons for this.

Not many years ago our elms became infected by a completely unexpected virulent race of Dutch elm disease (*Ophiostoma ulmi*). As a result, where elms grew in pure stands whole landscapes were destroyed. Where elms were growing in mixtures, other species were left to take over. Although we hope such a catastrophe will not be repeated, it always remains a possibility (Chapter 15). So mixed stands are an insurance.

In difficult conditions, such as when trees are being planted on old industrial waste heaps or old mine workings, it may be difficult to know which species will do well. Under these circumstances a mixture is a sensible insurance against failure.

A mixture of species also provides protection. In particular the more bushy edge species, such as hawthorn, can provide a better environment and general protection for the structural species. In places where vandalism, whether conscious or accidental, is expected, the more spiny species are excellent (Chapters 12 and 16). Where there is extreme exposure, wind-tolerant shrubs, such as sea buckthorn, will help more sensitive species to become established.

In the early stages of a planting, structural species contribute very little. There is therefore good reason to include rapid-growing pioneer species to create an

Figure 8.7
A mixed planting of native species at Warrington New Town. Ecologically based associations of species can be reliable and attractive, and require little or no maintenance.

Figure 8.8
The effect, in a very poor site, of the proximity of alder on the growth of companion species which do not fix nitrogen. Those trees closest to the alder have shoot extensions of 65 cm, those furthest away extensions of only 1 cm (redrawn from Kendle and Bradshaw, 1992).

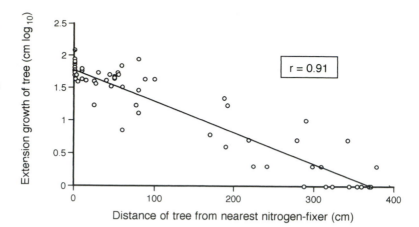

Table 8.5   *Examples of mixtures of species chosen to give maximum impact on the environment of urban areas. Short-and long-term success involves choosing species that complement one another*

For a good site

Fraxinus excelsior *Quercus robur* }	Structural species for long-term effect
Prunus avium *Corylus avellana* *Viburnum opulus* }	Filler species for decorative effect
Salix alba	Pioneer species for immediate effect – remove after 15 years

For a poor site

Fagus sylvatica	Structural species for long-term effect
Betula pendula	Structural species for medium-term effect
Sorbus aucuparia *Salix cinerea* }	Edge and pioneer species for immediate and decorative effect
Alnus glutinosa *Robinia pseudo-acacia* }	N-fixing pioneer species for rapid and soil fertility effect

For a site exposed to children and possible vandalism

Quercus rubra *Carpinus betulus* *Acer campestre* }	Structural and filler species for long-term effect
Crataegus monogyna *Prunus spinosa* }	Edge species for protection
Salix caprea *Salix viminalis* }	Pioneer species for immediate effect – but need not be removed. Extremely tolerant of vandalism
Alnus incana	N-fixing pioneer species and tolerant of vandalism

---

immediate impact. Many of them, such as *Salix caprea*, *S. cinerea* and *Populus canescens*, are able to grow particularly well on poor soils; they are species good at foraging for nutrients. Some important pioneers are nitrogen-fixing; they will be particularly valuable in supporting the growth of other species accompanying them in a mixture, as well as growing fast themselves (Figure 8.8) (see also Chapter 11).

Some examples of how mixtures can be made up are given in Table 8.5. There is no need to include more than about 10 species in total, otherwise the final product may have a rather confused character. Some of the finest mature woods in urban areas, as in the countryside, are dominated by just one species. When pioneer species are used in mixtures it is often considered that they be removed later. Except in the case of tall-growing species such as *Salix alba*, this is not always necessary; in informal plantings they can be left to disappear as the result of natural competition.

Usually it is sensible that such mixtures should be designed to copy natural mixtures of native species. In this way, communities will be created that are likely to be balanced and therefore to form a natural equilibrium. They are also most likely to be supportive of other wildlife, whether birds or small animals. Nevertheless there can be occasions when the nature of the site demands that aliens are introduced to help the developing community. An example is the use of nitrogen-fixing species such as *Robinia pseudoacacia* and *Alnus incana* in poor and exposed sites. In other situations aliens can be chosen for their particular all-round properties, such as *Quercus rubra* and *Acer pseudoplatanus*, with the expectation that they may ultimately dominate the planting.

8.9   Costs

There are only small differences in the cost of different species. These reflect the ease or difficulty with which the species can be raised. While most bare-root transplants or whips cost 0.02–0.05 tree units, a few species difficult or expensive to grow from either seed or cuttings, such as chestnut, beech, plane, blackthorn, oak and lime can cost 0.05–0.08 tree units. But this is still a very small sum. However, similar sized stock in containers is likely to cost 0.2–0.4 tree units.

Similarly, there are some species which, as standards, will cost more than 1 tree unit. Examples of these are hornbeam, beech and oak, which are not easy to raise to standard size. These are species which it is not advisable to transplant as standards. They will cost about 1.4 tree units. Uncommon species may cost more. There can also be variation in the prices offered by different nurseries; one nursery may have stock of a particular species which it is anxious to get rid of. But the purchaser should beware of buying poor stock (Chapter 7).

8.10   *No substitute for observation and experience*

In the end, to know which species and varieties are particularly suited for particular conditions, there is no substitute for experience. The best experience is acquired by carrying out actual planting schemes in different situations and then watching the subsequent performance of the different species involved. But it is also possible to learn from the performance of trees that other people have planted, whether in normal environments or where special conditions are operating. So every thoughtful arboriculturalist and landscape designer should spend time observing the performance of trees growing in city streets, parks and gardens, as well as in arboreta, in different parts of the country, paying special attention to trees in special conditions, whether these are paved streets, old mine workings or wind-swept boulevards (Figure 8.9). There are books to help the identification of unusual species and varieties.

The one problem of such tree watching is to be able to make proper allowance for effects which were the result of bad planting. The only real answer to this is to follow schemes from their beginning, or to talk to the people responsible to find out details of what went on. This will provide experience not only about the performance of species and varieties, but also about the effects of different treatments and maltreatments.

Figure 8.9
Successful trees such as this lime (*Tilia* x *europaea*) provide guidance for choice of species in similar areas.

References

Bradshaw, A.D. and Gill, C.J. (1990) The landscaping of reservoir margins, in *Landscape Design with Plants* (ed. B. Clouston), Heinemann Newnes, London, pp. 186–98.

Burdekin, D.A. (1980) Susceptibility of London plane clones to anthracnose, in *Research for Practical Arboriculture* (ed. D. Patch), Forestry Commission, Edinburgh, pp. 119–24.

Dobson, M.C. (1991) De-icing salt damage to trees and shrubs and its amelioration, in *Research for Practical Arboriculture* (ed. S.J. Hodge), Forestry Commission Bulletin **97**, HMSO, London, pp. 141–51.

Department of the Environment (1986) *Landfilling Wastes,* Waste Management Paper **26**, HMSO, London.

Gilbertson, P. and Bradshaw, A.D. (1985) Tree survival in cities: the extent and nature of the problem. *Arboricultural Journal,* **9**, 131–42.

Kendle, A.D. and Bradshaw, A.D. (1992) The role of soil nitrogen in the growth of trees on derelict land. *Arboricultural Journal,* **16,** 103–22.

Other reading

Beckett, K. and Beckett, G. (1979) *Planting Native Trees and Shrubs*, Jarrold, Norwich.

Building Materials Market Research (1994) *Plants and Landscape Materials Price Guide: The Green Book,* Building Materials Market Research, Brighton.

Burdekin, D.A. and Rushforth, K.D. (1988) Breeding elms resistant to Dutch elm disease. *Arboricultural Research Note* **2:88,** DoE Arboricultural Advisory and Information Service, Farnham, Surrey.

Clapham, A.R., Tutin ,T.G. and Moore, D.M. (1987) *Flora of the British Isles*, 3rd edn, Cambridge University Press, Cambridge.

Clouston, B. (1990) *Landscape Design with Plants,* Heinemann Newnes, London.

Hibberd, B.G. (ed.) (1989) *Urban Forestry Practice*, Forestry Commission Handbook **5**, HMSO, London.

Hillier (1978) *Hilliers' Manual of Trees and Shrubs*, Hillier Nurseries (Winchester), Romsey.

Ministry of Housing and Local Government (1967) *Trees in Town and City*, HMSO, London.

Phillips, R. (1978) *Trees in Britain*, Pan Books, London.

Ruff, A.R. and Tregay, R.J. (eds) (1982) *An Ecological Approach to Urban Design*, Department of Town and Country Planning, University of Manchester.

Tregay, R.J. and Moffatt, J.D. (1980) An ecological approach to landscape design and management in Oakwood, Warrington. *Landscape Design*, **134**, 33–6.

9

Planting techniques

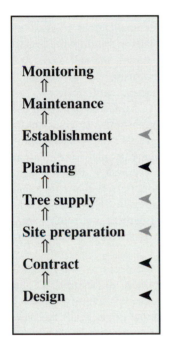

Monitoring
⇑
Maintenance
⇑
Establishment ◄
⇑
Planting ◄
⇑
Tree supply ◄
⇑
Site preparation ◄
⇑
Contract ◄
⇑
Design ◄

- The goal of successful planting is to allow trees to establish new root systems quickly so that they can exploit soil water and nutrient reserves and anchor themselves securely.
- Trees must be planted early enough to allow their root systems to become well established before leafing out.
- Their root systems must not be damaged by desiccation before and during the planting.
- Whatever the size of the trees the pits must be large enough for the roots to be spread out properly.
- Backfill can normally be the original material, but in difficult substrates this should be amended or replaced by high-quality material.
- The sides and bottom of the pits should be loosened to ensure hydraulic continuity and water movement into the pit soil from the surroundings.
- Pits must have adequate drainage, either natural or purpose built.
- Although root-balled or containerized material can be planted at almost any time, its continuous need for water must be met.
- Where trees are to be planted in purpose-built containers these must be large enough to maintain an adequate water supply in dry periods.
- Because of the damage to buildings on clay soils trees should not be planted closer to buildings than specific recommended distances unless the buildings have appropriate foundations.

There should be nothing more simple than planting a tree. Yet if any amenity planting in a town is examined, it is easy to see problems that have resulted from trees being planted badly – too deeply or too shallowly, or perhaps not planted upright. And far too often trees are planted much too late, well into April, so that they break into leaf before they have had a chance to develop any root system.

Each of the different types of tree stock requires a different method of planting, but the goal in each case remains the same. This is to allow the tree to establish a new root system quickly, by which it can exploit the soil water and nutrient reserves which it needs for growth and to anchor itself.

The tree's ability to exploit the soil reserves and become well anchored can be helped simply by using common sense. Firstly, the tree must be planted early enough to ensure that the root system has had an opportunity to re-establish before the tree breaks into leaf. Secondly it is imperative that the root system of the tree is not damaged in the transplanting process. Many people will think that the greatest need is to stop the roots being broken or crushed; in fact the most serious cause of damage is desiccation. Thirdly it is important to make sure that the roots are evenly spread within the planting pit; failure to do so can lead to poor tree stability in the future. Once the main roots of the tree are in place they remain and are not replaced, so distortions set at planting are there for the life of the tree.

Under no circumstances should the tree be planted too deeply or the metabolism of the stem and roots will be damaged. It is important to identify the true level of the base of the trunk and the root system and not just identify the level at which the tree was planted in the nursery. Any roots that might girdle the base of the tree later, a common occurrence in container-grown stock, should be removed at the time of planting.

Water loss and root desiccation, already discussed in Chapter 7, continue until the tree has been planted. All trees must therefore be kept moist from the time that they are lifted to when they have been planted. This means that bare-root material must be held in plastic bags (cost 0.02 tree units each), and container-grown and root-balled trees must be kept watered, until the moment they are planted out. Trees must not be laid out in their planting position on a dry day and then be planted half an hour or more later.

9.1   *Basic planting techniques*

The variety of forms in which rooted trees can be introduced into the environment have been outlined in Table 7.1. There is also the possibility of using seed and cuttings. Each type requires a different planting technique.

9.1.1 DIRECT SEEDING

The introduction of trees into a site as seeds can be a cheap and quick method (about 250 tree units ha^{-1} including cultivation, but 0.025 tree units per established tree). However it is not totally reliable, and great care must be taken to ensure that the seeds have a good chance to germinate and establish. Seed can either be surface sown or drilled or harrowed into the soil using conventional agricultural machinery. Harrowing or drilling gives the seed better protection, but may be difficult to carry out. Seed that has been surface sown can be protected by the use of a mulch. Careful herbicide use is important. In difficult areas it is possible to hydroseed, using a water-based slurry of seed, fertilizer, mulch, and sometimes soil stabilizer, sprayed onto the area in a single mixture. Hydroseeding can, however, be an expensive operation to carry out and does not

Figure 9.1
A seeded roadside in Gwent. Direct seeding of trees is possible where an informal layout is appropriate.

necessarily guarantee success although it costs 200 tree units ha⁻¹. It must be carried out with great care, because the seeds are very vulnerable to desiccation, and the fertilizers and stabilizers can inhibit the growth of young seedlings.

The general problem with direct seeding is that it is not possible to know precisely what the establishment rate will be as seed distribution can be variable (particularly with broadcast seed). The success of the scheme will be largely dependent on climatic conditions (a drought soon after germination will kill all the seedlings that have germinated). However on roadside and other areas where informal plantings are acceptable (Figure 9.1), it is a valuable new technique.

9.1.2 CUTTINGS

Certain species of trees can be introduced as unrooted cuttings (Table 7.3 in Chapter 7). The most widely used species are willows but the method also works for poplars. Dormant cuttings about 25 cm long, of new growth 10–20 mm in diameter, are taken. They can be planted at any time over the winter, although preferably in early spring. With willows and a damp soil much larger cuttings can be used, up to 2.5 m long and 5 cm diameter.

About three-quarters of the cutting is simply pushed into the soil, with large willow material about 50 cm. If the soil is rather firm, a crowbar can be used first. The length of the cutting ensures that its base is in damp ground, and that the roots are unlikely to suffer from spring drought. Growth from these cuttings can be quite spectacular, with up to 1 m of extension growth in the first season alone. Because only a few centimetres of the cutting are visible above ground, the newly planted material is unlikely to be vandalized. It is an extremely simple and inexpensive way of introducing a number of valuable species to a site and creating an instant effect (Figure 9.2) (planting cost about 0.01 tree units per

Figure 9.2
Willows planted from cuttings for quick effect on a reclamation site. Cuttings are an excellent planting technique for certain species.

Figure 9.3
Notch planting of small stock directly into the substrate is quick and simple, but it must be done with care.

tree). Since most of the species are pioneers (Chapters 8), a site exposed to wind or vandalism can be planted up using cuttings first, and then, after not more than 1 or 2 years, longer-lived structural species can be planted in the protection afforded by the pioneers.

9.1.3 NOTCH PLANTING

Most transplants are planted using the notch method. This is a very simple technique. Either a T-, L- or straight-shaped slit is made in the soil using a spade. The slit is held open whilst the roots of the tree are inserted. The slot is then closed and the soil firmed around the root system. It is important to make sure that the tree is planted at the correct depth, that the slot is big enough to contain all the roots, and that the layout of the roots is not distorted (Figure 9.3).

The technique is rapid and cheap (planting cost 0.02 tree units per tree), but since it does not allow any new soil to be added, it is most appropriate to good sites or those where a topsoil layer has been spread. If the soil is satisfactory physically but likely to be nutrient deficient, fertilizer can be spread around the root-zone of the tree after planting.

9.1.4 PIT PLANTING

The majority of whips and standards in the UK are planted as bare-root stock. This means that a pit must be dug that is large enough to accommodate the root system of the tree without deforming it in any way. As most standard trees are staked it is necessary to place the stake on the windward side of the tree before the tree is planted so that no damage to the root system occurs when the stake is driven into the ground. Once the tree has been positioned near the stake, the roots are spread evenly in the pit. Either the original soil or an imported soil can be used for the backfill. Care must be taken to ensure that backfill is settled around the roots and no cavities are left. This can be achieved by gently moving the tree up and down in the pit. The backfill should then be firmed by treading. For all this it is obviously important to have a pit of adequate size. It is not a cheap operation (cost about 1.5 tree units for a standard-sized tree).

Containerized and balled trees must also be planted in pits, but the planting technique required for these trees needs a slight modification. The tree should be placed in a rather larger hole, sufficiently large to allow the backfill material to be worked around the root ball so that no air pockets remain. Any roots of containerized material which have grown in a circle round the bottom of the container, must be unwound and spread out. It is also important that the base of the pit is not disturbed in order that settling and sinking of the tree is minimized. For large trees it may be necessary to construct a small hard platform immediately under the root ball.

9.1.5 TREE SPADES

For planting semi-mature or mature trees, although hand preparation and movement by crane is possible, a tree spade is far more satisfactory (Figure 9.4).

Figure 9.4
Large trees can be moved easily with special equipment such as this tree spade, but they must be given considerable care for the rest of the season.

The tree spade can be used not only to lift the tree and transport it to the planting site, but also to dig the hole. Using a tree spade is a skilled operation and is consequently expensive (at least 20 tree units).

Because these trees are so big, special care is needed after planting. The large canopy of the tree is supported by a very reduced root system. But the problems which arise from this can be overcome if water and nutrients are supplied almost continuously during the first year after planting; this is essential. To permit this, experienced contractors provide a positive drainage system for the pit so that excess water can be given without any fear of waterlogging.

9.2 *Backfill and soil amendments*

There is some debate as to the benefits or otherwise of using anything other than the original planting pit soil as the backfill. This is because the use of an imported substrate may cause an interface to form between the two substrates, which results in a disturbance in the flow of water between them. As a result water tends not to move easily between the planting pit material and the surrounding soil, until one of them is completely saturated. Thus the situation can arise where the planting pit may be completely dry whilst the surrounding soil is saturated. To overcome this, the sides of the pit should be loosened as the pit is filled, to ensure that the boundary between the two soils is broken down.

In many urban sites, however, the original substrate may be extremely poor in both its water-holding capacity and its nutrient supply, and the use of an imported backfill, usually topsoil, may be essential (Figure 9.5). If this is used, it should be of the highest quality obtainable, with a minimum organic matter content of 2% to ensure good water-holding capacity, and a minimum nitrogen

Figure 9.5
When a tree is pit-planted into a very poor substrate adequate amounts of a high quality soil should be provided for backfill: this will supply both water and nutrients in the early stages of growth.

content of 0.2%N to ensure long-term release of nitrogen (Chapter 11). It is not cheap, but is likely to be a good investment (extra cost about 1 tree unit). Practical experience shows that many materials sold as topsoil have been of a very poor quality; this must be guarded against.

Alternatively the original backfill material can be used, with its qualities improved by the addition of suitable amendments. It is extremely important that whatever the amendment used, it is well distributed within the backfill material. The use of amendments such as tree planting composts, to increase the water-holding capacity and the nutrient status of the substrates, are discussed in the following chapters. Whatever is done, it is essential that the water and nutrient requirements of the tree, discussed in Chapter 3, are provided for. To ensure that watering is effective, runoff should be prevented by ensuring that the planting area forms a slight hollow after planting has been completed (Chapter 10). If it is not, as much as 90% of the water applied can run off. There should be no likelihood of waterlogging if pit drainage has been attended to.

9.3   *Drainage*

Figure 9.6
All these trees had to be replanted because the pits were waterlogged. Underlying the pits was an impervious layer which had to broken with the help of a pneumatic drill.

The need for site drainage has already been discussed (Chapter 6). Equally important is adequate drainage for the individual planting pit. If the site is adequately drained, then all that will be necessary is for the base and sides of the planting pit to be sufficiently loosened so that any excess water can percolate away. In some urban sites it may be necessary to use a pneumatic drill to achieve this, because impermeable subsoil layers are often found overlying

well-drained deeper layers (Figure 9.6). Where drainage is likely to be a permanent problem, a proper drainage system for each tree pit must be installed before the trees are planted. Normal plastic or earthenware field drainage pipes are very effective.

The need for drainage cannot easily be seen by inspection unless the whole site is waterlogged. If waterlogging is suspected, the most sensible approach is to test for it by filling the tree pit with water and seeing how long it takes to drain away. If the water level falls at more than 2 cm min^{-1}, trouble is unlikely. However, after the test the bottom of the pit must be broken up again to ensure no sealing layer of mud has been formed. Waterlogging occurring after planting can be tested by the steel rod technique (Chapter 4).

9.4   *Planting pit design*

The process of planting must not only give the tree a satisfactory start to its life but also ensure that it does not run into problems later. The planting pit must, therefore, be not just a hole in the ground but a medium which will be adequate over a long period. Yet trees are often planted in small pits in very obdurate materials, such as in old road surfaces or the sites of old buildings. Normally the whole site should be upgraded (Chapter 6). But this may not always be possible, and the tree may end up in a very artificial situation, which requires careful attention at the design stage.

To ensure an adequate supply of both water and nutrients, the planting pit must be large enough and the tree roots be enabled to forage outside. Adequate

Figure 9.7
A prestige scheme beside a cathedral. It is useful to protect the soil of planting pits with a grid in areas where there is heavy pedestrian traffic.

Figure 9.8
Plane trees in the Mall leading to Buckingham Palace in London. The ideal planting site is an area where the planting pit is continuous within the soil around it.

drainage is essential. The imported soil used to fill the pit must be of high quality both physically and chemically. A clay soil is likely to cause trouble; a sandy loam giving good drainage will be optimal.

If the planting area has an impermeable surface, it is imperative to provide an uncovered space around each tree or group of trees, at least 1 m across for a young tree. In prestige schemes where the surface is impervious, it is valuable to provide a metal grid to protect the soil (Figure 9.7). It will at the same time prevent people stumbling over the planting area. For older trees in asphalt the bare area will need to be at least 2 m across. Asphalt should never be laid over areas where there are long-established trees for fear of causing their root systems irreparable damage.

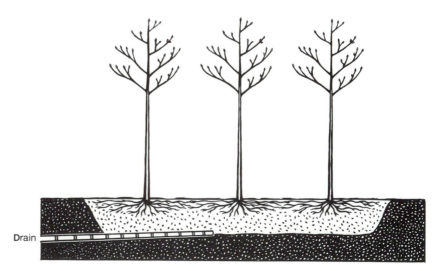

Figure 9.9
The expanded pit concept (redrawn from Hammerschlag and Sherald 1985). In restricted sites pits can be made larger by being continuous.

It is obvious that the larger the planting pit the better. This leads to the concept that tree planting should be concentrated in areas covered with grass or gravel set aside specifically for trees, such as along the Mall leading to Buckingham Palace in London (Figure 9.8). Where less space is available it is worth considering a continuous planting pit, which allows the individual trees a long if not a wide root run. It can be given a proper drainage system more easily than can a series of isolated planting pits (Figure 9.9).

In difficult areas, such as pavements which cannot be broken into, or in open spaces within buildings where there is a concrete slab underneath, it is becoming common for trees to be planted in large containers, usually of precast concrete. This allows trees to be planted where otherwise there could be none, and if it becomes necessary for roadworks, etc., the whole container can be moved. Trees may also be planted in more fixed structures, such as raised beds constructed of brick and lined with asphalt.

In these the critical problem is an adequate supply of water. Containers prevent the tree from foraging for water, so that unless water is provided, the

Figure 9.10
Unhappy trees in a prestige site in Washington DC, USA. Because they are completely isolated, containers are rarely satisfactory unless they can be provided with a reliable water supply.

tree has to rely entirely on what is caught by the container and stored within it. Trees use a substantial amount of water – 2 litres per day for an established standard (Chapter 10); and as the tree grows, its water use grows. At the same time its canopy prevents some rain from falling in the container.

Containers in which trees are expected to grow and prosper must therefore be large, at least three times the area of the expected canopy of the tree, unless a reliable watering system can be provided (Figure 9.10). More detailed analysis considering water losses and soil water supply suggests a more satisfactory figure should be in terms of container volume (Chapter 10).

9.5   *Buildings and services*

When trees are being planted, careful attention must be paid to their possible effects on buildings and services. The presence of drains can be considered a problem, but the only drains that become blocked by tree roots are those that are old, usually made of clay pipes, and in bad condition. Modern plastic drains are unlikely to suffer.

The major problem that has to be considered is the effect that trees can have on foundations. This means that all tree planting close to buildings should be planned carefully, so that the ultimate size of the tree and its root system is taken into account. But the critical factor is the depth of the foundations of the house and whether these are on a shrinking clay. Problems occur where the soil contains a high proportion of clay of the type which shrinks when it loses water. Then, if a tree develops roots which grow down under the foundations and in dry years remove water causing the clay to shrink, damage can result. This became very clear in the drought of 1982, when houses all over the country suffered damage. But in Manchester and London, for instance, the only buildings which suffered were those in the areas where clay soils occur.

Figure 9.11
An example of the guidelines now available relating soil type, foundation depth, and the minimum allowable distance from buildings, for trees with different water demands (redrawn from National House-Building Council, 1985). Trees can be safely planted close to houses even on shrinking soils if adequate foundations are provided or low water-demand species chosen.

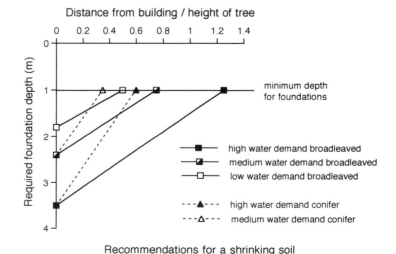

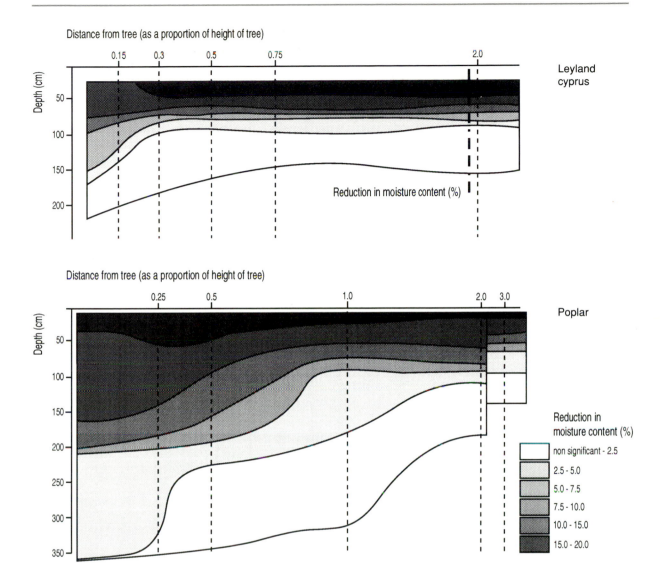

Figure 9.12
A comparison of the average reduction in soil moisture by Leyland cypress (top) and poplar (bottom) on clays at various sites in autumn 1983 (redrawn from Biddle, 1987). The area affected by the cypress is about 0.25 times the height and by the poplar about 1.0 times the height.

The solution is that the buildings should have had foundations deep enough, >2 m, to ensure stability on the soil type of the site. Unfortunately many houses have been built with foundations less than 1 m deep, even on clay soils. Tree planting close to these is likely to cause trouble, and should not be undertaken. Recently guidelines have been developed which relate soil type, foundation depth and the minimum distance from buildings trees with different water demands can be planted (Figure 9.11). The various sorts of *Sorbus* and Leyland cypress are examples of low water-demand species; oak, poplar and willow are examples of high-demand species. They can have very different effects in reduction of soil moisture content (Figure 9.12).

9.6   *Time of planting*

Practices vary widely and will depend on the type of material being planted. It is possible to plant containerized material throughout the summer so long as it is subsequently kept well watered, but bare-root stock should only be planted during the dormant season. Whatever the material, planting cannot take place when the ground is frozen.

In the UK nearly all planting is carried out during the autumn and winter when the trees are dormant. In our maritime climate this allows a long planting period, a luxury which countries with continental climates do not have. Therefore in the USA and elsewhere the practice is to plant throughout the growing season, which of course necessitates that the vast majority of tree stock is either container grown or root-balled.

There are good reasons to plant the tree whilst it is in a dormant condition, principally, of course, because there are no transpiration losses through the leaves. The tree is then not subject to the extreme water deficits which would otherwise be brought about by its truncated root system. There will be no damage to actively growing shoot material and leaf expansion will not be upset. This is extremely important, as it has been shown that even partial defoliation or pruning whilst the tree is in leaf will result in either a temporary reduction or even cessation of root growth (see Figure 14.6). If leaf development is disrupted by drought, the effect on root development can therefore be catastrophic. If possible, the tree should be planted early, so that the soil can settle well around the roots, and, importantly, root growth can take place during mild conditions occurring during the winter (Figure 9.13). As a result, when the tree comes into full growth there is already a well-developed root system, well integrated into the soil, and able to meet the demands of the leaves (Chapter 3).

Figure 9.13
The root growth at bud break and after leaf expansion of sycamore and birch planted in the autumn and in the spring (redrawn from Gilbertson *et al.*,1987). Early planting allows root establishment before the tree comes into leaf.

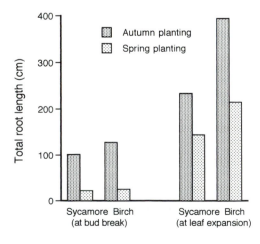

9.7 *Post-planting practices*

There are a number of practices that must be followed immediately following transplanting to ensure that the trees become established. These are dealt with in the following chapters. It is imperative that, if the soil is at all dry, the tree is watered immediately after planting, and that this irrigation practice is maintained for a considerable time afterwards (Chapter 10). Similarly, weed growth around the newly planted tree must be controlled to reduce competition for the limited water reserves (Chapter 13). Any dead or damaged branches should be removed immediately after planting and the tree pruned to the desired shape (Chapter 14). Some fertilizing may be required (Chapter 11).

References

Biddle, P.G. (1987) Trees and buildings, in *Advances in Practical Arboriculture* (ed. D. Patch), Forestry Commission Bulletin **65**, HMSO, London, pp.121–32.

Gilbertson, P., Kendle, A.D. and Bradshaw, A.D. (1987) Root growth and the problems of trees in urban and industrial areas, in *Advances in Practical Arboriculture* (ed. D. Patch), Forestry Commission Bulletin **65**, HMSO, London, pp. 59–66.

Hammerschlag, R.S. and Sherald, J.L. (1985) Traditional and expanded tree pit concepts. *Proceedings of the Conference of the Metropolitan Tree Improvement Alliance,* **4**, 33–44.

National House-Building Council (1985) *Building near Trees,* Practice Note **3**, National House-Building Council, Amersham.

Other reading

Bloomfield, H., Handley, J.F. and Bradshaw, A.D. (1981) Top soil quality. *Landscape Design,* **135**, 32–5.

Carpenter, P.L. and Walker, T.D. (1990) *Plants in the Landscape,* Freeman, San Francisco.

Clouston, B. (ed.) (1990) *Landscape Design with Plants,* Heinemann Newnes, London.

Hackett, B. (1979) *Planting Design,* E & F N Spon, London.

Lindsey, P. and Bassuk, N. (1991) Specifying soil volumes to meet the water needs of mature urban street trees and trees in containers. *Journal of Arboriculture,* **17**, 141–9.

Littlewood, M. (1988) *Tree Detailing,* Butterworth Architecture, London.

Putwain, P.D., Evans, B.E. and Kerry, S. (1988) The early establishment of amenity woodland on roadsides by direct seeding. *Aspects of Applied Biology,* **16**, 63–72.

Weddle, A.E. (ed.) (1967) *Techniques of Landscape Architecture,* Heinemann, London.

10 *The importance of water*

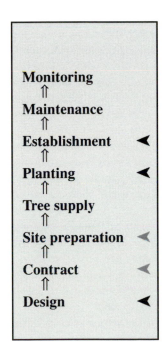

Monitoring
⇑
Maintenance
⇑
Establishment ◄
⇑
Planting ◄
⇑
Tree supply
⇑
Site preparation ◄
⇑
Contract ◄
⇑
Design ◄

- One of the major causes of death of newly planted trees is drought.
- About 1.7 million trees die annually from drought, amounting to a loss of about £4 million.
- Any measures and expense involved in overcoming the problem can therefore be readily justified.
- The amount of water held by soil is small and it is relatively immobile.
- At the same time water loss from a newly planted tree when in leaf is considerable, for a standard about 2 litres per day.
- The major reason for death due to drought is the inadequacy of the root system of the newly planted tree; this limits the volume of soil available to supply water to the tree during periods without rain.
- There is a simple relationship for a newly planted tree between the number of days that adequate water is available to the tree, and its root volume, soil water capacity and water uptake.
- From this it is clear that the major methods of overcoming tree water supply problems are:

  1. to plant trees with larger root systems to increase the soil volume available to supply water,
  2. to plant trees in the autumn to allow time for them to develop a larger root system before bud break,
  3. to use a soil ameliorant to increase water-holding capacity of the soil,
  4. to irrigate as required to restore soil water content before it reaches dangerously low levels, and
  5. to undertake dormant pruning since this reduces leaf area for a time after bud break although the effect is only temporary.

- It is imperative that one or more of these treatments is incorporated into tree planting specifications and becomes standard practice.

The surveys already discussed in Chapters 2 and 5 suggest that one of the major causes of death of newly planted trees in Britain is drought. If £10 million is wasted annually on newly planted trees which die during their first 3 years and if, as seems possible, 15% of these die due to drought (half those recorded as dying of stress in Figure 5.1), this amounts to a waste of nearly £4 million, when planting costs are included.

A walk through many urban parks in Britain during the summer months reveals how little the water requirements of newly planted trees are understood. The bedding plants within the park will be receiving irrigation, while any newly planted trees are unlikely to be given any irrigation at all. This scenario is not limited to trees in parks. It applies equally well to street, and even garden, trees. Yet in most European and North American cities, irrigation is carried out as a routine operation.

So why is there such a difference in our approach? The climates differ, but the greatest cause of transplant failure, drought, is common to both situations. The explanation would appear to be that because the British climate is essentially wet, the possibility that trees might suffer severe water shortage is not recognized.

One of the major difficulties is that the water demand of trees is not fully understood. Firstly, it is much greater than most people suspect. Secondly, the water requirements of trees are far from static; they change not only from day to day, but also from hour to hour. Thirdly, the water that the soil can supply varies from day to day, and from week to week. Since soil water is finite in amount, it may well be adequate for a few days and then become exhausted.

To understand the problem we must first understand the importance of water to trees and the amount they are likely to consume, and then examine different ways in which water can be managed in order to maximize growth.

10.1   *Importance of water*

Water is fundamental to the growth of trees. As was discussed in Chapter 3, it is not only required for all the biochemical functions necessary for growth, such as photosynthesis, respiration and transport, but also for the mechanical support of leaf and stem tissue. At the same time it is lost from leaves as an incidental result of the stomata being open to allow photosynthesis to take place.

So why is there ambivalence over the water requirements of newly planted trees? Is it the cost of irrigation? It certainly will be expensive to irrigate a tree, although the cost will depend upon the site. But in comparison with the value of

Table 10.1 *The effects of 10 weeks of drought on the growth of transplants of maple (Walmsley* et al. *1991). All aspects of the tree are affected including the roots, but the real effect on roots must be studied by more direct means (see Figure 10.1)*

	Shoot extension (cm)	Root dry weight (g)	Leaf area (cm^2)
Droughted	87	19.6	1387
Watered	377	52.8	6145

Figure 10.1
The effects of drought on root extension of sycamore transplants observed in glass-sided containers (Walmsley *et al.*, 1991). Extension rapidly comes to halt long before the trees die.

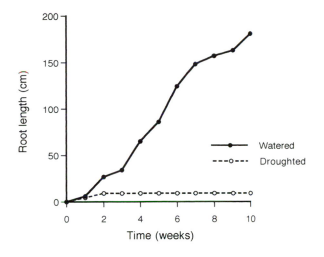

Figure 10.2
Droughted ash trees responding to irrigation at the Liverpool International Garden Festival 1984. Providing that a tree is not completely dead it can recover but its growth potential will have been severely weakened.

a mature standard tree in an urban setting, these costs will be quite insignificant. The real problem is that the effects that even a slight drought can have upon the growth of newly planted trees, although substantial, are rarely appreciated.

The effects of drought on leaf growth and shoot extension are clearly visible. The leaves stop expanding and the shoots stop elongating. Ultimately the leaves wilt and turn brown, or drop off. But long before this other changes occur that are just as important; in particular the stomata of the leaves close. This is the natural reaction of the plant by which moisture is conserved. But it prevents any further photosynthesis occurring.

All this has startling effects below ground as well as above (Table 10.1). At first glance these results would imply that root growth is less sensitive to disturbance by drought than shoot growth. But when actual root growth is watched, for instance in glass-sided containers and followed on a daily basis, a very different situation is uncovered (Figure 10.1). When a tree is subjected to drought, root elongation ceases almost immediately and does not resume for the duration of the drought. Root elongation is extremely sensitive to drought and root growth ceases very quickly as the water stress increases. Without new root growth, absorbtion of nutrients soon comes to a halt. As a result, the whole physiology of the tree comes under stress, not only from lack of water but also from lack of photosynthates and nutrients.

Although a tree can survive a limited period of water stress, particularly because of the closure of its stomata, there are serious implications for subsequent growth and development. An easily observable consequence of severe water stress is leaf abscission. It has been known for years that trees will produce new leaves if quickly given irrigation (Figure 10.2). The real problem will be, however, that the growth potential of the whole tree will have been seriously weakened. Not only will shoot development have been reduced, but, more importantly, so will root development. Because the size of the root system of a droughted tree will be much less than that of a comparable watered tree, there will be serious implications on the subsequent potential of the tree to exploit the soil water reserves and to tolerate further dry periods later.

It is therefore imperative that, during the establishment period, water stress is avoided. This means that the tree must be given an adequate water supply. For this, we need to know the tree's requirement for water.

10.2   *Water requirements*

Surprisingly, there is little information available on the water requirements of isolated trees. However, observed transpiration rates, the rates of water loss from leaves, are in the order of 6–14 g dm^{-2} day^{-1}. The area of the canopy of a newly planted light standard tree is about 1 m^2. This suggests that this sort of tree requires about 1 litre of water per day.

A more direct way to find out the water requirements is to determine the transpiration rate by weighing. If a whole tree is planted in a suitably sized container which is then sealed to prevent water infiltration or evaporation, any weight changes over time will be due to water lost from the leaves by transpiration. In an experiment in which small standard plane trees were grown outside in normal conditions in early summer, for the first 14 days the water loss from the system amounted to 1.2 litres day^{-1} (Figure 10.3). After this the rate of water loss fell off as the water in the containers began to be exhausted. Transforming this value to a leaf area basis gives a value of 11.7 g dm^{-2} day^{-1}, which is comparable with the values found by other workers.

To predict water use requires that the leaf area of the tree is known. This will

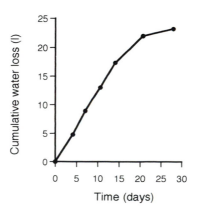

Figure 10.3
The cumulative loss of water from a standard plane tree in early summer (Walmsley *et al.*, 1991). The rate of transpiration until the water in the growing container became exhausted was 1.2 litres day^{-1}.

be dependent upon the species and the overall size of the tree. But the vast majority of newly planted standard trees have a leaf area of around 1 m², and it is unlikely that the leaf area of any standard tree is larger than 3 m². Therefore it can be assumed that the rate of water loss of most trees will lie somewhere in the range of 1–3 litres day⁻¹.

The problem is that the soil can only provide a certain amount of water. The significant supply will be that held in the soil in the immediate vicinity of the roots. Some water moves into the region around the roots from elsewhere in the soil, but the main way in which the water taken up by the roots is replenished is by rain. However, rain only falls intermittently, and there may be no rain for several days or weeks.

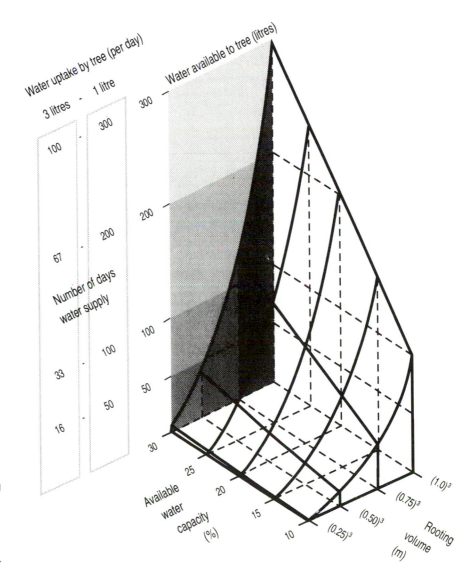

Figure 10.4
A model of the potential number of days that a limited volume of soil can supply water to a normal tree using 1 or 3 litres day⁻¹ (redrawn from Gilbertson *et al.*, 1987). The effects of different soil-available water capacities and different volumes of soil occupied by the roots are shown.

A fully established tree has a very large and diffuse root system. It has therefore available to it a very large store of water. But when a tree is transplanted it can lose about 90% of its root system. The problem that then arises can best be seen in a model in which it is assumed that the tree only has available to it the water held in the soil volume which contains the roots, which is effectively the volume of soil in the planting pit. Some water will come from outside this volume, but very little because the hydraulic conductivity of soil is poor. If a range of available water capacities for the soil and a range of root volumes are assumed, the number of days water supply for different situations can be calculated (Figure 10.4). This suggests that a newly planted tree, in the absence of rain or irrigation, is likely to experience water shortage quickly, certainly within one month and even within 10 days.

This model suggests there are two major ways by which this problem can be overcome. The amount of water available to the tree in its rooting zone can be increased, or the amount of water that is transpired can be reduced.

10.3   *Managing water supply*

A number of different approaches are possible. Firstly the volume of soil that the tree's roots can exploit can be increased by increasing the amount of root possessed by the tree after it has been transplanted. Secondly the amount of water that is stored in the soil around the trees roots can be increased by ameliorating the soil with substances that have a high water-holding capacity. Thirdly the tree can be irrigated when the need arises. Each of these different approaches is practicable; each has its own merits and drawbacks. Which should be adopted will depend on the particular situation of the tree being planted. What is crucial is that a method should be chosen positively, and the survival of the tree not left to the luck of good weather conditions.

10.3.1 INCREASING THE SIZE OF THE ROOT SYSTEM

There has been little evidence in the literature to suggest that the size of the root system of a transplanted tree has a direct relationship to the volume of water that is immediately available to the tree. Yet it can be shown that a transpiring tree reduces the soil water reservoir in the immediate vicinity of its roots very quickly. If, therefore, a tree with a small root system is planted occupying a soil volume of 50 x 50 x 50 cm (0.125 m^3; typical of the size of the pits dug for a light standard tree), if the soil has a water-holding capacity of 10% (not untypical of urban soils), and if the tree transpires 1.0 litre of water a day, all the available water will be exhausted within approximately 12 days. If the same tree had a larger root system occupying 75 x 75 x 75 cm (0.42 m^3), the available water would last 42 days (Figure 10.4). If the tree canopy was larger and was losing 2 litres of water per day, the available water would last half as long.

This model assumes of course that there is only slight, if any, movement of

Figure 10.5
Standard trees planted in a plastic tunnel house so that the moisture deficiencies which develop around the roots of newly planted trees can be studied critically (see Figure 10.6).

water within the soil profile. Perhaps it is best to verify the model by experiment. If rain infiltration into the soil surrounding trees is prevented by planting the trees sticking out of a plastic greenhouse (Figure 10.5), and the water tensions that develop in the soil around the roots of the trees are measured with a neutron probe, it is found that water is removed by the trees from a zone only very little larger than the volume occupied by their roots, i.e. trees with a smaller root system withdraw water from a smaller volume of soil than trees with a larger root system (Figure 10.6). These results show clearly that the volume of water available to a tree with a large root system is much greater than that to a tree with a small root system and that the model reflects reality.

The supply of water to a newly planted tree can therefore be increased simply by using trees with larger root systems. This is done by ensuring that (a) a larger root mass is excavated when it is transplanted (minimal cost), or (b) the tree is planted early enough in the winter to allow it time to develop a larger root

Figure 10.6
Water deficiencies after 21 days drought in the soil around standard trees with two different sizes of root system, determined by a neutron probe (redrawn from Walmsley *et al.*, 1991). Water has been taken by the tree only from the soil in the immediate region of the roots. The tree with the larger root system will have more water available to it.

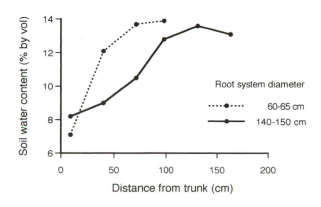

system before bud break (no cost) (Chapter 9). It also follows that it is very unlikely that the supply of water will be helped by using containerized or root-balled material unless the roots of such material occupy a larger soil volume, once planted, than bare-root material.

10.3.2 INCORPORATION OF AMELIORANTS

An alternative possibility of improving the water supply to a tree is to increase the plant-available water capacity of the soil in the rooting zone (Chapter 4). Increases in the water-holding capacity of the substrate can be achieved by mixing it with other materials. One such example is peat; compared to a normal urban soil which has a water-holding capacity of 10%, peat has a water holding capacity of 35% or more. If peat alone was used in the planting pit of the light standard tree referred to earlier, its water supply would in effect be increased from 12 days to 42 days (Figure 10.4). It is not usually sensible, however, to use as much peat as this because the stability of the tree will be affected; but a doubling of water-holding capacity is realistic (costing about 0.3 tree units per tree). The use of peat can be very effective (Figure 10.7), but this was not always found in other trials.

Peat is not the only material suitable for this practice. A variety of organic materials can be used. Coir compost, spent mushroom compost, and sewage sludge composted with straw are some examples of the materials becoming available. Recently a group of substances known as cross-linked polyacrylamide polymers have begun to be used. These are available under a number of individual names. They have in common a tremendous ability to absorb water – up to 500 times their own weight of distilled water. This value is however reduced as the amount of salts within water increases, as would be the case with soil water, but nevertheless polymers are available that have an ability to absorb 250 times their own weight of soil water .

A 0.2% addition by dry weight of polymer extends the supply of water in a given volume of soil by a factor of two (costing about 0.2 tree units per tree).

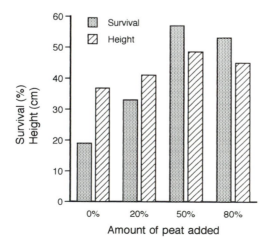

Figure 10.7
The effects of addition of different amounts of peat on the survival and growth of birch after three seasons (Davies, 1987). There were distinct beneficial effects in this trial although not in others.

Figure 10.8
The effects of soil amendment with 25% peat or 0.4% polymer (polyacrylamide) on the growth of sycamore transplants over one season under field conditions (redrawn from Walmsley *et al.*, 1991). The trial was set up in November so the materials had adequate time to become saturated.

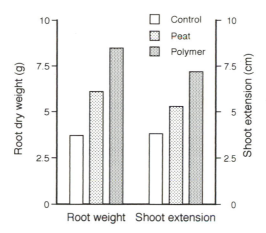

Figure 10.9
The root system of a transplant growing in a substrate amended with a polymer. The polymer increases root growth.

Even a tree with a relatively small root system occupying a volume of 0.125 m³ (50 x 50 x 50 cm) could, therefore, have its water supply extended from 10 days to 20 days, which would reduce substantially its chance of being upset by drought. This effect would be enhanced if the size of the root system were also increased. In trials polymers can give remarkable results (Figure 10.8). The effects on the rooting system can be impressive. So long as the polymer does not contain any toxic compounds, the roots tend to grow through the expanded polymer granules (Figure 10.9) and increase the growth of the root system substantially.

Some trials with both polymers and peat have been disappointing, perhaps because the materials did not become sufficiently wetted before drought set in. There is also the possibility that some polymers are slightly inhibitory of root growth. Although polymers may appear expensive, in conjunction with some irrigation during a prolonged drought a good polymer appears well worth using.

Analogous materials, usually organic, are often advocated as 'root dips'. It is suggested that these will aid establishment by improving the contact between the root system and the soil. While this is possible and may lead to improved establishment in some cases, in general root dips have not given positive results. Almost certainly this is because the real problem is lack of sufficient water to satisfy the developing needs of the tree, which the root dip can do little to overcome.

10.3.3 IRRIGATION

Irrigation is the traditional and most direct way of controlling the water supply to the tree. In agriculture, irrigation has been developed into a very sophisticated operation based on precise calculations of irrigation need. Because of their localized root systems exactly the same approach cannot be readily applied to amenity trees, although the same principles of calculation of need, based on water use and supply, can be applied. With the values given in Figure 10.4, the frequency at which water should be applied in a drought period can easily be calculated (an example is given in Table 10.2). At each application enough

Table 10.2   *An example of using Figure 10.4 to determine irrigation requirements for a set of standard trees*

1. Assess tree size and therefore likely water uptake.
2. Assess likely soil volume containing root system.
3. Assess likely soil water-holding capacity.
4. Read off from Figure 10.4 number of days water supply (if trees are medium standards using 2 litres of water per day assume the value is half the 1 litre value). This gives the number of days after leafing out before watering is required if maximum growth is to be maintained.
5. If rain has fallen allow 1 day extra for each 10 mm of rain.
   The minimum amount of water to be applied to the trees is the amount used (equivalent to the water available given on the vertical axis of the graphs); as a safety margin, to ensure soil is properly saturated, apply double this amount to each tree.
6. Repeat for any further drought period, allowing for the likely increase in size of the root systems (it can be assumed that there is no increase in size if the necessary watering has not been given).

Example 1 :   Light standards with roots occupying 50 x 50 x 50 cm pits, backfill ameliorated with 50% peat so water-holding capacity 25%; no rain since leafing out.
Water uptake 1 litre day^{-1}; water available 31 litres.
Water sufficient for 31 days.
Water each tree by the end of fourth week with about 60 litres.

Example 2 :   Heavy standards with roots occupying 75 x 75 x 75 cm pits, backfill not amended but poor topsoil with water-holding capacity of 15%; 3 inches of rain during month after leafing out.
Water uptake 3 litres day^{-1}; water available 63 litres.
Water sufficient for 21 days + 8 days contribution from rain.
Water each tree by the end of fourth week with about 120 litres.

water should be given to restore the rooting zone to field capacity. If this is calculated, a suitable excess can be given.

However irrigation has complications. Irrigation systems can be expensive. For example the installation of a permanent system in a planting bed might amount to 100 tree units for 300 m². This should rarely be worthwhile except in areas required to give special performance, such as a Garden Festival or exhibition site. It will be more usual to irrigate trees on an *ad hoc* basis as required, from a water bowser or hydrant. This can be costly (0.8 tree units per tree for a season), although various steps can be taken to simplify the operation, and it may only be necessary for the first half of the season because after this the roots should have grown sufficiently.

Whether applied by hand or machine, difficulties can be encountered in actually applying the correct quantity of water directly to the root zone. It is best to apply excess, but crucial to ensure that the water actually enters the soil. This is most readily achieved where the surface is loose and rough. Care must be taken on both flat and sloping ground to ensure that the water does not run off when it is applied rapidly by hand. A saucer-shaped depression with a rough surface around each tree is crucial (Figure 10.10). Slow application by sprinkler is better, so long as the rate of application does not exceed the infiltration rate

Figure 10.10
Formation of a hollow to prevent
water runoff of rain or when trees
are given irrigation. This is particularly important for trees on
slopes (redrawn from Littlewood,
1988).

Grade 1 in 5

into the soil. Sprinkler application has the added advantage of loading up the
water-holding capacity of the whole soil and not just localized areas. It can be
carried out very simply by either small-scale horticultural sprinklers or large-
scale agricultural equipment.

Difficulties can also arise because, whatever the system of application, the
water flows away from the root ball. This is especially the case where a different
planting substrate has been used in the pit itself. A physical boundary is created
at the junction of the pit and the planting compost. Depending upon the porosity
of each material, one area can become saturated whilst the other area remains
dry. The problem can be overcome if applications are repeated so that equilibra-
tion occurs. The problem is usually prevented if the sides of the pit are broken
up when the tree is planted, to give close contact between the soils of the
planting pit and the surroundings.

10.4   *Controlling water use by the tree*

There are two methods by which the water use of the tree can be reduced. Either the leaf area can be reduced, or the evapotranspiration from the leaves can be interrupted. Both can be valuable, but in practice neither are as effective as the methods already discussed.

10.4.1 PRUNING

Pruning would appear to be a promising way of reducing leaf area and therefore evapotranspiration. If this is done in the dormant period the tree usually only has a reduced leaf area for a relatively short time. The tree grows new shoots and develops a normal leaf area quite quickly. If pruning is done during the summer then indeed the tree has a lesser leaf area for quite a long period. There is experimental evidence to suggest that the moisture stress within the tree is reduced. However, photosynthesis will also have been reduced, at the same time as the tree responds by growing a new, second set of leaves, which makes extra demands on the metabolism of the tree. As a result the summer pruned tree could be seriously weakened, especially in its root growth, and this detrimental effect could have more important consequences to the tree than in the restriction of the amount of water that is transpired. Experiments confirm that the effects of drought are not relieved by summer pruning and there is a major negative effect on tree growth. There is, however, an indication that dormant pruning has some beneficial effects (Table 10.3). This pattern of results is found by several investigators and leads to a common European practice of pruning at planting. Pruning is discussed further in Chapter 14.

Table 10.3   *The effect of pruning, either before planting when the tree is dormant, or in early summer when the tree is growing, in combination with a droughting treatment, on the growth of transplants of maple. Dormant pruning appears to alleviate the effect of the drought on shoot growth, but summer pruning has a negative effect (Walmsley, 1989)*

Pruning	Root dry weight (g)		Shoot extension (cm)		Leaf area (cm²)	
	Droughted	Watered	Droughted	Watered	Droughted	Watered
Unpruned	20	53	87	377	1387	6145
Dormant pruned	19	59	178	459	2127	7012
Summer pruned	14	37	56	293	1033	4750

10.4.2 ANTI-TRANSPIRANTS

The other means by which the volume of water that the tree transpires can be reduced is by the use of anti-transpirants. These are materials which coat the leaf surface and reduce the evaporation of water from the stomata. Chemicals such as these have been used in the past. Whilst there is some evidence that these products can be used successfully, they can be costly (about 1.5 tree units per tree). They also have the drawback that because they limit the movement of all gases in and out of the leaves and other young tissue, they can limit photosynthesis and therefore the rate at which the plant itself grows. Their use can be warranted in the short term, for example when trees are being planted late, when the leaves are beginning to expand. But in the long term their use is of little value as a panacea for lack of water.

10.5   *Soil volumes for established trees*

An established tree has equivalent water requirements to that of a newly planted tree, only in considerably greater amounts. The great difference is that now the tree will have a large and ramifying root system able to pick up water over a wide area and soil volume. Indeed, the roots of the tree will have developed particularly in those areas where soil water is most readily available. An established tree does not therefore usually suffer from water shortage unless its root system is artificially restricted.

This situation will normally only arise when a tree has been planted in a container, although it can also arise if the tree is planted in a constructed area constrained by concrete foundations or walls or highly compacted impermeable materials. In these conditions there is good evidence that trees can suffer serious water shortage in dry periods (Figure 10.11). If the tree was given a reasonably large container, the problems will not be apparent when the tree is newly planted; they will only appear as tree grows and develops a large canopy.

In order to maintain an established tree, unless a permanent irrigation system is to be installed, it is clearly necessary to provide an adequately-sized container or planting pit. The size can be worked out in relation to the expected water loss of the tree. This will be related to the evaporative loss of water from a standard open pan; tree leaves lose water about one-fifth as fast as an open water surface. The leaf area of the tree can be calculated from the crown projection, by multiplying by a factor of four to allow for the fact that the ratio of leaf area to ground area (known as the leaf area index) is about four. Once the rate of water loss is known the size of container needed to sustain the tree over periods without rain can be determined. An example of such a calculation is given in Table 10.4.

If the available water capacity of the soil is 20% and water is re-supplied every 10 days, for north temperate climates a container of 0.12 m^3 is required for every 1 m^2 of crown area. And if, more correctly, it is expected that the drought periods could be 20 days, then the size of the container must be doubled

Figure 10.11
Established trees suffering from summer drought in a container bed too small to provide sufficient water in dry periods. The problem will only get worse as the trees get older.

Table 10.4 *Calculation of the water loss from a large established tree and hence the soil volume required to maintain it in satisfactory growth. A possible drought period of 20 days is assumed (derived from Lindsey and Bassuk, 1992)*

Water loss (in litres day^{-1}) =
crown projection[a] x leaf area index[b] x mean evaporation[c] x adjustment factor[d]

[a] Area of crown in m^2.
[b] Ratio of leaf area to crown projection area (usually assumed to be 4).
[c] Mean daily evaporation from a standard open pan in mm (for UK conditions = approx. 3).
[d] Because average tree leaf loses less water than open water surface (usually assumed to be 0.2).

Soil volume required =
$$\frac{\text{water loss}^{e} \text{ x number of days expected without rain}^{f}}{\text{soil-available water capacity}^{g}}$$

[e] From previous calculation.
[f] Could be expected to be 20 for UK conditions.
[g] Depends on soil material (normally expected to be 20%, i.e. 0.2).

Example: For a tree with a canopy of 20 m^2 (diameter of approx. 5 m):
Water loss per day = 20 x 4 x 3 x 0.2 = 48 litres.
Soil volume required = 48 x 20 / 0.2 = 4800 litres = 4.8 m^3.
This converts to 0.24 m^3 of soil per m^2 of crown area.

(0.24 m³ for every 1 m² of crown area) or the tree will begin to suffer. If an adequate-sized bed, or regular irrigation, cannot be provided, then planting should be limited to drought-resistant shrubs.

References

Davies, R.J. (1987) Tree establishment: soil amelioration, plant handling and shoot pruning, in *Advances in Practical Arboriculture* (ed. D. Patch), Forestry Commission Bulletin **65**, HMSO, London, pp. 52–8.

Gilbertson, P., Kendle, A.D. and Bradshaw, A.D. (1987) Root growth and the problems of trees in urban and industrial areas, in *Advances in Practical Arboriculture* (ed. D. Patch), Forestry Commission Bulletin **65**, HMSO, London, pp. 59–66.

Lindsey, P and Bassuk, N. (1992) Redesigning the urban forest below ground: a new approach to specifying adequate soil volumes for street trees. *Arboricultural Journal,* **16**, 25–39.

Littlewood, M. (1988) *Tree Detailing,* Butterworth Architecture, London.

Walmsley, T.J. (1989) Factors influencing the establishment of amenity trees, PhD thesis, University of Liverpool.

Walmsley, T.J., Hunt, B. and Bradshaw, A.D. (1991) Root growth, water stress and tree establishment, in *Research for Practical Arboriculture* (ed. S.J. Hodge), Forestry Commission Bulletin **97**, HMSO, London, pp. 38–43.

Other reading

Gilman, E.F. (1988) Tree root spread in relation to branch dripline and harvestable root ball. *Horticultural Science,* **23**, 351–3.

Kramer, P.J. and Kozlowski, T.T. (1979) *Physiology of Woody Plants,* Academic Press, New York.

Ministry of Agriculture, Fisheries and Food (1982) *Irrigation,* 5th edn, HMSO, London.

Scott Russell, R. (1977) *Plant Root Systems: their function and interaction with the soil,* Academic Press, Maidenhead.

Woodhouse, J. and Johnson, M.S. (1991) Water storing soil polymers and the growth of trees. *Arboricultural Journal,* **15**, 27–35.

11 *The need for nutrients*

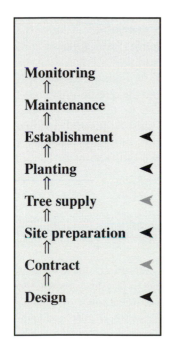

Monitoring
⇑
Maintenance
⇑
Establishment ◄
⇑
Planting ◄
⇑
Tree supply ◄
⇑
Site preparation ◄
⇑
Contract ◄
⇑
Design ◄

- Nutrients are essential for tree growth.
- Trees are good foragers and once fully established will usually find sufficient nutrients except on very poor soils.
- During establishment there will usually be a nutrient shortage, particularly of nitrogen and sometimes phosphorus, except on fertile soils.
- This can be provided by:
    1. good soil used as a site ameliorant,
    2. good soil used as a fill for the planting pit,
    3. high nitrogen fertilizer or organic manure added to the fill of the planting pit,
    4. similar fertilizer or manure applied around the tree after planting.
- Further high nitrogen fertilizer or manure should be added around each tree, normally by surface applications, for about a further 3 years.
- Normal fertilizers are cheap and convenient, but release nutrients very quickly; as a result either applications should be split or slow release forms or organic manures should be used.
- Nitrogen-fixing species are valuable in very poor sites either by themselves or as contributors of nitrogen to other species interplanted with them.
- Competition from weeds and grass, which will be encouraged by nutrient addition, must be eliminated.

Trees, like all other plants, will not grow without an adequate supply of nutrients. Nevertheless, the subject of fertilizing trees is sometimes confused. Simple questions such as what fertilizer should be applied, how much will be required, and how should it be applied, can result in conflicting advice from different people. The difficulty is that much of the information has been derived from research in the rather different disciplines of forestry and fruit production, and has only recently come from studies on amenity trees themselves. A lot of the information is not always interchangeable as the disciplines have different aims and, most importantly, involve very different types of site.

This chapter will not provide hard and fast rules on fertilizing trees, but will give the principles of managing soil fertility for trees and the questions that must be asked before decisions on nutrient applications can be taken. It will also suggest why differing effects of fertilization occur. It must be remembered that fertilizing trees is not a miracle cure for all poor growth; nutrients form only a part of the tree's requirements and must be in balance with the other factors controlling growth, whether water or physical factors.

11.1   *Nutrient requirements and soil supply*

Trees require an adequate supply of both macro- and micro-nutrients (see Chapter 3). Normal soils can supply all the nutrients necessary to support plant growth. Nitrogen and phosphorus are supplied by the breakdown of organic matter. Potassium, calcium, magnesium and phosphorus are readily available from the weathering of major soil minerals, whilst secondary soil minerals can supply both calcium and phosphorus.

Urban sites may have good soil derived from original topsoil, or topsoil brought in and spread, that can provide all the nutrients necessary for tree growth. However, as was discussed earlier (Chapter 4), urban soil is often composed of a mixture of only subsoil, bricks or concrete, and topsoil brought in can be of very low quality. Surprisingly, perhaps, all the nutrients required by the plant with the exception of nitrogen are usually available in adequate amounts in even these inhospitable substrates. Nitrogen is unique because it is stored in the soil entirely in the form of organic complexes, which may be almost completely absent in urban substrates, and very deficient in poor topsoil, whereas the other nutrients are contained in the materials which make up the substrate.

Trees require about 50–100 kg N ha^{-1}yr^{-1} (5–10 g N m^{-2} yr^{-1}) to maintain satisfactory growth. In urban soils, growth can be brought to an almost complete

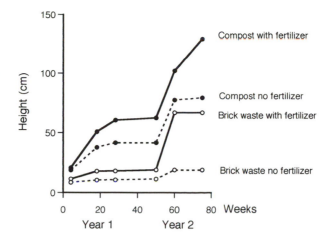

Figure 11.1
The growth of sycamore on urban clearance site material compared with growth on good soil (Capel, 1980 in Bradshaw 1981). Growth ceases if nitrogen fertilizer is not added.

halt without the addition of nitrogen (Figure 11.1). To provide an adequate supply, a minimum capital of nitrogen in the soil in the form of organic matter of about 1000 kg N ha^{-1} is required. By its natural decomposition at a rate of 5–10% yr^{-1}, this will then release 50–100 kg ha^{-1} of mineral nitrogen each year, which is readily taken up and is sufficient for satisfactory tree growth. Although the amount of mineral nitrogen in the soil can be measured, the values fluctuate greatly depending on supply (from organic matter) and demand (uptake by existing plants). As a result a satisfactory level is difficult to recommend. It is better to ensure that there is a good capital, measured as total nitrogen, so long as it can be assumed that this is capable of decomposition.

Phosphorus supply can vary widely in urban soils, but levels are usually high because of the amount that is contained in the clays which are used to make bricks, and is therefore in the soil. The main problem is that of availability. In calcareous or alkaline soils (pH above 7), common in urban situations, phosphorus may be complexed and rendered unavailable. A similar effect can occur in acidic soils, especially if these are high in iron. However the special fungi associated with tree roots, known as mycorrhiza, assist in overcoming this problem, so that it is usually not very important. Furthermore the nutrient requirements of trees for phosphorus are small, in the region of only 10 kg P ha^{-1} yr^{-1}. The important soil character to measure is available or extractable phosphorus.

It is very uncommon for there to be deficiencies in other nutrients, such as calcium, magnesium and potassium, because of their abundance in the raw materials that are found in most urban sites. As a result, since phosphorus is usually abundant, although it may not always be readily available, the response of urban trees is usually only to nitrogen (Figure 11.2). Recognizable visual symptoms of nitrogen deficiency, general yellowing and reduced growth of leaves, will only appear in very extreme conditions, but are very characteristic (Figure 11.3). Plant analysis, although complicated, is the only possible approach. A recent survey relating urban tree growth to site conditions found a significant relationship with tree nitrogen content and not other elements (Figure

Figure 11.2
Newly planted species in an urban area given combinations of nitrogen and phosphorus (Capel, 1980 in Dutton and Bradshaw 1982). The main response is to nitrogen.

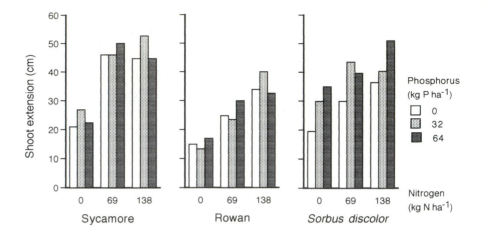

11.4). But because of the many other factors which can also affect tree growth, this relationship is not a very strong one.

Where trees have been planted into existing fertile, or moderately fertile, soil, this soil may provide such an adequate level of background nutrients that further additions of nutrients have no effect. Initial site treatments, where topsoil of good quality has been spread, can have a similar major effect on nutrient supply. But not all topsoils supplied by contractors are of good quality; some may be no better than subsoils. The possibility of nutrient deficiency should therefore not be ruled out even in treated sites. Established trees in apparent satisfactory sites may in fact have their roots almost entirely in poor tipped material and show considerable response to fertilizer addition (Figure 11.5).

Before applying nutrients to the soil it is, therefore, always important to know the nutrient status of the substrate. Simple soil analyses are relatively inexpensive and will show any nutrient deficiencies that may be apparent. In agriculture

Figure 11.3
Growth of sycamore on subsoil material with (right) and without (left) nitrogen. The trees without nitrogen become stunted and yellow.

Figure 11.4
The correlation between the growth of plane trees and their nitrogen content (redrawn from Colderick and Hodge, 1991).

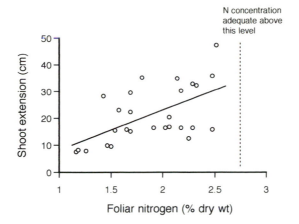

Figure 11.5
The effect of addition of nitrogen to 5-year-old standards of sycamore, maple and whitebeam planted on apparently satisfactory but mounded site (Capel, 1980). The considerable response to nitrogen suggests that the fertility of the underlying tipped material was very poor.

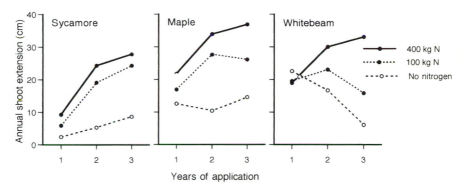

a farmer will have soil analyses carried out regularly for all the soils on which he grows crops. For amenity tree planting it is impracticable to obtain analyses for all the sites involved. But it can be carried out for all major sites, and for a selected sample of the rest, so that the likely range of soil variation is understood. With the appropriate knowledge, nutrient deficiencies can be corrected quickly and cheaply. Using the ADAS scale (Chapter 6; Table 6.1) correction should be given when the index is below 3 for phosphorus, potassium or magnesium. Nitrogen should be given when total nitrogen is below 0.2%.

Even with such knowledge there still remains the problem of the amount of nutrients which should be added. There is no point in adding excessive amounts. Experience from many different fertilizer experiments suggests the following will be satisfactory annual applications for all species:

Type of site	Nutrient Nitrogen (g m⁻²)	Phosphorus (g m⁻²)
Slightly deficient	10	5
Deficient	20	10
Very deficient	40	20

The amounts of fertilizer actually added must be adjusted in relation to the percentage of nitrogen and phosphorus they contain. The common nitrogen fertilizer ammonium nitrate (Nitram), for example, contains 35% N; a dressing of 20 g N m^{-2} therefore requires the addition of 57 g m^{-2} of ammonium nitrate.

11.2   *The response of trees to nutrients*

It is often stated that nitrogen, phosphorus and potassium affect different parts of the tree. In particular, nitrogen is commonly assumed to stimulate shoot development, and phosphorus and potassium to enhance root development. There is some experimental evidence to show that nitrogen will affect the partitioning of materials produced by photosynthesis, so that more energy is directed towards shoot growth than root growth. However any nutrient that is substantially deficient will restrict all aspects of growth. In poor soils, root growth is as responsive to nitrogen amendment as shoot growth (see Figure 3.3), and nutrient addition has a profound and important effect on overall growth (Figure 11.6).

The critical point is that, even if particular nutrients may have initial effects on particular aspects of a tree, because successful growth depends on the co-ordinated growth and functioning of all parts of the tree (see Chapter 3), it is

Figure 11.6
The effect of 3 years' nitrogen fertilizer application (left) compared with none (right) on the growth of a newly planted heavy standard ash. On a poor urban site with topsoil confined to the planting pit, fertilization has clear benefits; these may not be so marked elsewhere (but see Figure 11.5).

essential to ensure that no nutrient is deficient, or else the overall growth of the tree will suffer.

Response to nutrient addition can also be affected by the state of the tree itself. It is often held that trees do not respond to nutrient addition in their first year after planting. It is clear from recent work that this is not necessarily so; considerable responses to nutrients by newly planted trees can be demonstrated, as in Figures 11.1 and 11.2. However there is some indication that growth in the first year can be affected by internal reserves of nutrients and photosynthates. As a result a transplant which has been well fertilized in the nursery, and has a large root system (for nutrient absorbtion), is likely to be better able to tolerate poor growing conditions in its first year, and show less response than other material to nutrient addition particularly in the early part of its first growing season.

This provides an important reason for choosing well-grown stock. It also explains some of the conflicting results of different fertilizer experiments. But the effect is most unlikely to persist beyond the first growing season, and cannot be relied upon. So the application of nutrients must be contemplated for all plantings except those on the most fertile sites. However, if trees are growing in grass or surrounded by weeds, it must be remembered that most of the fertilizer will be taken up by the grass and weeds, so that the effects of fertilizing can be negative, another cause of conflicting results (see Chapter 13).

11.3 *Methods of nutrient addition*

11.3.1 USE OF GOOD SOIL

It has already been pointed out (Chapter 6) that nutrients can be provided by the application of a layer of soil, provided that it is of good quality. Since the element most likely to be in short supply is nitrogen, it can be used as a key to the amount of soil which is required. Table 11.1 shows the total nitrogen provided by different thicknesses of soil of different quality. The aim should be

Table 11.1 *The amounts of nitrogen (total and mineral fractions, assuming 5% release per year) which will be provided by layers of topsoil of different quality and different thickness (Bradshaw, 1989)*

Nitrogen content (%)		Depth of topsoil layer (mm)		
		100	200	300
0.02	Total N (kg N ha^{-1})	200	400	600
	N released (kg N ha^{-1} yr^{-1})	10	20	30
0.05	Total N (kg N ha^{-1})	500	1000	1500
	N released (kg N ha^{-1} yr^{-1})	25	50	75
0.1	Total N (kg N ha^{-1})	1000	2000	3000
	N released (kg N ha^{-1} yr^{-1})	50	100	150

to obtain a minimum of 1000 kg of total N ha^{-1}. If a soil containing 0.05% N is used, a layer of 200 mm will be needed. This will involve considerable expenditure; to purchase and spread it will cost at least 2000 tree units ha^{-1} or 0.4 tree units m^{-2} spread by hand. In large landscaping schemes, because grassland areas can be established without topsoil provided clover is included in the seed mixture to supply nitrogen, if any topsoil is to be used the most economic approach is therefore for it to be spread over the tree planting areas only, particularly where small stock such as whips are being planted.

Where standard trees are being planted, the planting pit has to be filled. With good stock the pit has to be quite large (Chapter 9). In this case the obvious approach is not to backfill with site material, but to use a good quality soil, preferably one containing at least 0.2% N. The nutrients are then immediately where they are needed, in close proximity to the developing root system. This will be sufficient to get the tree off to a good start, since the nutrients in the fill will be sufficient to satisfy the growth of the tree for several years. Then, as the tree grows, its developing root system will be able to forage for nutrients effectively over a wide area, so that it will not matter if the nutrients are at relatively low concentrations in the general substrate.

11.3.2 FERTILIZERS AND MANURES

The topsoil used for backfill may, however, be poor, or be unavailable, and the site materials equally poor. So for insurance or for necessity, the addition of nutrients by means of fertilizer has a great deal to recommend it.

There are many different types of fertilizers (Table 11.2). The most commonly available are granular, with the nutrients in soluble form but held in solid material. These types, when incorporated into the soil, will provide nutrients that are immediately available to the tree. If applied to the surface they become available only after rain. They are beneficial in quickly correcting any nutrient deficiencies that may be apparent, and are the most economical method of applying nutrients (about 0.02 tree units m^{-2} spread by hand or 80 tree units ha^{-1} spread by machine). Granular fertilizers commonly contain nitrogen, phosphorus and potassium. As these are released the phosphorus and potassium become absorbed by the soil, to be available later to the tree roots on demand. Nitrogen by contrast, particularly when in the form of nitrate, tends to be leached away from soils because it is an anion and not readily held by soil minerals. To overcome the problem of nutrient leaching, slow-release fertilizers, which gradually release nutrients over a specific period of time, are available. These are more expensive, but can be very effective.

Many different types of organic manures are also available (Table 11.2). These release nutrients only by decomposition, and are therefore usually slow release. They may be made of wastes from food processing, such as dried blood, hoof and horn, bone meal, and fish meal. These have the advantage that they are relatively concentrated, but they are becoming difficult to obtain and are always expensive (about 5 times more than normal fertilizers) in relation to the quantities of nutrients that they contain. High-volume manures, particularly farmyard manure, spent mushroom compost, and sewage sludge, are more likely to be

Table 11.2 *Fertilizers and manures suitable for urban trees*

Fertilizer	Composition (%)				Special characteristics
	N	P	K	Other	
Fast release fertilizers					
Ammonium nitrate	35	0	0		Balanced NH_4/NO_3
Nitrochalk	25	0	0		Contains lime
Superphosphate	0	8	0		
Potassium sulphate	0	0	41		
Compound 17:17:17	17	8	14		
Compound high N	25	4	8		The most suitable compound for trees
Slow release fertilizers					
Sulphur-coated urea	32	0	0		Rather fast release
Magnesium ammonium sulphate	5	10	8	Mg 10	Very satisfactory release
Urea formaldehyde	38	0	0		Release slow in cold weather
Isobutylidene diurea	31	0	0		Expensive but good
Osmocote	18	4	7		Expensive but very effective
Rock phosphate	0	13	0		Only released in acid soils, cheap
Organic manures					
Chicken manure	2	1	1		Variable, high ammonia when fresh
Farmyard manure	0.6	0.1	0.5		High water content
Pulverized domestic refuse fines	0.7	0.3	0.5		Variable
Proprietary mushroom/peat compost	1.2	0.3	3		Composition depends on supplier
Digested sewage sludge	4	2	0.4		Values for dry material, only 5% dry solids when fresh

available and have the advantage that they not only contain good slow-release supplies of nutrients but also organic matter which can considerably improve water supply to the roots (Chapter 10).

There are many different ways fertilizers (F) and organic manures (M) can be applied to trees:

1. surface broadcast (F and M)
2. included in backfill on planting (F and M)
3. injected into the root zone (F)
4. placed in auger holes (F)
5. as fertilizer spikes (F)
6. as injections into the trunk of the tree (F)
7. as a foliar spray (F).

At the time of planting, if organic manures are being used, it is most sensible for them to be incorporated in the backfill. With fertilizers, because of their solubility, there appears to be no reason why they should not be applied on the surface, by broadcasting. Subsequently, surface application will be the easiest method of application, for both fertilizers and manures. However they may have little effect if applied to trees growing in grass, since the nutrients may well be intercepted and taken up by the grass, leaving little or none for the trees. Indeed on young trees the effect may be to increase the competition from the grass for water so much that the tree actually grows worse rather than better. This is discussed further in Chapter 13. For this reason the insertion of a fertilizer spike or injection of nutrients under pressure directly into the rooting zone is often advocated. The results are mixed, perhaps because the nutrients have not always been placed in a position where they are accessible to the absorbing roots (see Section 3.2). Nevertheless there are situations, for instance where trees are planted directly into a pavement, where the use of injection or a spike is the only practicable method. For situations where there can be a choice and there is no grass competition, experimental evidence suggests that there is negligible difference between sub-surface placement and broadcasting.

Foliar sprays, widely used on fruit trees, have limitations for amenity trees in that their application is a skilled operation and can lead to damage of non-targeted plants, as well as causing annoyance to passers-by. Injections directly into the trunk have not proved very successful and leave a wound which is prone to infection.

A serious problem with normal fertilizers is that the component nutrients, particularly nitrogen, are very soluble. If a single large fertilizer application is used, the tree is likely to suffer an immediate excess followed by shortage as the nutrients are leached away, out of reach, into the lower parts of the soil profile and streams and other water bodies. Repeated fertilizer applications throughout the growing season, although a little more costly, are likely to be more effective. Simply put, it can be better to apply nutrients in smaller doses throughout the

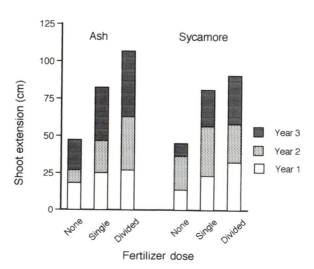

Figure 11.7
The effect of the addition of fertilizer to newly planted trees when the dose is divided into three, applied at different times in the growing season (Capel, 1980). Growth is improved but the cost of application may make two doses preferable.

growing season rather than as a single dose once a year (Figure 11.7). However the gain in growth may not be worth the cost of the extra application. Perhaps the optimum method is for the annual dose to be split into two, given in spring and summer.

These problems are not associated with the use of specially formulated slow-release fertilizers, or organic manures which are essentially slow release. Both tend to release nutrients in relation to prevailing weather conditions, particularly when temperatures improve in the spring, in tune with the requirements of the tree. However some organic manures, especially freshly produced sewage sludge, may contain high levels of ammonium nitrogen, not only in excess of tree requirements, but sufficient to be toxic. This can be obviated if the sewage sludge is allowed to weather for 3–6 months before use. The elevated levels of heavy metals sometimes found in sewage sludge are not a problem; they will only cause trouble when applications are repeated over a large number of occasions.

In general terms, slow-release fertilizers and organic manures are more beneficial to trees than normal fertilizers, especially if they can be incorporated into the pit at planting time, when handling is less difficult. However, it is essential to ensure that an excessively high price is not being paid for them in relation to the nutrients they contain.

11.3.3 NITROGEN-FIXING SPECIES

Nitrogen is the nutrient most likely to be in short supply. A very inexpensive way in which it can be contributed to the soil is by nitrogen-fixing plants such as legumes. White and red clover can fix 100 kg N ha^{-1} yr^{-1}, which is equivalent to

Figure 11.8
A comparison of the growth of alders (in the background) with various species of *Sorbus* and *Quercus* (in the foreground) on a very poor site after 8 years. The growth of the nitrogen-fixing species is about 10 times greater than the growth of the others.

Figure 11.9
The performance over 10 years of sycamore growing on a poor substrate close to a nitrogen-fixing species, alder (redrawn from Kendle and Bradshaw, 1992). Growth can be enormously improved by release of nitrogen from the alder, although this effect may take some time to build up; over the same period the growth of the alder remains considerable.

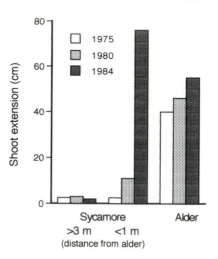

the application of 500 kg ha^{-1} yr^{-1} of a nitrogenous fertilizer such as sulphate of ammonia. Legumes sown in a tree planting area can therefore ensure long-term nitrogen supply; for this they can be sown at not more than 10 kg ha^{-1}, but must be provided with adequate phosphorus. In the short term, however, they can compete with newly planted trees for water, particularly when combined with grass, and so must be kept away from the rooting zone by the use of herbicides (see Chapter 13). As a result they are not very valuable for new plantings in the first 2 years, when reliance must be placed on fertilizers, manure or good quality soil.

In sites where there is a great deficiency of nitrogen, such as on mine or quarry wastes, tree species which are themselves nitrogen fixers, such as alders and false acacia, can be used. They will grow much faster than non-fixing species (Figure 11.8). If planted in mixed stands they will improve the growth of non-fixing species considerably by their contribution of nitrogen (at least 100 kg ha^{-1} yr^{-1}), although this effect may take some time to materialize because of the initial slow rate of release of nitrogen from the woody tissues (Figure 11.9). The nitrogen-fixing species which are valuable for interplanting on infertile sites are given in Table 11.3.

Table 11.3 *Nitrogen-fixing species suitable for use in poor sites in urban areas*

Trees	Shrubs
Alnus glutinosa (common alder)	*Cytisus europaeus* (broom)
Alnus cordata (Italian alder)	*Hippophae rhamnoides* (buckthorn)
Alnus incana (grey alder)	*Lupinus arboreus* (tree lupin)
Robinia pseudo-acacia (false acacia)	*Ulex europaeus* (gorse)

References

Bradshaw, A.D. (1981) Growing trees in difficult conditions, in *Research for Practical Arboriculture* (ed. Anon), Forestry Commission, Edinburgh, pp. 93–108.

Bradshaw, A.D. (1989) The quality of topsoil. *Soil Use and Management,* **5**, 101–8.

Capel, J.A. (1980) The establishment and growth of trees in urban and industrial areas, PhD thesis, University of Liverpool.

Colderick, S.M. and Hodge, S.J. (1991) A study of urban trees, in *Research for Practical Arboriculture* (ed. S.J. Hodge), Forestry Commission Bulletin **97**, HMSO, London, pp. 63–73.

Dutton, D.A. and Bradshaw, A.D. (1982) *Land Reclamation in Cities,* HMSO, London.

Kendle, A.D. and Bradshaw, A.D. (1992) The role of soil nitrogen in the growth of trees on derelict land. *Arboricultural Journal,* **16**, 103–22.

Other reading

Atkinson, D. and Ofori-Asamoah, T.E. (1987) The growth of the nursery tree root system and its influence on tree performance after transplanting, in *Advances in Practical Arboriculture* (ed. D. Patch), Forestry Commission Bulletin **65**, HMSO, London, pp. 32–7.

Bradshaw, A.D. and Chadwick, M.J. (1980) *The Restoration of Land*, Blackwell, Oxford.

Bernatsky, A. (1978) *Tree Ecology and Preservation,* Elsevier, Amsterdam.

Gilbertson, P., Kendle, A.D. and Bradshaw, A.D. (1987) Root growth and the problems of trees in urban and industrial areas, in *Research for Practical Arboriculture* (ed. D. Patch), Forestry Commission Bulletin **65**, HMSO, London, pp. 59–66.

Harris, R.W. (1992) *Arboriculture*, Prentice Hall, New Jersey.

Putwain, P.D. and Evans, B.E. (1992) Experimental creation of naturalistic amenity woodland with fertilizer and herbicide management plus lupin companion plants. *Aspects of Applied Biology,* **29**, 179–86.

Tromp, J. (1983) Nutrient reserves in roots of fruit trees, in particular carbohydrates and nitrogen. *Plant and Soil,* **71**, 401–13.

Walmsley, T.J. (1989) Factors influencing the establishment of amenity trees, PhD Thesis, University of Liverpool.

12 *Support and protection*

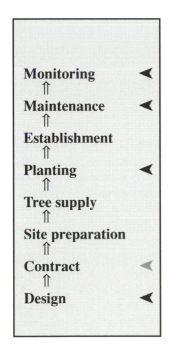

Monitoring ◀
⇧
Maintenance ◀
⇧
Establishment
⇧
Planting ◀
⇧
Tree supply
⇧
Site preparation
⇧
Contract ◀
⇧
Design ◀

- Because of their truncated root systems, most trees larger than whips will need support for a period after planting.
- Artificial support restricts the development of supporting, reaction, wood so that when support is removed the trees will be less able to stand upright.
- Minimizing support encourages reaction wood formation, reduces maintenance of ties, and is cheaper.
- The simplest way of minimizing support is to plant small trees.
- With larger trees it is best to use the shortest stake which will keep the stem upright.
- Ties must be examined at least twice a year to ensure they have not broken and are not strangling the stem.
- The most effective protection against vandalism is to design schemes so that trees are not immediately accessible to people.
- Tree guards are valuable for very exposed trees but stem damage will occur if the tie breaks, which can be difficult to observe and rectify.
- Where grass surrounds the tree, there can be serious mower and strimmer damage which can pass unnoticed; it can be obviated if the grass is controlled by herbicides or mulches.
- Tree guards and shelters can be valuable in protecting trees from the effects of wind, animal and mower damage; tree shelters also increase rates of early growth.
- Damage by road salt is best avoided by design, planting away from roads and paths, and channelling salt-laden runoff away from the planting pit, rather than by the use of soil ameliorants.

Large trees that have been transplanted often need to be supported until they have developed a new root system. At the same time trees may need to be protected from a variety of damaging agents, including animals, vandals, wind, mowers, strimmers and cars. Protection measures can be free standing, but often they will need to be attached to the device which supports the tree itself. Experience has shown that if careful maintenance is not employed, support and protection measures can become a lethal combination.

12.1   *Benefits and problems of support*

Trees growing in natural situations do not require artificial support. They are sometimes blown over in extreme winds, especially where rooting is restricted to shallow depths by unfavourable soil conditions, but root systems usually develop to anchor the above-ground parts securely as the tree grows. In contrast, transplanted trees, with truncated roots and an unnatural shape, especially if they are standards, may take some time to achieve stability. Thus some interim support is often required; but this is not always so.

Potentially the problems caused by supporting trees outnumber the benefits, (Table 12.1). Therefore the first question which arises is whether or not to support trees at all. Transplants, whips and feathers, because of the size of the root system relative to the shoot, are securely anchored by simple pit, notch or slit planting (Chapter 9). This may also be true for half and light standards, though support may be needed in windy sites, and at the top of this size class.

Table 12.1   *The potential benefits and problems of supporting newly planted trees: the problems outnumber the benefits*

Potential benefits	Potential problems
1. Stabilizes transplanted trees, which have truncated root systems 2. Provides anchorage for protection devices	1. Alters tissue distribution in stem and roots 2. Weakens stem at attachment point 3. Requires careful regular maintenance 4. When removed, the tree may be less able to stand upright than a tree which was unsupported from planting 5. Expensive

Small trees should be planted wherever they can satisfy the design criteria for the site, avoiding the need for support.

In many situations, however, small trees are unsuitable. In streets, for example, larger trees may be needed to provide an instant visual impact and to deter their removal by vandals. These trees will need supporting. The question then becomes how to minimize any problems resulting from the means of support.

12.1.1 STEM AND ROOT GROWTH

As pointed out in Chapter 3, the growth of trees is not limited to extension growth. Each year existing wood increases in girth by a ring of new tissue. The trunk therefore thickens every year, tapering upwards from the base (Figure 12.1a), so that stable support is provided for the canopy, including the lateral branches. Trees growing naturally move in the wind, swaying about the base of the trunk. Tensions created in the stem, which decrease with distance from the base of the tree, can lead to extra thickening of the stem and roots. This 'reaction wood' enhances the ability of the tree to withstand high winds.

The amount of reaction wood produced depends on the degree of sway the stem experiences. Trees growing individually in open situations often experience high wind speeds with little or no shelter. Production of reaction wood is relatively high, and canopy growth tends to take a spreading form at the

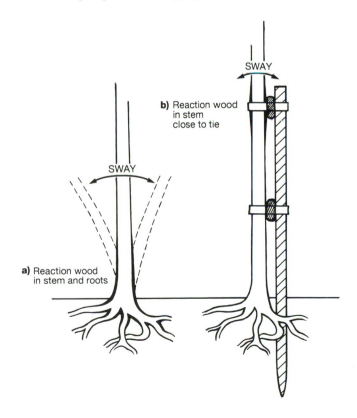

Figure 12.1
(a) A free-standing, open-grown tree allowed to sway about at a point near to the ground with its stem and roots strengthened by the formation of reaction wood. (b) A fully supported tree swaying about a higher fulcrum so that reaction wood only forms close to the point of attachment. If the stake is removed the stem will not be in a good condition to support a large canopy.

Figure 12.2
The damaging effects of over-supporting trees. This tree does not have a strong enough root system to support itself now that the stake has rotted.

expense of height growth. In contrast, trees growing close together in woodlands experience lower wind speeds and reduced light input to the canopy. Consequently height growth is encouraged at the expense of canopy spread, with lower stem diameter growth and a relatively low level of reaction wood production.

The result of this is that trees growing in natural woodlands and in mass plantings have different shapes to open-grown trees; but in both cases the growth form is always closely linked to the environment in which the tree is growing, and the stems will be strong enough to support their canopies.

Artificial support interrupts this link. Evidence suggests that, compared with unsupported trees, lower stem thickening tends to be reduced at the expense of canopy growth. Close to the highest attachment point, however, reaction wood is produced, as this is the new fulcrum about which the tree sways (Figure 12.1b). None of this is necessarily a problem whilst the tree remains adequately supported. When, however, the support breaks or is removed, the trunk will be less able to support the large canopy because it is top heavy. Such a tree is prone either to snap in high winds or to develop a pronounced lean (Figure 12.2).

12.1.2 TIE AND STAKE DAMAGE

Attaching a tree to its support is fraught with problems, and damage to tree stems by stakes and ties is all too common in urban areas (Figure 5.2). On the one hand the tree must be held firmly enough to stand upright in windy conditions. If it is too loosely held, the stem will be damaged by banging against the support, and by rubbing against the tie. On the other hand, if the tie is too tight, it will pinch the stem, as well as prevent the beneficial effects of swaying already mentioned. In severe cases tie strangulation can restrict stem growth so much that swellings form either side of the tie (Figure 12.3). Alternatively the tie snaps, allowing the tree to rub and bang against the support (Figure 12.4), or even blow over.

Where ties constrict the stem abnormal growth can replace the normal pattern of tracheids and fibres. The changes occurring may result in reduced transport of water, nutrients and photosynthates, leading to impaired growth. In most situations, however, this is unlikely to be the major problem. In one survey tie and stake damage to the stem were, in fact, positively correlated with shoot extension. This is not as peculiar as it sounds, as it is those trees which establish and grow quickly which expand and become constricted by the tie most rapidly.

The good growth of these trees which suffer stem damage will, however, hide more important problems stored up for the future. In the long term, the strangulation can only lead to a weakened stem. The sight of trees which have snapped at, or close to, the tie point is common in urban areas. This is often presumed to

Figure 12.3
Ties left too long on an otherwise healthy tree can cause severe stem damage. Note the swellings both above and below the tie.

Figure 12.4
If a tree tie snaps or is not adjusted correctly, the stem may rub and bang against the support. In this instance the tie had been replaced but no cushion had been placed between the tree and the stake.

be due to vandalism, which is frequently untrue. The usual cause is a strong wind which is responsible for applying the final blow to a tree weakened at the tie point. However vandalism, may be helped by such weakness.

12.1.3 METHODS OF SUPPORT

Different methods of support may be more suitable for different tree sizes and situations. In all cases support should be minimized, for a number of reasons. Firstly, support is expensive. Secondly, there are benefits in allowing some tree sway, as already discussed. Thirdly, minimizing support usually reduces the amount of maintenance required to prevent damage to the stem. Minimizing support should include its removal as soon as the tree can stand upright unaided, as well as using the least rigid support from the outset.

Whenever support is required, this should be as low to the ground as possible. Rather than a tall stake, with two attachment points (cost about 1 tree unit), a short stake should be used with only a single tie (cost about 0.7 tree units) (Figure 12.5). A 'short stake' is perhaps best defined as the minimum height of stake which will support the stem vertically. This method of staking will induce reaction wood close to the tree base by allowing the tree to sway. A tree grown with this form of support will be better able to stand upright when the stake and

Figure 12.5
A short stake is the best support for most standard trees since it allows the tree to flex which encourages the development of reaction wood.

Figure 12.6
The results of an experiment to test the use of no support, short stakes, and tall stakes, on standard plane trees. Although the planting site was extremely windy, the trees supported by short stakes remained upright and showed greater stem diameters than the fully staked trees.

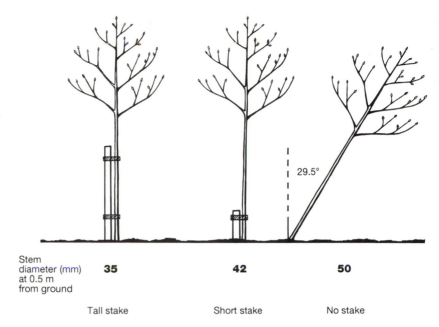

Stem diameter (mm) at 0.5 m from ground

35   **42**   **50**

Tall stake   Short stake   No stake

tie are removed. Figure 12.6 shows the results of an experiment using three levels of support on standard trees. Even though the site used was extremely windy, short stakes supported the trees as well as tall stakes and allowed excellent stem thickening.

When stakes are used, great care should be taken to ensure that they are not placed too close to the stem. At the same time they must be close enough to allow the tie to be firmly attached. Rubber blocks placed between the stake and the tie act as a cushion, but should not be nailed to the stake, as is sometimes the case. The potential benefits of elastic, expanding and biodegradable ties remain unproven.

An alternative to the single stake is to use more than one support, each placed slightly further away from the trunk, with separate ties all at the same height (cost about 2 tree units). This allows the stem to expand without strangling at the tie, and will allow tree sway, even when tall stakes are used.

Ties should be adjusted or removed along with the stake as soon as the tie becomes tight on the tree trunk. If a tall stake has been used, but the tree cannot stand upright unaided after one growing season, the upper tie should be removed. A new attachment point can then be found at the lowest possible point which will still maintain the tree upright. The stake can then be shortened accordingly. This should be reviewed later, and the support removed as soon as possible. Ties must be inspected at least twice a year.

Very large trees, usually root-balled, are unsuitable for staking. Guys or some method of underpinning may be necessary. Guys, however, can produce many of the problems caused by ties, such as stem abrasion, as well as obstructing mowers, tripping pedestrians and inviting vandalism. Some form of underpinning is usually preferable. Planting semi-mature trees on a raised platform in the

Figure 12.7
Diagram of underpinning specimen trees. Large root-balled trees can be securely anchored by driving stakes into the ground close to the root-ball and fastening wires between them. The technique is easy to apply, inexpensive and invisible.

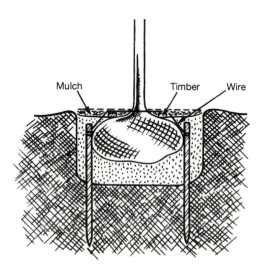

Mulch   Timber   Wire

middle of the pit can aid stability (Chapter 9), and this can be supplemented by driving three or four stakes into the ground close to the root ball and wiring the roots down as in Figure 12.7. This method is sufficient to hold most trees steady, and has the benefit of being cheap and invisible. More elaborate and expensive systems are available, but their superiority has not been established.

12.2 *Problems of protection*

Many different agents can damage trees. Measures taken to protect trees can be very effective; but they can also be very expensive, and require maintenance to prevent them from damaging the tree as it grows. None of these problems will arise if steps are taken at the design stage to isolate trees from the cause of damage.

12.2.1 VANDALISM

In towns the most common objective is to protect trees from attacks to stem and canopy by vandals. The available evidence suggests that this emphasis is often misplaced (Chapter 5). But, none the less some protection may be thought essential, frequently involving elaborate and expensive measures.

Trees can be most effectively protected from vandals by proper design at the planning stage. In areas that are heavily used by people, trees should be placed in areas where they are least accessible (Figure 12.8). Damage is considerably reduced when trees are placed in flower beds, or better still in shrubberies (see Figure 5.4), and need little or no protection. Trees are most susceptible when they are young. So where trees are in a group, a simple fence, made of chestnut paling (cost 1 tree unit per linear metre), placed around the planting area for the first 5 years, may be necessary.

Figure 12.8
Protection by design. Trees planted amongst shrubs are less accessible and more protected.

It is possible to create plantings that are effectively vandal tolerant, by mass planting of small stock, i.e. transplants or whips. These have great powers of recovery and regrowth after damage, and losses are covered by the growth of other trees. A combination of prickly shrubs with a mixture of whips and standards can provide both vandal protection, resistance and immediate effect.

The most severe vandalism involves snapping the stem. Tall staking is often suggested as the answer to this problem, but may in fact make matters worse. Pulling on a tree is likely to be less damaging when most of the stem can flex, and therefore absorb the strain. Supporting trees with tall stakes prevents this flexing, increasing the likelihood of the stem snapping close to the fulcrum, the upper tie. This will, of course, be exacerbated if tie strangulation has already occurred. It is worth pointing out that even where the tree is snapped off close to the ground, all may not be lost. If a species has been chosen which will shoot from the base (Chapter 8) the tree may not die, although the instant visual impact of the standard tree will have been lost.

Another common method of protecting trees from vandalism is the use of a tree guard. This comes in several forms, but the simplest is a cylinder of wire mesh placed around the stem, anchored by nailing it to the stake (cost 1–1.5 tree units). Damage to the trunk, for instance by penknives, used to strip bark, is more difficult with a guard in place. Guards can, however, present numerous problems. Ties placed on the tree before the guard is fixed are difficult to adjust to prevent stem strangulation. If ties snap they cannot be replaced, and the stem will not only bang against the stake, but can swing round and round against the top of the guard, effectively sawing itself in half (Figure 12.9). In some cases, if not removed, the tree may even grow around the guard, which becomes embedded in the wood. Occasionally, guards can actually attract vandalism. They act as litter traps, filled with rubbish, waiting to be set alight (Figure 12.10).

Figure 12.9
When the tie snaps inside a tree guard the tree may saw itself in half against the guard. The damage will not usually be noticed until it is too late.

Figure 12.10
Rubbish stuffed into a tree guard. The means of protection has become a focus of vandalism.

Large trees are sometimes planted in order to make vandalism more difficult. Semi-mature trees can achieve this aim, but they are very expensive if all the correct planting and cultural practices required to produce healthy trees are employed. If further protection is required, a wide range of attractive free-standing guards is available (Figure 12.11), but again these are very expensive (cost 10 tree units).

The cheapest and most effective way to minimize vandalism remains design – not planting trees in areas likely to be a focus for attack – and planting larger numbers of trees together in dense groups rather than as isolated individuals. Design solutions effectively cost nothing. Where this cannot be done, a pragmatic approach is essential. It is, for instance, worth considering a change of species, for example replacing a smooth-barked tree such as *Acer plantanoides*, whose bark is relatively easy to strip, with a species possessing a rougher trunk, such as *Crataegus monogyna*, which will resist vandalism. These two species are very different; but if it is possible to accommodate the change in the landscape, it should be considered. As mentioned earlier, another alternative is to plant species tolerant of vandalism, such as birch or willow which will shoot from the base. Where an individual is persistently vandalized it may be advisable to conserve time and resources by bowing to the inevitable and not replanting in that position.

12.2.2 MOWER AND STRIMMER DAMAGE

Where weeds are allowed to grow close to the base of trees, efforts are often made to tidy up the site by mowing. Cutting weeds can improve the visual appearance of a site, but it does not alleviate the detrimental effects of the weed competition especially where the weeds are mainly grass (Chapter 13). Equally important is the amount of damage that can ensue.

Figure 12.11
Free-standing tree guards are effective and attractive but also expensive.

Figure 12.12
Damage by mowers and strimmers used to cut grass close to trees is a common and serious result of poor maintenance which is often difficult to see

Recent observations suggest that strimmers and mowers have become a major factor causing poor growth or death of urban trees. Indeed if mowers and strimmers pass close to the tree, untrained and careless operators can strip the bark and underlying wood from the trunk without realizing it (Figure 12.12), often affecting a high proportion of the trees on a site. The damage may go unnoticed by the supervisor since the trees do not usually die but go into decline because root growth is inhibited. Despite these problems, mechanical methods of weed control are still favoured by many in charge of tree maintenance.

There are few protection measures available to prevent this form of damage. Smaller trees can be protected by shelters and guards designed principally for other purposes, i.e. to prevent animal and wind damage. Anti-vandal guards may be effective in protecting larger trees. But the best method for protecting trees from mowers and strimmers is to remove the offending vegetation by herbicides, mulches or mats (see Chapter 13), obviating the need for cutting. These methods are relatively cheap and allow mowing to proceed much faster in the neighbourhood of trees.

12.2.3 ANIMAL DAMAGE

Animals can cause severe damage to the stem and shoots of trees. Small trees can be killed by rabbits, mice, voles, etc. feeding on bark, new buds and shoots. Mass plantings in urban fringe areas are particularly vulnerable. Some protection is afforded by the use of tree shelters (see later), but there is also a variety of purpose-made guards available. Some of these are designed to expand as the tree grows. Care must be taken, however, to ensure that the animal guard is securely fastened to a suitable support, or the tree and guard will be blown over in high winds. Often animals can be excluded by fencing off tree areas, which removes the need for any guards. If this approach is taken, however, great care must be taken to ensure the integrity of the entire boundary.

In the unlikely event of larger trees requiring protection from animals such as deer and cattle in urban areas, elaborate measures can be taken to protect them using large barriers around individual trees, as in the British parks tradition. They are, of course, very expensive (over 3 tree units each).

12.2.4 WIND DAMAGE

High wind speeds often occur in urban areas, as described in Chapter 5. The scorching of tree canopies by strong winds, exacerbated by salt spray in shore areas is, however, often overlooked in the design of urban plantings. Only small trees can be effectively protected from this type of damage because their growth is within the boundary layer of slow-moving air close to the ground. If mass planted they will then protect each other as they grow up. Plastic windbreaks are effective, but are unsightly. Trees less than 0.5 m in height can benefit from the use of tree shelters. These are essentially hollow tubes of semi-transparent plastic placed over the tree (costing 0.3 tree units each, installed). Ideally they should be sufficiently tall and durable to allow 3 years protected growth. Shelters slightly reduce solar radiation input to the canopy, but significantly

Figure 12.13
The effect of tree shelters on growth of small trees (Potter, 1991). Growth can be significantly enhanced and the trees are given protection from animals and wind.

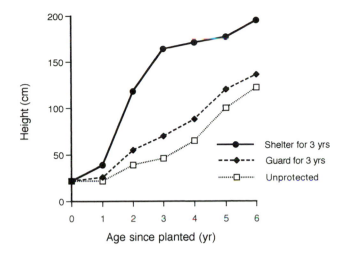

increase air temperature and humidity. The result is an enhancement of photosynthesis. Thus shelters will not only protect trees from wind, but have been shown to actually aid establishment and growth (Figure 12.13). They are, however, highly visible and attractive to vandals.

For larger trees, no effective protection against wind damage is possible. Recognizing site conditions and adapting planting designs, choosing the most tolerant species (see Chapter 8), possibly even replacing trees with shrubs, or building up defence in depth with a graduated set of species, is the only realistic alternative to one-sided, scorched and stunted tree canopies.

12.2.5 ROAD SALT

As with vandalism and wind damage, the best protection lies in avoiding road salt before it becomes a problem, by appropriate planting design. The simplest method is to place the trees at a sufficient distance from the source of the salt, thus ensuring that damaging concentrations of spray or soil salt do not develop. In urban areas where traffic speeds are relatively low, a distance of 3 m is sufficient. This means, unfortunately, that on roads where heavy doses of salt are used, the curb-side tree can no longer be justified. Street trees must be planted at the back of the pavement or in open areas free from concentrated salt unless given special protection.

Design detail is, however, paramount. Pavements which may themselves be salted must be designed so that salty melt-water does not drain into tree rooting areas (Figure 12.14). If there is any chance of drainage towards the planting pit then the immediately surrounding paving should be elevated to slope away from the pit, or the pit provided with a low but effective curb (Figure 12.15).

There are additional steps which can be taken to protect roots from road salt. It has been suggested that calcium-rich compounds such as gypsum and limestone can be added to the soil in the planting pit to ameliorate the effects of the sodium ions in road salt. Experimental results, however, are inconclusive.

Figure 12.14
This tree had to be replaced because of salt damage. Bad design means that salt water draining from the pavement goes into the tree pit.

It may be more effective to use a surface layer of organic material covering the pit. This has long been the practice in countries such as Sweden and the Netherlands. Materials such as straw, coarse peat and bark mulches can absorb large amounts of road salt; but good evidence of their benefits is scant. In Denmark during the winter rubber mats are fixed round the bases of trees exposed to salt. There is also some limited potential for selecting salt-tolerant species (Chapter 8). However, the real answer is to limit salt use.

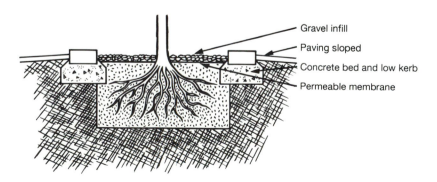

Gravel infill

Paving sloped

Concrete bed and low kerb

Permeable membrane

Figure 12.15
Design for a tree pit in a paved area to minimize the chance of salt water entering the pit. Good design is the best way to achieve protection.

Reference

Potter, M.J. (1991) *Tree Shelters,* Forestry Commission Handbook **7**, HMSO, London.

Other reading

British Standards Institute (1991) *Guide for Trees in Relation to Construction,* BS 5837:1991, British Standards Institution, London.

Brown, I. R. (1987) Suffering the stake, in *Advances in Practical Arboriculture* (ed. D. Patch), Forestry Commission Bulletin **65**, HMSO, London, pp. 85–90.

Cowan, M. (1964) *Inverewe*, Geoffrey Bles, London.

Dirr, M. A. (1976) Selection of trees for tolerance to salt injury. *Journal of Aboriculture,* **2**, 209–16.

Dobson, M.C. (1991) *De-icing Salt Damage to Trees and Shrubs,* Forestry Commission Bulletin **101,** HMSO, London.

Fayle, D.F.C. (1968) *Radial Growth in Tree Roots,* Faculty of Forestry Technical Report **9**, University of Toronto, Canada.

Gilbertson, P. and Bradshaw, A.D. (1985) Tree survival in cities: the extent and nature of the problem. *Arboricultural Journal,* **9**, 131–42.

Hunt, B., Walmsley, T. J. and Bradshaw, A. D. (1991) Importance of soil physical conditions for urban tree growth, in *Research for Practical Arboriculture* (ed. S.J. Hodge), Forestry Commission Bulletin **97**, HMSO, London, pp. 51–62.

Littlewood, M. (1988) *Tree Detailing*, Butterworth Architecture, London.

Malcolm, D.C. (1974) Root development and tree stability, in *Tree Growth in the Landscape*, Wye College, Kent, pp. 77–82.

Patch, D. (1987) Trouble at the stake, in *Advances in Practical Arboriculture* (ed. D. Patch), Forestry Commission Bulletin **65**, HMSO, London, pp. 77–84.

13 *Weed control*

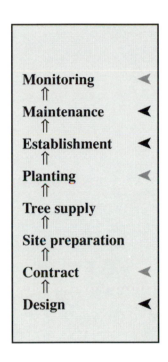

Monitoring ◄
⇑
Maintenance ◄
⇑
Establishment ◄
⇑
Planting ◄
⇑
Tree supply
⇑
Site preparation
⇑
Contract ◄
⇑
Design ◄

- Competition from weeds can have serious effects on the growth of newly planted trees.

- Grass, whether sown or arising naturally, constitutes one of the most serious weeds, particularly because its root growth is normally much greater than that of the trees.

- The major mechanism of weed competition is by depletion of soil water resources, so that weeds can have major effects on standard trees as well as on transplants.

- The effect of addition of nutrients is only to increase weed competition by increasing weed growth.

- Herbicides are the most effective and economical method of weed control.

- A range of herbicides with immediate or long-term effects for use with urban trees is available.

- Mulches are an alternative, but are best combined with an effective herbicide.

- With grass, mowing or cutting is not an alternative because it does not reduce the competition by the grass.

- Because competition is mainly for water by the weed roots, the weed-free zone around each tree should be at least 1 m in diameter.

Rarely is it possible to achieve good establishment and good growth rates with trees grown in the presence of weeds. Although many people think that this refers only to normal agricultural and garden weeds, it applies equally well to grass, which can have just as serious effects and is undoubtedly the dominant component of urban landscapes. It is common for trees and grasses to be used

Figure 13.1
Standard trees affected by lack of weed control. Larger trees are as susceptible to weed competition as smaller stock.

together in planting schemes. Trees are either planted directly into existing grass, or grass is sown around newly planted trees.

As a result, there is a great deal of misunderstanding about the effects that weed growth can have, not only on the growth of trees but on their ultimate survival. Until recently, weed competition had been ignored as a major factor in the death of urban trees, even though foresters and fruit growers have recognized for many years the devastating effects that weed growth can have upon tree growth.

Today the design of tree planting schemes is changing. There is a movement away from planting standard trees and grass together, to mass planting of whips and transplants. The importance of good weed control under these circumstances is now widely accepted and indeed practised. It is perhaps easy to understand the effects that weed growth can have upon smaller trees; but the same dramatic effects can be observed with larger trees (Figure 13.1).

It is not just newly planted trees that can benefit from weed control. There are many examples in older schemes where trees that have been kept in check by weed competition have grown well after the weed growth has been suppressed.

Weed control is not an optional extra that can be incorporated into the planting specification if sufficient funds are available. It has to be an integral part of all specifications that trees are kept free from weeds for at least 3 years after planting.

13.1 *Effects on survival and growth*

Planting failure rates of 80% are not uncommon when weed control is not practised. This situation can be greatly exacerbated with poor planting stock and bad planting technique; under these circumstances failure rates of 100% have been recorded.

Subsequent growth of the trees can also be severely impaired if weed competition is not controlled in later years. Halving of height increments and reduction in shoot extension growth by a factor of 10 are common responses to weed growth. But it is not shoot growth alone that responds to competition from weeds; root growth is equally as sensitive.

13.1.1 MECHANISMS OF ACTION

It is now clear that water supply is usually the major factor that affects the growth of newly planted trees and their consequent ability to exploit more of the soil water reserves (Chapter 10). Weed competition exacerbates the problems of water supply. Grasses, for example, probably the most vicious of all weeds, are in an ideal position to exploit the limited supply of water available to newly planted trees. Their roots are more abundant than tree roots and have a greater length and total weight (Table 13.1). In addition, the roots of weeds occupy the layer in the soil which is not only the first to receive precipitation but also warmth in the spring, all the conditions that allow weeds to begin growth early,

Table 13.1   *The root weight (g) in summer of grass and trees in an experiment set up in late autumn to examine competition by grass under different conditions. Grass has a more aggressive root system than newly planted trees*

	With water and nutrients	With water no nutrients	No water, with nutrients	No water, no nutrients
Grass roots	145	49	45	53
Tree roots (no grass)	34	45	17	26
Tree roots (in grass)	15	25	13	21

well in advance of the tree. Table 13.1 also shows that when competition occurs, the root growth of the trees is severely affected, which exacerbates the situation.

It can be demonstrated that competition for water is the major mechanism by which weeds inhibit the growth of trees. If the water loss from containers in which trees are growing with or without grass is assessed, for any given volume of soil the grass is able to utilize soil water reserves twice as quickly as the tree (Figure 13.2). The trees growing in the presence of the grass show symptoms of water stress much earlier than those growing without grass. Eventually the trees with grass wilt and die earlier. But before this, a more sensitive indicator that the trees growing with grass are in trouble is that their stomata close while the stomata of the trees growing without grass are behaving normally.

In the field the interaction between the presence of weeds, rainfall and soil moisture in an area planted with trees is very clear when continuous recordings of soil moisture deficiencies are made (Figure 13.3). During periods without rain, severe moisture tensions build up under grass. This does not occur if the grass and other weeds are excluded by either herbicide or mulch, despite the presence of the trees.

Apart from the resulting severe competition for the limited water resources

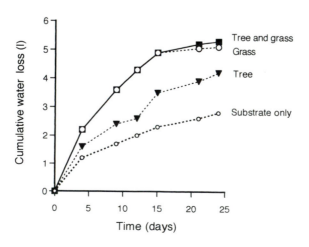

Figure 13.2
The effects of weed competition on the utilization of water from a limited volume of soil. Water is used up twice as quickly when grass is present.

Figure 13.3
The soil moisture tensions developing in an area planted with trees and given different surface treatments (Davies, 1987a). In dry periods the severe tensions do not build up when grass and other weeds are excluded.

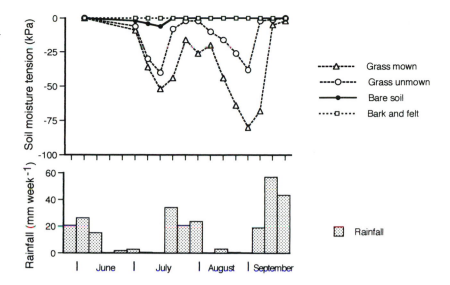

that the growth of the grass imposes, a most noticeable feature of such experiments is the deleterious effect that the addition of nutrients has on water loss from the soil, because of increased growth of the grass. In particular, grass root growth is increased (Table 13.1). The consequent increased water stress in the tree can easily be demonstrated. Under field conditions, fertilizing trees growing without weed control can quickly devastate a planting scheme (Figure 13.4). Although there is some competition by the weeds for nutrients, this appears to be only a minor mechanism by which the presence of weeds affects tree growth.

Perhaps the most critical effect that competition has on trees is on their root system. This can be demonstrated in simple experiments (Figure 13.5). Even if the trees manage to survive, those that experience the most severe competition – from grass that has been fertilized – are left in a very poor state to re-establish their root system and begin their next years growth.

The fact that grass growth can have such a powerful effect on the growth of even standard trees, confirms that the major competition must be below ground,

Figure 13.4
The effect of weed growth and fertilizer on the growth of transplants under field conditions (Gilbertson *et al.*, 1987). Tree performance is disastrously affected where fertilizer is given without weed control.

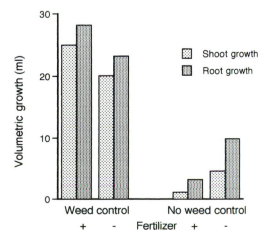

Figure 13.5
A simple experiment showing the severe effects that competition can have on root growth of young trees. Treatment from left to right: +grass +fertilizer, +grass -fertilizer, -grass +fertilizer, -grass -fertilizer

since under these circumstances there cannot be competition for light. Undoubtedly, however, there are situations where small stock has been planted, e.g. transplants or willow pegs, where competition for light may be a problem. This situation can become worse during subsequent years, following the die-back of the weeds, where a mat of dead material is formed over the trees, further restricting light. Where weed control is not applied over the whole site, but only around individual trees, problems of light may also occur. However this situation may, in the end, be beneficial in some cases, as a result of the shelter from wind that the growth of the weeds can give over the whole of a planting site.

Another mechanism that has been suggested for weed action is allelopathic toxicity. Some species may contain in their roots, or release from them, substances that are inhibitory to the growth of other plants. But this theory is not well proven, and certainly not for urban trees.

13.2   *Methods of weed control*

To be successful, any weed control measure must eliminate weed competition rather than just suppress it, and it should be as permanent as possible. It is not much use if, after good weed control in the spring, there is a major infestation later when water deficiencies are likely to be greatest. Equally, it is important that weed control is carried out sufficiently early in the season to ensure that the store of water in the soil is not reduced by the weeds in advance of the spring growth of the tree. Soil moisture deficits usually begin to appear in May. Weeds left in position during April can therefore have an effect which carries over throughout the growing season.

13.2.1 PHYSICAL REMOVAL

The traditional, but most expensive, method of controlling weed growth is by the physical removal of the plants. In grassland it has been normal practice for a

Figure 13.6
The traditional method of eliminating grass competition is effective but expensive.

bare area to be maintained by hand around individual trees. In the past many of the trees in our urban parks were tended to using this technique; it creates a neat and positive impression (Figure 13.6). But with limited resources now available this practice has almost ceased, and it is rarely applied to new plantings (costs are about 0.07 tree units m^{-2}). It is not actually the most efficient method of weed control. Shoots can quickly sprout with vigour from the edges of the cleared areas or from rhizomes left in the soil. So the effects of trimming, pulling or hoeing can be quite short lived. Over-enthusiastic hoeing may, in fact, damage tree roots growing near the surface.

13.2.2 CUTTING AND MOWING

A simpler method of control of weeds would appear to be to cut them, at a cost of less than 0.02 tree units m^{-2}. This will destroy many tall broad-leaved weeds. But grass responds by forming a denser, more low-growing sward. Since weed competition is mainly for water, cutting will do nothing to alleviate the situation in grass (Table 13.2). It is common sense that cutting a lawn does not prevent it growing; thus the water used by the grass will not be significantly reduced. Replacing the grass with a nitrogen-fixing legume such as white clover similarly has no effect.

Table 13.2 *The growth of silver maple transplants in the first season when surrounded by different surface coverings (Davies, 1987a). Grass and/or clover can arrest growth completely whether mown or not*

	Height increment (cm)	Diameter increment (mm)
Grass/clover sward (unmown)	1	-0.1
Grass/clover sward (mown)	-1	0.3
Pure clover (unmown)	0	0.4
Grass/clover sward + herbicide 1 m diam.	38	5.0
Grass/clover + polythene 1 m diam.	41	5.8
Complete area herbicide	58	7.8

Yet schemes are still planted today where the only weed control measure is to mow the grass around the tree. This is likely to be more detrimental to the growth of the tree than leaving the grass uncut, as there is a strong possibility that the tree will suffer severe damage from the mower or strimmer used, as discussed in Chapter 12.

13.2.3 HERBICIDES

The use of herbicides remains the only effective method of totally eliminating weed growth. However the use of herbicides does have a number of significant drawbacks. Herbicides are not always environmentally friendly; recently for instance permission to use a valuable group of herbicides, the triazines, in amenity and domestic areas has had to be withdrawn because of potential contamination of water supplies. None are naturally occurring products. Some can be hazardous to the health of the operator and skilled application is essential. Indeed there are strict rules on who can actually use herbicides, and their use now falls under the COSHH legislation.

Many different herbicides are available, and it is commonplace for the same materials to be marketed under different brand names; glyphosate, for instance, is known as 'Roundup' in agriculture and 'Tumbleweed' in the domestic market. It is important to know the active chemical compounds which any herbicide contains. Their mechanisms of action fall under three broad categories. **Contact herbicides**, as their name implies, are effective mainly on the part of the plant with which they come in contact (e.g. paraquat); others, **systemic herbicides**, have a more general effect because they are translocated around the plant (e.g. glyphosate); others, the **residual herbicides**, are taken up from the soil, in which they can remain effective for a long period of time (e.g. propyzamide, dichlorbenil). The materials are relatively simple to apply, either scattered as granules or sprayed as a liquid.

Care must be taken in selecting the appropriate herbicide. The first priority is to select the correct herbicide to combat the specific weed growth on site. Some herbicides will act against certain grasses, but not others, whilst some will kill broad-leaved weeds whilst only checking the growth of grasses. The correct herbicide must be selected for pre-planting spraying, as some remain active within the upper soil surface and could well affect the growth of any trees planted into it. In addition, different tree species respond differently to different herbicides and, indeed, differently at different times of the year. Paraquat, for example, can be applied safely onto relatively immature bark with no effect to the tree, whilst an application of glyphosate to the same immature bark will

Table 13.3 *The different herbicides most suitable for use with urban trees (Williamson and Lane, 1989, with modifications)*

Contact herbicides

> **Paraquat.** Action by foliar contact, weeds must be green. Not selective. Since not translocated rhizomatous plants will regrow. Poisonous so appropriate precautions must be taken. ('Gramoxone', 'Dextrone x')
>
> **Glufosinate ammonium.** Similar to paraquat but not so poisonous. ('Challenge')

Translocated herbicides

> **Glyphosate.** Action is contact and systemic. Apply to weeds by spray when actively growing, good on grasses, even rhizomatous species. Care must be taken not to apply to tree foliage or young bark. Very safe, inactivated by soil contact. ('Roundup')
>
> **Alloxydim-sodium.** Action is contact and systemic. Particularly controls grasses. Best in cool conditions. ('Clout')
>
> **Dalapon.** Action is contact and systemic. Apply as spray. Major effect is on grasses. ('Dalapon')

Residual herbicides

> **Propyzamide.** Action is by soil, volatilizes in cold soil, affecting surface rooting plants. Apply as granules or wettable powder October–December. Lasts 3–6 months. Do not apply immediately before or after planting. Very safe on broad-leaved trees. ('Kerb')
>
> **Dichlorbenil.** Action is by soil, less active in cold soil than propyzamide. Apply as granules January–March and autumn. Problems if over-application. ('Casoron G', 'Prefix')

Residual herbicides only able to be used in forest or nursery areas

> **Atrazine.** Action is by both foliar contact and soil. Products containing atrazine are unsuitable for use on very light soils, those prone to waterlogging, and poorly structured soils including recently constructed sites. It is also unsuitable for use after planting on poorly planted or unhealthy trees. ('Atroflow', 'Gesaprim 500FW')
>
> **Atrazine with dalapon.** Action as atrazine alone, but increased effect on coarse grasses. Apply mid-March to May. ('Atlas Lignum')
>
> **Cynazine with atrazine.** Action as atrazine alone but more effective on broad-leaved weeds. Apply only when trees dormant. ('Holtox')
>
> **Terbuthylazine with atrazine.** Spray. Action is by foliar contact and soil. Only on ash, beech, oak and sycamore, and when dormant. ('Gardoprim A500FW')

quickly lead to the death of the tree. Some residual herbicides become volatile in the soil as the ground warms up. This causes no problems whilst the trees remain dormant but new foliage can quickly be killed.

It is not difficult, however, to select the correct herbicide for the right job. Advice is readily available from the Forestry Commission who have published flow charts for the correct selection of herbicides. A simplified set of herbicides for use with broad-leaved trees in forest and urban areas is given in Table 13.3. These represent the most widely accepted herbicides: it is unfortunate that triazines can no longer be used in urban areas. Clearly the list is far from exhaustive, and particular situations or types of weed problem may merit the use of a less commonly used herbicide, often with very specific applications, for which specialist advice should be sought.

When herbicides are being used care must be taken, especially the directions relating to handling and dose. Despite popular misconceptions, health and environmental hazards are negligible if the materials are handled correctly. What is important, however, is to use the dose and method of application appropriate for the weed situation concerned. Spray drift can cause problems; under-application can lead to poor weed kill, over-application to wastage or tree death. Manufacturers test their products rigorously and if there is any doubt about the use of any herbicide, the manufacturer should be contacted and asked for advice.

Herbicide application is probably the most efficient and economical method of weed control. Average costs including application are about 0.02 tree units m^{-2}, although this can vary depending on the herbicide and the size of the area. This is a very small fraction of the total planting costs, even if repeated over 3 years. Herbicides can be applied without difficulty to isolated trees in grassland (Figure 13.7). Because they can be so effective and long lasting, repeat treatments are reduced. In new areas they have a further advantage over many other weed-control methods in that they allow the planting of trees into weed-free ground.

Figure 13.7
Herbicide applied as a spot treatment to standard trees in grassland is the most effective method of weed and grass control for isolated trees.

Figure 13.8
A mulch becoming ineffective as a result of weed invasion. The combination of mulch with a residual herbicide is more effective.

13.2.4 MULCHES

The next most common method of controlling the growth of weeds in urban areas, and one that is becoming increasingly popular, is the use of a mulch. There are many different kinds of mulches available, from the common organic types such as chopped bark to inorganic plastic mulches; indeed 'weed mats' are now marketed widely. Mulching has the disadvantage over herbicide treatment in that it suppresses rather than eliminates the weeds. Thus when the mulch cover is damaged, weed competition rapidly returns (Figure 13.8). Mulches also tend to be relatively expensive; the average price including application is about 0.3 tree units m^{-2}. They are often difficult to maintain. Loose mulches such as shredded bark are often blown by the wind; plastic mulches can be degraded by the action of sunlight and are often torn by animals. It is essential that damaged mulches are repaired or they will quickly become ineffective.

However many of the mulches used in the urban environment have the advantage over herbicide treatments in that they are considered to be relatively friendly to the environment. Many, such as chopped bark, are from renewable resources. In addition they tend to have an attractive appearance, perhaps one of the reasons why they are being used so widely.

Mulches can also have other consequences for the rooting environment of the newly planted tree. They can reduce the rate of evaporation of soil moisture and retain the warmth of the soil, undoubtedly beneficial factors that other weed control regimes cannot offer.

The use of mulches alone is less effective than when used in conjunction with a herbicide. Application of a herbicide to eliminate the weed competition followed by a mulch to prevent light infiltration and reduce the germination of weed seeds is an ideal combination. Without occasional herbicide treatment single weeds can grow up through the mulch and have almost as much effect as a large number.

13.3   *Area of treatment*

If weed competition were predominantly by light exclusion then it would be necessary to keep only a small area clear around each tree. Once it is realized that competition is mainly underground, by roots, and for water, it can be seen that it is crucial to keep a much larger area clear of weeds, related to that from which the tree is likely to draw water as its root system develops.

There is clear evidence of a direct relationship between the size of the treated area and the growth of the tree. Not only is shoot growth directly proportional to the area treated but so too is root growth (Figure 13.9). Considerable improvement in growth is achieved as the size of the area is increased, even up to 1 m diameter.

This obviously has specific implications in terms of establishment where the priority is the rapid restoration of the size of the root system. In practice, if complete weed control cannot be achieved over the whole site, an area with a

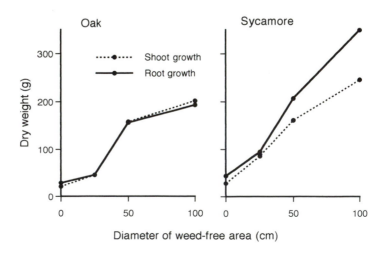

Figure 13.9
The effect of the size of the herbicide-treated area on the root and stem growth of oak and sycamore transplants (Davies, 1987b). The considerable improvement that occurs even up to a maximum of 1 m diameter has important implications for normal practice.

Figure 13.10
In mass plantings total herbicide
treatment is simplest and most
effective.

diameter of 1 m around transplants, and of 1.5 m around standard trees, should
be kept weed free. In mass plantings this means that complete weed control will
usually be preferable (Figure 13.10).

References

Davies, R. (1987a) Weed competition and broadleaved tree establishment, in *Advances in
Practical Arboriculture* (ed. D. Patch), Forestry Commission Bulletin **65**, HMSO,
London, pp. 91–9.

Davies, R. (1987b) *Trees and Weeds: weed control for successful tree establishment,*
Forestry Commission Handbook **2**, HMSO, London.

Gilbertson, P., Kendle, A.D. and Bradshaw, A.D. (1987) Root growth and the problems
of trees in urban and industrial areas, in *Advances in Practical Arboriculture* (ed. D.
Patch), Forestry Commission Bulletin **65**, HMSO, London, pp. 59–66.

Williamson, D.R and Lane, P.B. (1989) *The Use of Herbicides in the Forest,* Forestry
Commission Field Book **8**, HMSO, London.

Other reading

McCavish, W.J. and Insley, H. (1992) Herbicides for sward control among broad-leaved
trees. Arboriculture Research Note **27:92**, Arboricultural Advisory and Information
Service, Farnham.

Walmsley, T.J., Hunt, B. and Bradshaw, A.D. (1991) Root growth, water stress and tree
establishment, in *Research for Practical Arboriculture* (ed. S.J. Hodge), Forestry
Commission Bulletin **97**, HMSO, London, pp. 38–43.

14 *Pruning*

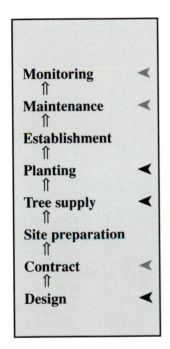

Monitoring ◄
⇑
Maintenance ◄
⇑
Establishment
⇑
Planting ◄
⇑
Tree supply ◄
⇑
Site preparation
⇑
Contract ◄
⇑
Design ◄

- Pruning is an unnatural process but is necessary for various training and remedial purposes, particularly to control shape, but also disease in larger trees.
- It must be carried out with care, the cuts made in a way which optimizes healing.
- In the nursery, pruning can ensure a satisfactory growth form.
- On planting, pruning can be used to assist the tree to regain its natural root:shoot ratio, but this should be done with caution and not after the tree has leafed out because this severely disrupts root growth.
- Pruning at the planting stage can be used to reduce wind resistance, valuable in exposed sites to prevent trees being blown over.
- Subsequent pruning should be minimal, although crown lifting is nearly always necessary.
- The need to control plant size is a common problem; it must be carried out carefully, not by crude lopping or topping.
- However since the fault is usually in the choice of species or site, it is these which should be remedied.

There are a number of reasons for pruning. When trees are mature the principle reason is to maintain the health of the plant, and its shape where this is necessary. When they are past maturity they may need remedial action to keep them safe. When trees are young pruning is often carried out with the aim of aiding its establishment and stability following transplanting. These are all good practical reasons for pruning. However there are aesthetic reasons also, that stem from our desire to create decorative or convenient shapes, often paying little attention to the effect on the structure and health of the tree.

Pruning is a totally unnatural phenomenon that the tree would not normally experience. It can be argued that the self-thinning and branch loss, which occur

Figure 14.1
Pollarded trees: a long-established tradition in parts of Europe.

Figure 14.2
Multi-stemmed willows in a
Norfolk car park are an excellent
contribution to the landscape.

throughout the life of a tree, are a self-pruning mechanism, occurring because of some form of stress, whether shade, disease or drought. Nowhere in nature, however, apart from where trees are subjected to grazing or extreme exposure, are the structure and shape so altered as when a tree is pruned.

Pruning has been practised for centuries. Evelyn in his treatise of 1678 states:

> Prune off the branches, and spare the tops; for this does not only greatly establish your plants by diverting the sap to the roots; but likewise frees them from the injury and concussions of the winds, and makes them to produce handsome streight shoots, infinately preferable to such as are abandon'd to nature and accident, without this discipline.

Pruning has developed over a long period into an often quite elaborate art form. The pollarding of plane trees (Figure 14.1), for example, and the ancient bonsai techniques of the Japanese are two of the most extreme examples. Pollarding used to be carried out in country areas to allow the production of poles and withies for fencing and baskets, etc. on trees accessible to grazing animals. In amenity situations the need to lift the crown of the tree as it develops to reduce shading and obstruction by branches is the most common reason for skilful pruning. To many people an equally important reason for pruning is the simple removal of branches in order to make trunks of good shape. This is understandable where the ultimate objective is to produce timber of high quality, but in amenity situations a curved, multi-stemmed, tree may be preferable and more effective from a design point of view (Figure 14.2).

14.1   *Principles of pruning*

Pruning is not the straightforward procedure that it may appear. It could be assumed that because all trees have a similar biology, they would all react to the effects of pruning in a similar manner. This is not the case. Some species, such as lime and plane, are capable of surviving even the harshest of pruning treatments, whilst species such as birch and cherry may well perish after similar treatment; some conifers are particularly sensitive. Cuts made in one way can allow natural healing to occur quickly; made in another way the tree may become invaded by a decay fungus and ultimately die.

Pruning is therefore a skilled operation which should be carried out by properly trained personnel. There are too many examples where misplaced eagerness by a novice or, even worse, ignorance by some of the less scrupulous firms advertising their services as tree surgeons, has resulted in the early demise of trees. Moreover, with mature trees, pruning is often a dangerous task, certainly when large heavy branches are being removed from a considerable height in the canopy. It is not in the scope of this text to examine the technical methods by which large trees are pruned. This chapter will be restricted to the pruning of young trees.

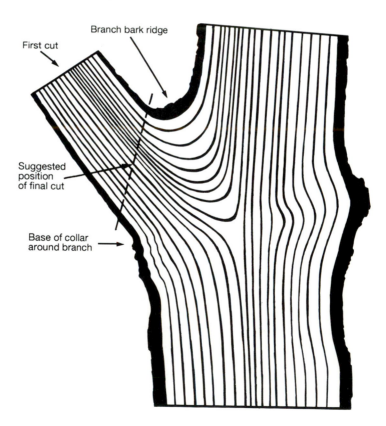

Figure 14.3
'Target' pruning (Lonsdale, 1993). The importance of pruning the tree in the correct place cannot be over-emphasized.

Trees are pruned using a number of different tools, from pruning knives (for small shoots), hand pruners (for shoots up to 15 mm in diameter) and bow saws (for intermediate sized branches), up to chain saws (for branches over 80 mm in diameter). Whatever the tool being used, it should be sharp to give a clean cut. Hygiene is also of primary importance to stop transmission of disease. It is recommended that tools are chemically sterilized before use on a different tree.

The general requirements for any cut are quite clear. On smaller shoots, a bud is selected that is facing in the direction of required growth. The stem is then cut just above the bud, in parallel with the direction of its growth. If the cut is made too far away from the bud the wound created may not heal, and there can be die-back. If it is made too close to the bud, the bud itself may be damaged.

For the removal of larger branches, it is usually necessary to take the whole branch right back to the stem or back to a suitable lateral. In either case it is important that the cut is **not** flush with the stem or lateral, but is made 1–2 cm out, just above the collar of tissue, where it is present, which surrounds the branch at its point of departure, so-called 'target' pruning (Figure 14.3). By doing this the size of the cut area is minimized and the development of callus tissue over the wound to seal the cut encouraged. If the cut is made too far from the stem, the development of the callus tissue will be restricted; if it is made too close to the stem the bark of the stem may be damaged. Proper pruning technique is much more effective in minimizing infection and decay than any sealants applied to the wound, none of which appear to have positive effects.

14.2   *Nursery pruning*

Pruning trees in the nursery to select a healthy leader and form a well-structured crown is undoubtedly of importance when trees are going to be planted in urban areas. The liabilities that can arise following damage to people and property due to the falling of a badly situated branch can be considerable. Training of the tree in the nursery is one way of reducing the possibilities of this occurring.

The overall aim must be to produce stems that are structurally sound, and bear well-supported branches. This is achieved if the branches leave the stem at an angle of not less than 20°. At smaller angles than this, a weak crotch nearly always develops, because bark tissue becomes trapped between the stem and the branch as they grow.

Nurserymen and -women are skilled in the practice of pruning trees. They watch the trees growing and have time to notice their potential problems. They will direct growth into one main leader, removing the possibility of two leaders. They will also take a great deal of care to build up the crown. Weak growth will be removed and a tree with a vigorous, healthy and structurally sound shoot system produced (Figure 14.4).

Sometimes, however, in the interests of rapid production, nurseries may produce a tall, lanky tree with a stem which is far too thin. Such stock should not be purchased. If this is tending to happen, a good nursery will drastically trim the branches and allow the tree to grow on for 2 or 3 years before selling it.

Figure 14.4
Nursery pruning (from Bentley, 1991). Correct pruning in the nursery will result in a well-structured tree.

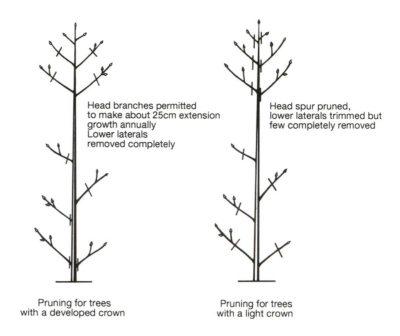

Head branches permitted
to make about 25cm extension
growth annually
Lower laterals
removed completely

Head spur pruned,
lower laterals trimmed but
few completely removed

Pruning for trees
with a developed crown

Pruning for trees
with a light crown

14.3 *Pruning at planting*

Of prime importance to the establishment of the newly planted tree is the restoration of the natural root:shoot ratio which existed before transplanting, already discussed in relation to the problem of water in Chapter 10. This, of course, necessitates the vigorous development of a new root system, but it is commonly argued that it can be helped by the reduction of the size of the crown at planting. Die-back is one common feature of tree growth in the urban environment and is really a self-pruning mechanism by the tree itself, to restore the balance between the shoot and root systems (Figure 14.5). Unfortunately this produces a tree that can be aesthetically unappealing for several years. Pruning at planting would appear to be the answer.

However, there is an opposing theory, that pruning is of little or no value or is actually detrimental to the growth of the tree. It is suggested that by disrupting the crown of the tree, the physiological processes of carbohydrate production and auxin release, and subsequently root regeneration, are disrupted, and that this has more important consequences than the development of water stress discussed in Chapter 10.

There is no doubt that summer pruning of a tree will disrupt physiological processes and ultimately root regeneration. A simple experiment comparing the effect of dormant and summer pruning on root growth of sycamore transplants (Figure 14.6), shows that root growth essentially ceases for several weeks following summer pruning, while trees that receive dormant pruning treatment show similar rates of root development to unpruned trees. At the

Table 14.1 *The effects of dormant pruning on the leaf development of standard plane trees. Pruning results in fewer leaves and a reduced leaf area (Walmsley, 1989)*

Pruning treatment	Leaf area (cm^2)		Leaf number	
	Mid May	Mid July	Mid May	Mid July
Unpruned	5365	5256	292	142
Moderate	4592	4412	215	113
Severe	536	3894	54	100

Figure 14.5
Die-back is a common feature of many urban trees. This self-pruning mechanism in response to the stress of bad planting creates an unsightly appearance.

same time the pruning appears to have no effect in alleviating the effects of drought.

However, during the early period immediately following planting, the effects of dormant pruning are not only to delay bud burst but also to reduce the leaf area of the tree, principally by a reduction in the number of leaves (Table 14.1). Although the evidence is not altogether clear, this can have an effect on the subsequent development of moisture stress. At the same time dormant pruning leads to an invigoration of shoot growth (Figure 14.7).

What can be said with certainty is that it is important not to prune a newly planted tree once it has leafed out. The disruption in root growth following a summer pruning will only exacerbate the vicious circle whereby, because the tree is planted with a small root system, the volume of water available to the tree will be reduced, which in turn will reduce root growth and the volume of water available to the tree the following season.

Pruning the tree at planting can also be used to reduce the wind resistance of the tree. This will be important when trees are being planted in exposed sites, whether between buildings or near coasts. If the wind load can be reduced significantly then trees that might otherwise have required staking may be capable of being established without a stake. The problems associated with staking trees have already been discussed in Chapter 12.

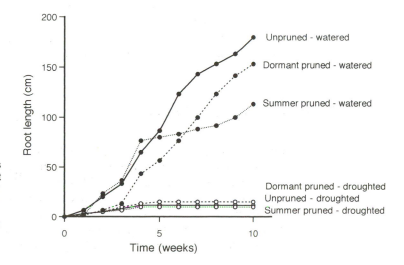

Figure 14.6
Root growth of maple transplants in relation to pruning and drought (Walmsley, 1989). Neither winter nor summer pruning relieves the effect of drought on root growth, and summer pruning inhibits root growth in trees not suffering drought.

Figure 14.7
Shoot growth after different levels of dormant pruning (Walmsley, 1989). The new growth leads to invigoration of the shoot system. (Vertical lines indicate means.)

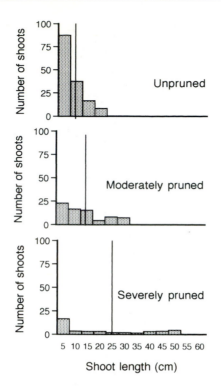

Whatever the reason for pruning at planting, it is common practice not to prune the tree until it has actually been planted. However this puts the onus onto the planting contractor. It would be better if the plants were pruned in the nursery where this could be carried out by skilled operatives. The pruned trees would then be available for inspection before they are purchased. Disease problems that might be a consequence of unskilled pruning will be less. An additional benefit is that damage to the shoots of the tree during transit to the site will be reduced because of the shortened shoot system, and pruning to remove damaged shoots should not be necessary. In parts of Europe it is common practice to reduce the crowns of heavy standards substantially before planting. The tree responds by making excellent growth in the first year, but retains a balanced small crown (Figure 14.8).

14.4   *Pruning for shape*

Correct pruning in the nursery will significantly reduce the necessity to prune trees once they have been transplanted into the urban landscape. However there are several reasons why trees may still be pruned.

Crown lifting is nearly always required, even within a few years after planting. The lower branches of the tree are removed. This increases the clearance between the lowest branches of the tree and the ground, prevents any problems of obstruction to either people, vehicles, or buildings, and makes vandalism to the canopy

Figure 14.8
Early growth of a newly planted tree in Berlin which has been heavily pruned to reduce crown size before planting. This common practice leads to a tree which is well balanced in its early years.

Figure 14.9
Stability and pruning. Pruned trees have less dense canopies than unpruned trees and are less likely to be damaged by severe storms.

less likely. Such pruning does not normally have to be severe; the branches removed are usually already becoming suppressed, and are being replaced by branches directly above, so the disruption to the shape of the tree is minimal.

The crown of the tree may sometimes be pruned to remove dead or damaged branches. This is referred to as crown cleaning. It reduces the risk of infection and significantly reduces the possibilities of accidents being caused by falling branches. It is an inevitable feature of planting trees in urban areas that because of the situations in which they are placed some damage to branches occurs.

Sometimes the whole canopy of the tree is thinned to allow more light penetration and also to remove branches that might eventually touch or cross. This practice is known as crown thinning. The overall size and shape of the tree is not affected. It results in a tree with a reduced wind resistance. This obviously has implications on the stability of the tree, which is less likely to be blown over in severe storms than trees with a denser canopy (Figure 14.9). However if the pruning is too severe the tree may respond by a dense growth of new shoots, nullifying the original intention.

14.5   *Controlling plant size*

One of the commonest reasons why trees are pruned is to control the size of the tree. It is a difficult operation to carry out satisfactorily because the real problem lies in an incorrect choice of species. Far too often the wrong tree has been planted in the wrong place, with the result that it becomes too large for its position. This is an important reason why correct species selection is essential. But with the inevitable changes in land use that occur in cities, the nature of a site may be changed so dramatically that the size of a mature tree could well be too large for the new use of the site. The result of both of these problems is that the tree will have to be heavily pruned to bring it back to a desired size.

Heavy pruning is extremely difficult. Often the tree is merely 'lopped' or 'topped'; the whole crown is cut back to the trunk (Figure 14.10). This makes the tree grossly misshapen and prone to infection and subsequent decay. Some

Figure 14.10
Although lopping is sometimes necessary to reduce tree size, it leads to misshapen trees with increased liability to disease. It would be better to replace the tree.

species of tree will not tolerate such harsh treatment, and problems will inevitably occur, such as branch loss from the subsequent regrowth of the shoot system. In fact further pruning to restore the crown of the tree (restoration pruning) will usually be essential. It is therefore a practice that should be prevented at all cost. It is much more practical to carry out controlled pruning. This should not be carried out at one time, but the size of the tree reduced over a number of seasons. This will significantly reduce the need for subsequent restoration pruning.

Sometimes because the tree is too old or the wrong species, the task of reduction is too difficult. In this case it is better to remove the tree and replace it with a more suitable species, or with the same species in a more suitable place. Properly planted it will soon make the same contribution to the environment, or better, than the over-pruned tree it replaced.

One important consideration before any tree is pruned is to make sure that the tree is not covered by a Tree Preservation Order. If it is, permission from the local planning authority will be required before any work can be undertaken.

Pruning a large tree can be a very expensive operation (20 tree units). Careful thought should, therefore, be taken in firstly deciding if the work is really required and secondly in considering who should actually carry it out. Correct choice of species will help in reducing the need for large-scale pruning in our towns and cities. Species should be chosen which will suit the site. Trees should not be expected to outgrow their positions, even at maturity, and the species chosen should not be prone to problems such as disease and premature breakage of branches.

References

Bentley, R.A. (1991) Plant production: tree training, in *Research for Practical Arboriculture* (ed. S.J. Hodge), Forestry Commission Bulletin **97**, HMSO, London, pp. 23–8.

Lonsdale, D. (1993) A comparison of 'target' pruning, versus flush cuts and stub pruning, Arboriculture Research Note **116:93**, Arboricultural Advisory and Information Service, Farnham.

Walmsley, T.J. (1989) Factors affecting the establishment of amenity trees, PhD thesis, University of Liverpool.

Other reading

Capel, J.A. (1987) *A Guide to Tree Pruning*, Arboricultural Association, Romsey.

Davies, R.J. (1987) Tree establishment: soil amelioration, plant handling and shoot pruning, in *Advances in Practical Arboriculture* (ed. D. Patch), Forestry Commission Bulletin **65**, HMSO, London, pp. 52–8.

Harris, R.W. (1990) *Arboriculture*, Prentice Hall, New Jersey.

Lonsdale, D. (1987) Prospects for long term protection against decay in trees, in *Advances in Practical Arboriculture* (ed. D. Patch), Forestry Commission Bulletin **65,** HMSO, London, pp. 149–55.

Kozlowski, T.T. (1975) Effects of transplanting and site on water relations of trees. *American Nurseryman,* **141**, 84–94.

15 *Pests, diseases, damage and decay*

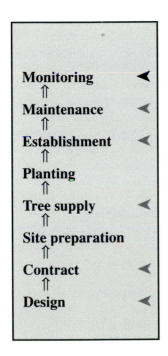

Monitoring ◄
⇑
Maintenance ◄
⇑
Establishment ◄
⇑
Planting
⇑
Tree supply ◄
⇑
Site preparation
⇑
Contract ◄
⇑
Design ◄

- Pests and diseases are not usually a problem with newly planted trees.
- Nevertheless the disaster caused by Dutch elm disease gives us warning of the need for constant vigilance against the possibility of new disease or pest epidemics.
- In Britain there are a number of existing diseases which can cause trouble under certain circumstances.
- Each of these has its own characteristics and control measures.
- In nearly all cases the only effective treatment is the removal of the infected part, or the whole tree.
- At present there are no pests causing serious problems.
- Damage is always likely to occur unless it is prevented by design.
- Damage associated with constructional work should be anticipated and effective protective measures taken beforehand.
- Decay is essentially a problem of older trees, but its initiation in younger trees can be prevented by ensuring vigorous growth and minimizing major or recurrent damage.

A cursory inspection of the trees in our cities suggests that there are few problems due to pests and diseases. Indeed this is not an unfair observation. On the whole, examples of poor growth or death are nearly always due to other factors, which have already been discussed. So do we need to bother about pests and diseases? The simple answer is yes, and the best example of why we must continue to pay attention is the devastation which was wrought by Dutch elm disease. The elm was one of the most important amenity trees in southern Britain before the outbreak of the disease in the late 1960s. The elm dominated areas of the countryside in hedgerows and woodlands. Selected cultivars were widely used as street trees because of their potential for majestic and trouble-free growth. Now these have disappeared from all but a few towns, killed by a disease which effectively spared not a single tree, cultivar or species (Figure 15.1).

This example is, mercifully, the only one of its kind affecting amenity trees. But there are major examples of the destruction which can be wrought by a new disease in other species, especially crop plants. The coffee crop of Ceylon was destroyed by the leaf rust fungus, *Hemileia vastatrix*, in the 1880s and had to be replaced by tea. Currently serious damage to fruit crops in California is being caused by the Mediterranean fruit fly. In all of these cases the situation has been the same. In undisturbed conditions pests and diseases are, except in very rare cases, in equilibrium with their hosts. This has come about by long evolution towards a balanced relationship in which the pathogen does not eradicate its host, because this would mean its own death.

This equilibrium is, however, only between coexisting pathogens and hosts. It does not necessarily occur between pathogens and potential hosts that have not previously coexisted. A pathogen which is in equilibrium with host species in its own country may be totally destructive to species of another country. When a pathogen escapes into a new country it can cause immense damage. With a pest there is also the possibility that it was in equilibrium in its own country because other organisms controlled it. If these are left behind when the pest is introduced into another country, there is the possibility that it can be much more damaging.

In the case of Dutch elm disease the situation was more complex because it appears that the disease changed its characteristics when it was introduced into North America from Europe. Although benign in Europe, it killed all the elms in North America. Then when it was reintroduced into Britain it showed that it had become a very different, lethal, disease. Exactly what had happened to it is still not certain. But the history is worth telling because it shows that in modern conditions, in which materials, and potential pests and diseases, are moved all over the world despite quarantine, original balances between pests/pathogens and their hosts can be upset.

Figure 15.1
Elms in the Midlands dying of elm disease in 1972. We should never forget the lessons from this catastrophe.

Control of the movement of pests and diseases by strict quarantine measures is therefore essential, and operates in all countries. But pests and diseases can still escape, and constant vigilance is essential. For this reason it is crucial that any signs of serious damage which are unusual and not immediately explicable should be investigated and then reported to the Forestry Commission at its Alice Holt Research Station.

However, there are a number of pests and diseases already existing in this country, which can have serious effects in some situations. Some of them appear when trees are, for one reason or another, in a weakened condition due to some other stress factor. Others appear because of infection from other trees in the vicinity. Since the effects and control of pests and diseases are individually specific, they will be dealt with individually.

15.1   *Diseases*

15.1.1 BEECH BARK DISEASE

This is apparently due to the combined attack of the beech scale insect, *Cryptococcus fagisuga,* and a fungus, *Nectria coccinea,* although other factors may be important. The insect lives by sucking the sap from below the bark and kills small patches of phloem and cambium so that the fungus enters through the wounds into the inner bark. The result is sap exudation, and blackish spots on the bark more than 2 cm in diameter (Figure 15.2a). These can spread and cause large areas of the bark to die and flake off. If these girdle the stem then translocation of nutrients and photosynthates is stopped and the tree slowly dies. If a branch is infected, the wood itself may rot and the branch break off.

Control is difficult. An insecticide can be used to kill the insect, and surgery can remove the fungus. But wound wood growth is slow and uncertain. It was thought that the disease was becoming epidemic, but it now appears that it is only serious on trees that have already been weakened by other factors, such as drought or old age.

15.1.2 DUTCH ELM DISEASE

Although this disease, caused by a fungus, *Ophiostoma ulmi,* seems to have been present in this country for a long time, it never caused any serious harm until the advent of a new aggressive strain which was imported from America in the late 1960s in elm logs. The first signs of the disease are a wilting and yellowing of the leaves of a single branch or shoot, usually high up in the tree. These symptoms may spread rapidly so that the whole tree dies by the end of the season, or it may be several years before the whole tree is dead. Characteristic brown stains can be seen in the outer wood of affected branches and twigs (Figure 15.2b).

Much to the disappointment of many people, cure seems impossible, although some expensive injections have staved off the problem for some years. The disease is spread by bark beetles which breed in the bark of dying trees and then feed in the crotches of healthy trees. Although removal of infected trees did not stop the spread of the disease in the centre of the epidemic where elm trees were dense, there is no doubt that a sanitation policy of rapid removal slows down the spread of the disease considerably. This allows the catastrophe to develop more slowly, so that the expense of replacement is spread over a number of years. But it requires both vigilance and rapid action. There are now new resistant clones appearing, such as *Sapporo Autumn Gold,* from hybridization of European elms with the Siberian elm, *Ulmus pumila,* and the Japanese elm, *Ulmus japonica,* which should provide the long-term answer.

15.1.3 FIREBLIGHT

This disease was first reported in the UK in the 1950s, on pears. It is caused by a bacterium, *Erwinia amylovora.* The initial effects are a wilting of young leaves, flowers and shoots; these then turn black as if they had been scorched by fire (Figure 15.2c). The infection spreads slowly through the tree over a few years and the whole tree may die. The disease appears to be able to attack a wide range of members of the family *Rosaceae*, including both cultivated and wild hawthorns and *Sorbus* species. Whitebeam (*Sorbus aria*) is particularly susceptible, usually dying within 6 months, but mountain ash is more resistant.

At the present time the disease is still spreading slowly from its original centre in the southeast of England, and it is uncertain what the final outcome will be. The disease is carried by insects which feed on the slime exuded from infected branches. Infections and the spread of the disease can be limited if any infected branches are removed to a point at least 50 cm below the infection and burnt. If a whole tree is dying it should not be left to die, but grubbed up and burnt without delay. It is important to keep a watch out for the disease at the present time, since it may be spread more widely by the transport of infected material.

15.1.4 ANTHRACNOSE (LONDON PLANE)

This is a disease caused by the fungus *Apiognomonia veneta*. Dormant buds are initially infected; when these die the infection spreads into the adjacent twigs, resulting in a canker. If these are large enough to girdle twigs they cause die-back. During the growing season whole shoots, up to 10 cm long, can be damaged. The infected shoot, including the leaves, turns yellow, and the leaves fall off as if it were autumn. Brown patches can also be seen on individual leaves (Figure 15.2d).

Although the damage can sometimes be severe, particularly when a cold winter is followed by a cold wet spring, the disease does not usually cause much damage. There are no practical control measures. If the damage occurs early, there is usually recovery later by a new flush of leaves. It appears that some clones of plane are more resistant than others. The oriental plane (*Platanus orientalis*) is resistant.

15.1.5 OAK WILT

This is a disease which so far is only a threat. It is caused by a fungus, *Ceratocystis fagacearum*, related to that causing Dutch elm disease. It causes wilting of branches and, in susceptible species, progressive and rapid death (Figure 15.2e).

At present it is confined to North America, spreading slowly from its point of original appearance in Wisconsin. The only control is by the removal of diseased trees. This is proving quite effective because transmission is only through root contact and rather immobile insect vectors. It has not appeared in this country, because there is a very strict quarantine and sanitation policy. Oak logs may only be imported if all bark has been removed and the logs treated to kill the fungus. But a careful watch must be kept in case this control policy fails.

Figure 15.2
Symptoms of different diseases: (top left, page 218) beech bark disease, (top right, page 218) elm disease, (top left, page 219) fireblight, (top right, page 219) plane anthracnose, (bottom left, page 218) oak wilt, (bottom right, page 218) poplar canker, (bottom left, page 219) weeping willow anthracnose, (bottom right, page 219) willow watermark.

15.1.6 CANKER

This disease of poplar is caused by a bacterium, *Xanthomonas populi*, which enters the tree through wounds. It causes cankerous growths on the main stem or on branches. These can remain small, or develop into rough outgrowths as much as 30 cm across. The large growths can girdle and cause die-back of the branch or stem infected. Although the whole tree does not usually die, it will become disfigured and misshapen (Figure 15.2f).

No treatment is possible. But the disease is only prevalent on certain species, such as the aspen (*Populus tremula*), and certain clones, such as of the hybrid black poplars and balsam poplars especially *Populus trichocarpa*. If these are avoided, and resistant clones, such as ' Robusta', 'Serotina', 'Scott Pauley' and 'Fritz Pauley' used instead, the problem is minimal. The very distinctive and widely planted Lombardy poplar is very resistant, which has, no doubt, contributed to its popularity.

15.1.7 ANTHRACNOSE (WEEPING WILLOW)

This is caused by the fungus, *Marssonina salicicola*. Small brown or purple spots appear in the spring on leaves and new shoots, which become distorted and die (Figure 15.2g). Most of the crown can be damaged. Some recovery can occur later, but rarely as much as with anthracnose in London plane. The whole tree may die.

There is no control once the tree is infected. If the attack is severe, the tree should be removed and burnt to prevent infection of other weeping willows. Stock may be received already infected in the nursery. Infection can be prevented by spraying with a fungicide such as benomyl, but this will only be worthwhile for special individuals.

15.1.8 WATERMARK DISEASE

This disease of willow, rather similar to the previous, is caused by a bacterium, *Erwinia salicis*. It infects the wood, causing a progressive die-back, firstly of individual branches, then eventually of the whole tree (Figure 15.2h). Its name comes from the characteristic stain that appears in infected wood. It spreads only locally, except where infected stock is moved.

It is most serious at the moment only on certain cultivars of the white willow, *Salix alba*, notably the cricket bat willow cultivar which seems particularly susceptible. In regions of East Anglia where the cricket bat willow is grown in monoculture whole plantations have been wiped out. The worry is that it may spread over the country into the many recent amenity plantings of white willows, which include other susceptible clones such as 'Liempole' and 'Drakenburg'. No treatment is possible, but a strict sanitation policy has kept the disease under control so far in East Anglia. This was not carried out in the Netherlands where there is now a severe outbreak. Infected trees must be removed and burnt as soon as symptoms occur.

Figure 15.3
Honey fungus growing under the bark of a tree. The fungal strands are characteristic and are the means by which the fungus spreads.

15.1.9 HONEY FUNGUS

This is a root disease caused by the fungus *Armillaria mellea* and its very close relatives. It survives in dead stumps and root systems from past trees, and spreads out a distance of 1 or 2 m, or more, into the surrounding soil by means of complex cords called rhizomorphs, rather as dry rot fungus in buildings, and infects new root systems. It grows slowly and may only affect some roots. If it girdles the root collar then the tree dies. White sheets and brown strands of fungus can be seen under the bark (Figure 15.3).

Despite claims, no chemicals yet give satisfactory control. The only solution is to dig out the infected or dead tree completely, and hope that the lack of a food source will make it difficult for the rhizomorphs to spread far. Obviously the infected area should not be replanted with the same species until many

Table 15.1 *Species and genera susceptible and resistant to honey fungus,* Armillaria *spp. (Grieg et al., 1991)*

Susceptible	Resistant	
Acer	*Ailanthus altissima*	*Prunus laurocerasus*
Betula	*Carpinus betulus*	*Prunus spinosa*
Juglans	*Crataegus*	*Quercus*
Pinus	*Fagus sylvatica*	*Robinia pseudoacacia*
Prunus	*Fraxinus excelsior*	*Sambucus nigra*
Rhododendron	*Ilex aquifolium*	*Taxus baccata*
Salix	*Nothofagus*	*Tilia*
Ulmus	*Platanus x acerifolia*	

years have elapsed. Species do, however, vary in resistance; birch, horse chestnut, and Lawson and Leyland cypresses are very susceptible, and London plane very resistant (Table 15.1). Gaps can therefore be planted with resistant species.

15.1.10 *PHYTOPHTHORA* ROOT DISEASE

This disease is caused by a number of different species of the fungus *Phytophthora*. All that is usually visible is yellowed or small leaves followed by the death of the tree, but the roots will be found to be dead and fingers of dead bark often extend up the stem. The disease occurs mostly where the ground is wet or waterlogged, and is quite widespread, attacking a number of species (Table 15.2).

No treatment is possible. The disease can be avoided by ensuring good drainage, and this can allow infected trees to recover. Many species are resistant, in effect all those not included in Table 15.2. These can be used where there is trouble, for instance Leyland cypress instead of Lawson cypress.

Table 15.2   *Tree and shrub species susceptible to* Phytophthora *root disease (Strouts, 1987a)*

Azalea and rhododendron	Lawson cypress
Apple	Lime
Beech	Southern beech
Eucalyptus	Sweet chustnut
Flowering cherry	Yew
Horse chestnut	

15.2   *Pests*

We are lucky that apart from their role in transmitting or assisting diseases, there are no serious pests of amenity trees in Britain. The situation is very different in North America, where there have been invasions by aliens such as the Japanese beetle, *Popillia japonica*, and the San Jose scale, *Quadraspidiotus perniciosus*, both on many species, and the Gipsy moth, *Lymantria dispar*, on oak. But this is not to say that there are no pests in Britain.

Perhaps the pest that comes most quickly to mind is the aphid, *Eucallipterus tiliae*, which attacks the common lime, *Tilia* x *europaea*, causing it to produce abundant honeydew which falls onto cars and whatever else is underneath. Sycamore is similarly attacked by *Drepanosiphon platanoidis*. But in both the result is only annoyance; the trees themselves are not damaged. Other species of lime are attacked less often and can be used if problems are expected.

Horse chestnut, plane, lime and sycamore are sometimes attacked by a scale insect, *Pulvinaria regalis*, which forms white woolly masses. But these do not harm the trees significantly. Oaks are sometimes defoliated by the larvae of various species of moths. Although the damage can appear severe by late spring, there is usually rapid recovery by the summer with the growth of new shoots.

15.3   *Damage*

Any tree is liable to physical damage and, as a result, to decay. The possible causes of physical damage are many and various (Table 15.3). Damage that occurs above ground is usually very obvious. The ways in which extrinsic site factors such as air pollution, vandalism and mowing can have their effects have

Table 15.3   *The major causes of damage likely to lead to decay*

Cause of damage	Area of tree affected
Ties, guards and posts	Trunks
Grass mowing machinery	Trunk bases
Motor vehicles	Above trunk bases
Vandalism – fire	Trunk bases
Pruning	Branch bases
Storms	Branch bases, trunks
Construction and services	Roots, trunks

already been discussed (Chapter 5), and also how they can be guarded against (Chapter 12). Pruning is a source of damage; but if it is carried out carefully, serious problems need not arise (Chapter 14). Most serious damage arises from construction and development work.

Most incidental damage above ground, whether due to vandalism or the mishandling of vehicles and machinery, involves damage and loss of bark. When this occurs on a small scale, the tree has a well-organized process of natural recovery. The cambium, the place where new growth occurs in the stem, becomes active and new tissues begin to form at the edge of the damaged area. These tissues spread sideways, to form a new covering of bark, at a rate which can be as much as 10 mm per year (Figure 15.4). As a result, the damaged area can become covered up in a few years if it is not too large. However this process is not effective at covering large areas of removed bark.

There appears to be no way in which this process can be assisted, except by ensuring that the tree is growing vigorously. If the damaged area is very large, then redevelopment of the bark may take many years. Even if decay fungi do not enter, it is likely that the stem will be misshapen and have a permanent structural weakness at this point. In this case it may be better to remove and replace the tree. Often, however, rot may begin and spread, so that after 10–15 years the tree becomes unsafe and has to be removed. What might have been a casual accident substantially shortens the life of the tree.

Another major region of damage is below ground, to root systems. This

Figure 15.4
Bark regrowing over a damaged
area: the tree has natural
recovery processes.

damage almost entirely arises due to excavations for the construction of new
buildings or trenches for services, but on construction sites it can be due to the
passage of heavy machinery. Trenches are the commonest source of trouble,
because most contractors have little idea of the havoc that a trench passing close
to a tree can cause (Figure 15.5). As we saw earlier (Chapter 3) the root system
of a tree has diffuse and scattered feeder roots which are constantly growing and

Figure 15.5
A trench for cable television
being cut far too close to a beech
tree. The result is that large
numbers of roots have been
damaged (the shredded roots
are on the waste heap) and the
bark has been torn off roots that
have not been broken.

Figure 15.6
Cutting a trench in relation to a tree and its likely root distribution. If more than one-third of the roots are not to be damaged, the maximum distance that the trench should approach the tree is one-third of the radius of its canopy or of the distance specified in BS 5837 (see Table 15.4).

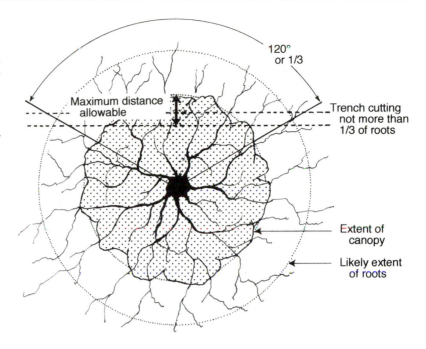

120°
or 1/3

Maximum distance allowable

Trench cutting not more than 1/3 of roots

Extent of canopy

Likely extent of roots

regrowing. A proportion of these can be damaged without causing serious problems for the tree. But if the disturbance is close enough to the tree to damage one or more of the main roots then serious trouble can arise, because these roots do not regenerate themselves and healing is limited.

If the damage is within 1 m of the base of the tree, the stability of the whole tree is likely to be permanently weakened. The tree may not blow over immediately, but will be liable to topple in a storm. If the damage is further away, the damaged tree is less likely to blow over but its growth is upset. The tree suffers from a partial and localized water and nutrient shortage. Branches may die, particularly on the side of the tree where the roots have been damaged, so that the tree becomes lop-sided. Recovery is usually slow or may never occur.

There is no treatment, only prevention. The feeder roots of a tree occupy an area about 50% greater in radius than the crown of the tree. Empirically it appears that a tree is likely to suffer if more than one-third of its roots are cut. This will occur if the segment of the roots removed approaches closer to the trunk than two-thirds of the radius of the crown, which is effectively the recommendation of the British Standard BS 5837 (Figure 15.6). If a trench has to be cut closer than this for services, either it must be dug carefully by hand and the roots avoided, or the service taken past by newly developed remote techniques without disturbance, or the service re-routed. The latter is often an easy option if the problem is realized in time. If a wall or something more substantial is to be constructed, this same distance needs to be observed. Care must also be taken to exclude heavy vehicles from the rooting area, since these can damage surface roots. It should be mandatory that BS 5837, for trees in relation to construction, be respected. It recommends that protective fences should always be erected in construction sites, at distances given in Table 15.4.

Table 15.4   *Minimum distances for protective fencing around trees on construction sites (British Standards Institute, 1991)*

Tree age	Trunk diameter (mm)	Minimum distance (m)	
		If tree vigorous	If tree not vigorous
Young (< 1/3 life expectancy)	< 200	2.0	3.0
	200–400	3.0	4.5
	> 400	4.0	6.0
Middle aged (1/3 to 2/3 life expectancy)	< 250	3.0	5.0
	250–500	4.5	7.5
	> 500	6.0	10.0
Mature	<350	4.0	6.0
	350–750	6.0	9.0
	> 750	8.0	12.0

Alternatively the fencing should be erected at a distance equal to the spread of the branches or half the height of the tree, whichever is the greater.

All this considers the effect of services and buildings on trees. The reverse problem of the effect of trees on buildings has already been considered in Chapter 9.

15.4   *Die-back*

Within our heritage of older trees it is very easy to find trees which appear to be dying back from the top. Sometimes the whole tree appears moribund. But sometimes only the top has died and there is a reasonably vigorous growth of branches and leaves lower down, without any signs of disease or damage. Such trees from a distance often look 'stag-headed'. The condition is most common in oaks and ash (Figure 15.7).

A great deal of concern has been expressed about these trees, that their condition may be due to some unrecognized pollutant. But the most significant fact is that trees showing die-back are commonest in hedgerows in country districts; they are not common in towns except in development sites. This hardly suggests that pollution is the cause.

No single cause has been identified. Die-back can certainly be due to old age and associated death and decay of roots and parts of stems. Many of the trees showing the most extreme symptoms are over 150 years old, planted at the time of the Napoleonic wars. But the fact that many of the trees are in hedgerows between arable fields suggests that an important cause is damage to roots caused by recent ploughing, analogous to construction damage. The trees developed their main root systems either when the adjacent fields were pasture, or were ploughed only to a shallow depth. Modern machinery has allowed ploughing to

Figure 15.7
Oak die-back is most common in rural areas where the roots of hedgerow trees have been damaged by modern deep ploughing.

a much greater depth and can cause considerable damage to previously established root systems. In these circumstances it is difficult for the tree to establish an adequate new root system to meet the demands of the original canopy, and a smaller new canopy is formed. The same effect can be obtained if the drainage and water relations of the surrounding soil have been greatly altered. All this can happen on development sites.

15.5   *Decay*

Decay is hardly a problem of newly planted and young trees. Yet, because it can begin in a tree early due to mismanagement or damage, it is a matter that needs attention.

Decay is caused by a large number of different fungi, which enter the wood and decompose it, so that the structure of the tree is weakened. The end result is that the affected branch breaks and falls, or the stem is so weakened that it breaks in a high wind when other trees remain standing. Below-ground fungi may enter a damaged root and destroy it progressively towards the base of the tree, and render it unsafe.

Infection depends on the bark of the tree being damaged, so that a spore of a decay fungus can germinate and penetrate into the unprotected wood. Although

Figure 15.8
Rot at the base of an oak tree heavily damaged by fire 20 years previously. Rot can take many years to develop.

trees have natural protectants in their wood, especially when the wood is alive, this protection disappears slowly once damage has occurred, so that fungal entry becomes easier. The older wood of a tree, the heart wood, which is usually recognizable by its different colour, is itself fairly resistant.

Trees naturally shed lower branches not receiving sufficient light; this is most obvious in forests and close plantings. It is interesting that the broken stumps of these branches rarely become rotten because natural defences are developed within the cells of wood that has died by natural processes. Even when a tree has been artificially damaged, the bark regrows to cover the damage. Nevertheless, it is in these places that infection seems most likely to occur, particularly if the tree is already weak, if the healing processes are prevented for any reason, or if conditions are particularly suitable for spore germination and growth.

Infection is likely therefore (a) where the tree is old or already subject to some environmental stress, (b) where such a large wound has occurred that complete healing is taking many years, or (c) where the surface of a wound is kept wet, such as near the ground or in a crotch (Figure 15.8). Because old trees are likely to show the slowest rates of healing, it is not surprising that they are the most likely candidates for decay. But younger trees which suffer damage, for instance from a mower or from a fire, are also candidates, although such wounds will usually heal if the tree is not maltreated a second time and is growing vigorously (Figure 15.4).

A great deal of work has been done to find treatments, such as paints, that can be applied to a wound to prevent or reduce the chance of infection. Inoculation by fungi which are antagonistic to other decay-producing fungi is even being tested. So far no treatment has given convincing results. Indeed many paints seem to increase the chance of decay, perhaps by making conditions better for spore germination behind the treatment or by preventing natural healing processes. This being so, the best approach is to treat all wounds in such a way as will maximize natural healing and minimize the opportunity for spore germination.

When pruning is undertaken, cuts should be simple and clean, positioned to ensure rapid healing (see Chapter 14). Wounds should be made clean and tidy. Where decay has started, the affected piece should be removed, to a point where healing can occur rapidly. Heavy pruning of an established tree, often called lopping or topping, leaving a wound that can only heal over 10–20 years will almost always lead to decay in the long term.

But most problems can be avoided if correct planting and management techniques are employed. If the design is correct little damage should be caused (see Chapter 12), and if the tree is growing vigorously recovery from damage should always occur.

References

British Standards Institute (1991) *Guide for trees in relation to construction, BS 5837: 1991*, British Standards Institute, London.

Grieg, B.J.W., Gregory, S.C. and Strouts, R.G. (1991) *Honey fungus*, Forestry Commission Bulletin **100**, HMSO, London.

Strouts, R.G. (1987a) *Phytophthora* root disease, Arboriculture Research Note **58:87**, Arboricultural Reseach and Advisory Service, Farnham.

Other reading

Burdekin, D.A. and Rushforth, K.D. (1988) *Breeding elms resistant to Dutch elm disease,* Arboriculture Research Note **2:88**, Arboricultural Reseach and Advisory Service, Farnham.

Clouston, B. and Stansfield, K. (1981) *Trees in Towns,* Architectural Press, London.

Hibberd, B.G. (ed.) (1989) *Urban Forestry Practice,* Forestry Commission Handbook **5**, HMSO, London.

Hull, S.K. (1991) Ash dieback in Great Britain: results of some recent research, in *Research for Practical Arboriculture* (ed. S.J. Hodge), Forestry Commission Bulletin **97**, HMSO, London, pp.129-38.

Phillips, D.H. and Burdekin, D.A. (1992) *Diseases of Forest and Ornamental Trees,* 2nd edn, Macmillan, London.

Sinclair, W.A., Lyon, H.H. and Johnson, W.T (1987) *Diseases of Trees and Shrubs,* Comstock, Ithaca.

Strouts, R.G. (1987b) *Fireblight of ornamental trees and shrubs,* Arboriculture Research Note **118:94**, Arboricultural Reseach and Advisory Service, Farnham.

Strouts, R.G. and Winter, T.G. (1994) *The Diagnosis of Ill-Health in Trees*, HMSO, London.

Turner, J.G., Guven, K., Patrick, K.N. and Davis, J.L.M. (1991) Watermark disease of willow, in *Research for Practical Arboriculture* (ed. S.J. Hodge), Forestry Commission Bulletin **97**, HMSO, London, pp.152–60.

16 *Urban forestry*

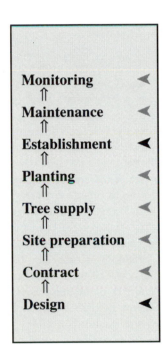

Monitoring ◄
⇑
Maintenance ◄
⇑
Establishment ◄
⇑
Planting ◄
⇑
Tree supply ◄
⇑
Site preparation ◄
⇑
Contract ◄
⇑
Design ◄

- The term urban forestry can best be applied to tree planting on reasonably sized blocks of land, normally more than 0.25 hectare (0.5 acre).
- From these areas of land economic returns are possible even if the trees are planted mainly for amenity and environmental purposes.
- The land involved will usually be either parcels awaiting development in the long term, or derelict land, but sometimes areas intended for long-term amenity.
- The types of planting possible are:
    1. short term using poplar or willow for biomass,
    2. medium term using species that can be coppiced,
    3. long term using normal timber species,
    4. or combinations of these.
- The better soils should be chosen for (1) and (2) to ensure rapid growth.
- Choice will depend on the types of outlet available for the product, although these can be developed from new in relation to potential markets.
- The possibility of disturbance and vandalism must be considered and steps taken to counter them.
- Community involvement will normally be very important.
- Amenity uses can be combined with commercial use, especially in long-term plantings.
- All woodland plantings have an important nature conservation role, in restoring habitats in which specialized woodland wildlife, whether plant or animal, can prosper.

So far in this book we have concentrated on the growth of trees for amenity purposes, whether as isolated trees in streets or gardens, or as groups of trees within parks. However trees can be planted in urban areas in larger blocks, where suitable areas of land are available. Under these circumstances urban trees can not only have amenity, but also economic, value. Today it has come to be recognized that urban trees can provide a valuable source of income as timber or other products such as wood chip mulch. Growing trees on such areas can be considered as urban forestry.

Recently some people have taken urban forestry to cover all trees grown in, and close to, urban areas. Most of these trees have previously been thought of as the remit of arboriculture, or horticulture. There is therefore confusion. It would seem best to keep the term forest to apply to 'an extensive tract of land covered with trees and undergrowth ...', and forestry to apply to 'the science and art of forming and cultivating forests, management of growing timber' (Oxford English Dictionary, 1971). It is perhaps most sensible then to think that what can be called an urban forest should have a minimum size of 0.5 acre (0.25 ha). Trees on such an area will not only form a recognizable and practicable small woodland, but it is also the minimum size for which a Forestry Commission grant is available.

The character of size is an important aspect of the areas of land and trees involved, because from these areas some sort of economic return can be possible. This will usually be an economic return in respect of timber or other wood products, but it could also involve attracting tourists or creating areas where sport or recreation can be undertaken. The Oxford English Dictionary definition of forest includes '... sometimes intermingled with pasture'.

Urban forestry is unlikely to be conventional forestry as we have come to know it. The constraints placed upon forestry in the urban area, particularly the constantly changing demand for land within the urban conurbation, means that normal long-term forestry cannot usually be practised. A private landowner with a piece of land that may in the next 25 years become valuable for development, is unlikely to want to plant a long-term woodland on the site. Therefore some other method of employing the land for commercial wood production must be considered. The landowner might be interested if the land could be used for a short-term tree crop, if one could be found. Not only would the land be cared for, but an economic return would be forthcoming

In some cases long-term forestry may be possible, particularly in areas owned by local authorities. Here a different consideration, that of use of the areas for amenity, arises. Forests and woodlands can provide high-class areas for a wide variety of amenity uses. There is no reason why these should not be combined with economic forestry.

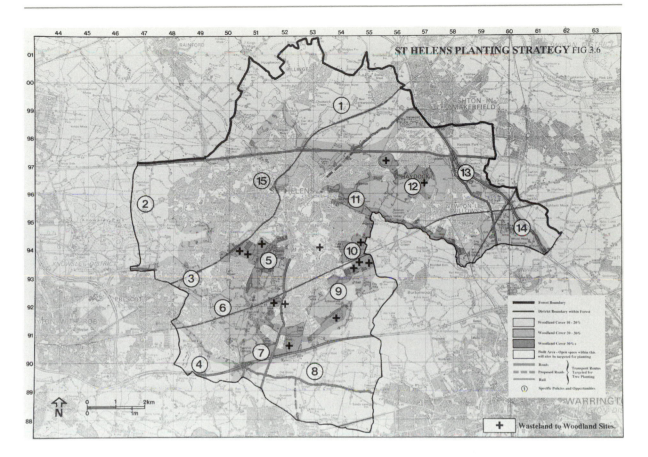

Figure 16.1
The master plan of afforestation of under-used land in the borough of St Helens. Nearly all the land is on the urban fringe awaiting development.

With the guidance from this definition of what constitutes an urban forest, it can be seen that a complex pattern of afforestation can arise in urban areas, with small and large forest areas, in some cases privately and in some cases publicly owned, with amenity uses in some parts and not in others, but with the whole development contributing to the overall landscape, amenity and environmental aspects of the region (Figure 16.1).

This is very much the thinking behind the development of the 12 new Community Forests throughout England. Jointly developed by the Countryside Commission and the Forestry Commission, their mission is 'to develop multipurpose forests which will create better environments for people to use, cherish and enjoy'. Through the creation of each of the community forest plans it will be possible to have a strategic approach to the development and, more importantly, subsequent management of new and existing woodland plantings in urban forests as a whole.

To understand what is generally possible we must first look at the opportunities and the constraints in more detail.

16.1   *Land available for urban forestry*

For reasons of economics the land most suitable for urban forestry must be in relatively large, by normal urban standards, blocks of 0.25 ha or more. Such large areas are often available. Within the urban fringe there is always land which has less potential for development. This will principally be farmland where conditions of slope or drainage make building difficult. But it can also be better areas, for instance where for special reasons planning permission for development is not given but agriculture is no longer a possibility.

Also, in an area such as an industrial estate, where development has been approved, land can often lie vacant for many years waiting for speculators to decide on an appropriate time for development. The time scale could be a matter of a few years or as much as 20 years. If the period is more than 10 years then urban forestry is possible (Figure 16.2).

Beside those areas where farming took place until quite recently, there can be other large areas where industry has been active in the past but has since ceased. These areas can be sand and gravel pits, waste heaps, old railway lines or even old factory areas. Land in urban areas tends not to be static. Industries come and go; particular resources such as coal and sand and gravel become used up. During recession large tracts of land may become available for redevelopment as companies go into liquidation.

Land that is not far removed from agricultural use is likely to have its original soil intact and be highly suitable for forestry. Where the soil has been grossly disturbed, or even destroyed, by industrial activity, the situation is very different. The material can be so skeletal, or even toxic, that tree growth is out of the question. Other areas may have soils which although not impossible, are just difficult for tree growth.

Figure 16.2
Land in the urban fringe now disused and awaiting development. These areas of land are very suitable for short rotation forestry.

Urban substrates have already been shown to be sometimes far from hospitable (Chapter 4). This will pose problems for any type of tree growth, but where it is required that a good return on investment is generated, as in the case of urban forestry, the problems can be particularly serious. Nevertheless, good tree establishment and growth has been achieved on a wide range of degraded soils, such as in sand and gravel pits, and on colliery spoil heaps, if ground preparation and species choice are carried out with care.

All these problem factors indicate that if urban forestry is proposed for an individual piece of land, great care must be taken. Nevertheless because of the individual adaptations and tolerances of different species, urban forestry is a viable option in many urban areas, even in those which are at first sight unpromising.

16.2 *Types of planting*

What sort of planting schemes are likely to provide a return on capital both in the short, medium and long term? There are in essence three major alternatives: (1) short-term rotation of species such as willow and poplar for production of biomass, (2) medium-term rotation coppice crop for production of roundwood poles, and (3) long-term forestry for production of valuable timber crops and related by-products. There is a fourth option also, in which no planting is done at all but trees are allowed to develop naturally. These alternatives can readily be combined. In lowland forests there is, for instance, a long-standing tradition of coppice-with-standards, producing both medium- and long-term rotation products.

16.2.1 SHORT-TERM ROTATION

The use of willow, poplar and similar species to provide a quick sustainable crop is far from being a new idea. This short-term rotation cropping is now often given the grand title of woody biomass production, where the use of the term biomass emphasizes that it is the mass of what is produced, rather than its nature, that matters. Rapid growth is important. This places particular demands on the system.

Species of rapid growth are chosen. They are necessarily species with a relatively high demand for nutrients and water. This means that the sites chosen should have soils of reasonable fertility and moisture, and usually therefore are areas derived directly from farmland. But areas where domestic refuse or sewage sludge have been deposited are equally ideal, because of their inherent fertility. Modern landfill sites with substantial clay capping for gas control may not be so suitable unless provided with a deep (>1 m) soil cover. Any damp areas not completely waterlogged are also suitable. Where there is moisture in urban areas there is usually a good supply of nutrients.

Planting can easily be carried out by insertion of willow or poplar sticks which are very cheap (0.02 tree units per tree planted) (Chapter 9). But the

Figure 16.3
Willows newly planted on a fertile moist site; an excellent combination for biomass production.

overall costs of such plantings can be high because of the high density of planting (cost 220 tree units ha^{-1}), as well as the necessity to fence against rabbits (cost 0.75 tree units m^{-1}). In more agricultural areas the trees are normally placed not more than 1 m apart. However in more urban areas the trees may be as little as 50 cm apart in the row to achieve a quicker return (Figure 16.3). Care must be taken to ensure that the correct spacing between rows is achieved in order to facilitate ease of harvesting and weed control. Unless some form of mechanical harvester is used, it is not easy to achieve a viable financial return. Crops can be taken every 3–5 years. The range of uses of the products is enormous. The material is commonly chipped and then used as a fuel source, or as a mulch substituting for peat. But the end use of the crop will depend upon both location of the source of material and economic factors prevailing at the time.

Production from such short-term rotations can be impressive. Willow, which has so far been found to be the most productive genus, commonly yields 12–15 tonnes of dry matter per hectare per year and, exceptionally, yields of 17 tonnes have been obtained.

Management of this type of system is more intensive than ordinary forestry systems and perhaps has more in common with arable farming. For example, because the nutrient cycle within the plantation will be disrupted by continual harvesting, it will be necessary to monitor soil nutrient levels and amend with fertilizers when required.

Depending on the use for which the wood is required, crops can be taken on very short rotations; stems required for basket weaving can be taken every year. For chipping or fuel crops the rotation may be as long as 3–5 years. Nevertheless the length of time required to generate income from the land is relatively small.

This type of rotation is obviously most suited to land which may be developed in the short term, as well as to land that is relatively fertile. But it is particularly applicable to poorly drained soil for which it may be difficult to find any other use.

16.2.2 MEDIUM-TERM ROTATION

Medium-term rotations of tree crops can be approached from two very different directions. Production can be from a coppice system, in which many slender stems are produced from a basal stool, with a cutting rotation time of 12–15 years depending upon species. Alternatively, production can be from plantations of single stemmed trees, with a medium rotation, harvested after 12–20 years. Obviously the latter has the disadvantage in that the area must be replanted once the trees have been felled.

The emphasis is again on rapid growth. Soils must, therefore, be relatively fertile if reasonable returns are to be achieved. Exactly what soils are appropriate depends on the species chosen. Or, reversing the argument, because a wider range of species is possible, not just willow and poplar, a somewhat wider range of soils can be used than for biomass production (Figure 16.4).

Trees can be managed with a coppice system, either as pollards, where the stem is allowed to develop before the head is cut back, or with the true coppice system where the stems are cut back to ground level. The pollard system is used in areas where cattle are allowed to graze; a famous example is Epping Forest. It has the drawback in that the size of the tree will undoubtedly reduce the amount

Figure 16.4
Traditional hornbeam coppice is a viable medium-term rotation on poorer soils.

of available light and therefore will restrict the number of trees that can be planted in a given area; and harvesting is more difficult. However access through the forest is much easier.

The straight roundwood poles cut from coppice or pollarded trees can be utilized in a number of ways depending upon the species from which they are cut. Certain species, such as sweet chestnut, produce poles that can be used for fencing; hazel can be used for hurdles. Coppiced wood is an ideal raw material for the production of charcoal. Today there is a revival in locally based charcoal making. This not only has the effect of promoting woodland management but also acts as competition for imported charcoal, the majority of which comes from non-sustainable sources.

When coppice areas are planted, the trees are usually planted 2–3 m apart (costing 150 tree units ha^{-1}). As with all tree planting, it is imperative that weed competition around the tree is suppressed. The first cut should not be undertaken until the trees have established and there is sufficient production for the cutting to have some value.

Harvesting is normally carried out during the winter. With the stool system the stems are normally cut as close to ground level as possible in order to encourage shooting from the root system and not only the stool itself.

This medium rotation crop is perhaps best suited to areas of land that have some development potential but are unlikely to be developed within the foreseeable future. The products have a wide range of markets.

16.2.3 LONG-TERM FORESTRY

Planting long-term woodland crops in the urban environment is likely to be the least attractive scheme to the developer or landowner, at least in economic terms. It is unlikely that any long-term commitment to such a scheme would be given, unless the land has previously been damaged or degraded in the past. However, once the amenity value of such long-term plantings are recognized then this option becomes more promising. It is particularly relevant to perimeter plantings around rather dull industrial sites, where planting would not only lead to an increase in the amenity appeal of the area but be followed by an increase in the value of land to developers. The reason for this is quite simple; industrialists have now come to realize the importance of having areas of high visual amenity surrounding their buildings.

Long-term planting is equally valid for areas of land owned by local authorities which have a long-term amenity value. Although young plantations are not particularly attractive, maturing woodland has great attractions for young and old. If attractive woodland flowers such as bluebell, yellow archangel, red campion and wood anemone (depending on soil conditions) can be encouraged, such woodlands can become extremely popular. At the same time selective felling can provide a limited income.

Because immediate rapid growth is not so important, long-term forestry is possible on an even wider range of soils than the two previous options. Successful forests can be established on mine wastes and old quarries, as well as on poor acid and alkaline soils, providing appropriate species are chosen

(Chapter 8). On poor acid soils conifers are an obvious choice, but the site will have to be free from interference and vandalism.

Planting techniques do differ from other types of amenity planting, since it is imperative that costs are kept to a minimum. This means that typical commercial forestry techniques must be used, using bare-root transplants bought in bulk. These will normally be planted rapidly using the notch technique at 2500 plants ha^{-1} (cost including planting is less than 0.05 tree units per tree or 125 tree units ha^{-1}). Spacings for the plantings would normally be at 2 m centres. It is equally possible that direct seeding can be used, especially on subsoil and derelict land materials. It is not expensive (about 250 tree units ha^{-1}) and can give very naturalistic patterns of establishment and excellent early growth so long as the seedlings have been given the right establishment conditions by the use of herbicide and fertilizer.

It is imperative that all young forest trees are free of competition for at least 3 years after planting. This will necessitate careful herbicide treatment (Chapter 13). Fencing will also be necessary to exclude grazing animals (at 0.75 tree units m^{-1}). Tree shelters, the transparent plastic tubes fastened to a stake, are an alternative possibility (Chapter 12), with the added advantage that they will increase the rate of early growth.

16.2.4 WILD WOODLAND

There is another sort of urban forest that must not be forgotten. This is those woodlands which have not been planted, have not been managed, and have, in many cases, developed by natural colonization on pieces of forgotten wasteland. They may be in old quarries or sand pits, on deserted railway lines, or on corners of farmland that escaped development.

Figure 16.5
Woodland at Hampstead Heath developed by natural processes in an old sandpit. It is now a much valued amenity area.

Figure 16.6
Dense sallow, alder and birch developed within 20 years of the closure of a railway. The area is now a country park and an important wildlife habitat.

In the light of commercial pressures, it seems surprising that any should still be present. But they can appear quite rapidly following the onset of disuse, such as on old railway lines, or develop more slowly where an industry has disappeared, as in an old sandpit (Figure 16.5). Once, however, they have appeared, they are taken over for public enjoyment. In the case of Hampstead Heath, the area had become so attractive following the cessation of sand winning, that when the owner tried to obtain permission for development there was such an outcry that he was refused and the area was bought by public subscription.

Unlike the previous systems of urban forestry, these areas have come to be what they are without human intervention, except desertion. Tree development has been the result of natural processes of colonization. The part played by pioneer species, such as sallow and birch, discussed further in Chapter 8, is very apparent. The growth is often very dense (Figure 16.6) and spectacular. In older areas the pioneer species may have given way to dominants such as oak.

Despite, or even because of, the lack of human intervention, such areas are most attractive. They are admirable places to follow the processes of nature, and therefore for ecology and natural history studies. But their lack of apparent order gives them a romantic appeal to many. No management is needed, and therefore almost no costs. Nature can be left to its own devices, although amenity uses may require some simple manipulations.

16.3 *Choice of species*

Where new areas are being set up, choice of species will depend upon a number of factors:

1. How long the land is available for the planting and the type of rotation being chosen.
2. Soil conditions on the site.
3. The need for high growth and maximum economic returns.
4. How exposed the site is to interference and vandalism; for example it is unlikely that in a large conurbation, conifers even slightly resembling the typical Christmas tree will survive over the Christmas period.
5. Whether the planting is required to match the species composition of any natural or semi-natural woodland already present in the area. This will be particularly important in the suburban fringe.
6. The need for disease resistance.
7. The market potential for the product.
8. Any amenity requirements.

All these factors have to be balanced before the final choice is made. What species are chosen is, therefore, determined essentially by the situation and the type of forestry that is possible. A list of the most useful species is given in Table 16.1.

Table 16.1   *Species suitable for urban forestry: the correct choice is important for commercial success*

	Requirements	
	Fertility	Soil pH
Short-term rotation		
Populus nigra	high	neutral
Populus x euamericana	high	neutral
Salix alba and hybrids	high	neutral
Salix viminalis and hybrids	high	neutral
Alnus glutinosa	medium	neutral
Alnus incana	medium	neutral
Nothofagus procera and *obliqua*	medium	neutral/acid
Eucalyptus niphophila and *nitens*	medium	neutral/acid
Medium-term rotation		
The above and the following:		
Acer campestre	high	neutral
Acer platanoides	medium	alkaline/neutral
Acer pseudoplatanus	medium	alkaline/neutral-acid
Betula pendula	medium	alkaline/neutral-acid
Carpinus betulus	medium	neutral/acid
Castanea sativa	medium	neutral/acid
Corylus avellana	high	neutral
Fraxinus excelsior	medium	alkaline/neutral
Prunus avium	high	alkaline/neutral
Long-term rotation		
Any of the structural species listed in Tables 8.1 and 8.2		

16.4   *Economic viability*

It is clear that there are, potentially, a great many uses for the timber produced from urban forestry (Table 16.2). However, as with any other business, there is a certain risk factor. This concerns not only the growth of the trees themselves under the stressful conditions found in the urban and suburban environment, but also the market conditions prevalent at the time the crop comes to maturity. In general, with correct design and management it should be possible to create vigorous tree plantations within the urban environment, even though extrinsic site factors such as vandalism can prove a major problem. The greatest risk, therefore, will come from the market available for the crop at the time of harvest.

It is difficult to provide specific recommendations about markets, because these will vary, depending on local economic and social factors. Table 16.2 suggests that there are both more likely options, such as garden mulch and fence wood, and less likely options, such as turnery and charcoal (Figure 16.7).

Table 16.2   *Possible uses for the material produced by urban forestry. There are many opportunities to be exploited*

As biomass (i.e. chipped or shredded whole material)
Fuel for wood-burning stoves and industrial appliances
Production of fuel brickettes
Mulch for horticultural purposes
Mulch for footpaths and play areas
Surfaces for equestrian gallops
Panel board (if mill close by)

As wood or timber
Fuel logs
Charcoal
Fencing
Gates
Garden furniture
Garden and park features (steps, paths, bollards, edging, etc.)
Turnery
Pallet wood
General sawn timber
General roundwood timber
Paper industry (if mill close by)

As planting stock
Especially willows and poplars

Figure 16.7
Charcoal burning. Charcoal production is an interesting economic possibility for urban forestry.

However the latter may be very successful if the right enthusiast appears to take the wood. Similarly it is common to see little potential in a tree like sycamore, yet a well-grown specimen can have considerable value for veneer. Wisely based opportunism is all-important.

Regardless of whether or not a tree crop is grown on a piece of land, under current economic conditions it is likely that the value of the land will rise. Any crops taken from the land will, therefore, provide extra income and will in no way damage the land or reduce its resale or development value. It must be remembered, too, that in the urban environment, trees, regardless of their end use, will have a value for amenity. By providing a more pleasant environment they will make an area more attractive to investment. This value ought therefore to be included in the profit side of the equation.

Because of the often small size of the pieces of land on which urban forestry can be practised, the full commercial viability of a project is unlikely to be realized unless there is some form of co-operative agreement on the management of the woodlands once they have been planted. How this is achieved depends on local circumstances. Whether the local authority can play an active role in this management, or whether it is best left to private contractors, is a matter which will need investigation.

16.5   *Nature conservation value*

All the different types of forest described have considerable conservation value. Firstly, although perhaps the least important reason, they constitute substantial blocks of native tree species. Secondly, even small blocks of trees are large enough to provide food and shelter for a wide variety of small mammals and birds, and large blocks will provide suitable habitats for more specialized animals such as tawny owls, green woodpeckers and badgers. Thirdly the trees will provide the protection and microclimate suitable for woodland plants, which cannot tolerate open country. These include species already mentioned, such as wood anemone, yellow archangel, and bluebell, but also unusual species such as ramsons, sanicle and dog's mercury. Some, such as wood anemone, primrose and wild strawberry, are particularly favoured by the environmental variation produced by coppicing and other regular cutting. These species are all part of our heritage from the days of the wildwood.

Animals are mobile, and if the right habitats are created, they will come into the woods created. But for plants it may be necessary to undertake carefully managed and recorded introductions, from seed produced by specialist suppliers. This is all very different to the problems of a city street, but it is just as much part of a consideration of trees in the urban landscape.

16.6   *Amenity value*

Finally, the significant contribution urban forest areas can make to local amenity is very important. Since such areas are close to centres of population, it is inevitable that they will acquire an amenity function, even if only a commercial function was intended. The peaceful atmosphere of woodland areas attracts many people, and the more unruly young find woodlands a lure for games of all sorts. It therefore seems unlikely that the amenity function can be disregarded. Indeed there is no reason why amenity and commercial uses cannot be combined, as so well demonstrated by forests of the Forestry Commission, particularly those near urban areas (Figure 16.8).

This does require, however, a positive approach to the needs of those who come to enjoy the areas. Not only need there be paths, to allow access and encourage people not to wander all over the area and cause unnecessary damage, but some of these must be wide enough for people to feel that there are areas in which they can walk without fear of being molested. There will need to be some open areas, perhaps with picnic tables. There will also need to be litter receptacles, and perhaps toilets.

If the area is large and interesting enough, it will merit wardens and a warden's centre. Once an area takes on an amenity function, to exploit it fully requires positive investment, but then it will be thoroughly appreciated by the

Figure 16.8
Amenity use of a commercial forest close to a conurbation. Sherwood Forest has been heavily used by the people of the Midlands for many decades.

public. At the same time, wild areas are perceived by some people as appropriate places to dump rubbish, and once this begins, it escalates as others follow. The simple answer is fencing, or the equivalent, on the perimeter to define the area, and proper maintenance, which in this case is nothing more than effective litter and rubbish collection. In view of the very small investment needed to allow urban forests to be used for amenity, efficient cleansing is a small ongoing cost to pay.

Finally, the positive role of the community in urban forests must not be forgotten. Because urban forests are so close to people, they should as far as possible be community forests. They should be forests with which people can identify; forests that can be 'their' forests. An urban forest has a great deal to give to, but it also has a great deal to receive from, local communities. Given the right supervision, local people, children as well as adults, can participate in the planning, planting and maintenance of their local forest. By this they will learn to understand and appreciate trees and forests. The work that they put into the forest will give them self-esteem and a sense of belonging. Forestry seedlings are of a size that can be readily planted and cared for by children. So children can see it as their forest; this is a proven way in which vandalism is decreased. It is in urban forests in particular that we can gain a new relationship with our environment.

Other reading

Emery, M. (1986) *Promoting Nature in Cities and Towns*, Croom Helm, London.

Forestry Commission (1984) *Silviculture of Broadleaved Woodland,* Forestry Commission Bulletin **62**, HMSO, London.

Forestry Commission (1985) *A Guide to the Reclamation of Mineral Workings to Forestry*, Forestry Commission Research and Development Paper **141**, HMSO, London.

Forestry Commission (1988) *Farm Woodland Practice,* Forestry Commission Handbook **3**, HMSO, London.

Forestry Commission (1991) *Forestry Practice,* Forestry Commission Handbook **6**, HMSO, London.

Grey, G.W. and Deneke, F.J. (1986) *Urban Forestry*, 2nd edn, Wiley, New York.

Hibberd, B.G. (ed.) (1989) *Urban Forestry Practice,* Forestry Commission Handbook **5**, HMSO, London.

Peterken, G.F. (1981) *Woodland Conservation and Management*, Chapman & Hall, London.

Putwain, P.D. and Evans, B.E. (1992) Experimental creation of naturalistic amenity woodland with fertiliser and herbicide management plus lupin companion plants. *Aspects of Applied Biology,* **29**, 179–86.

17 *The integrated approach*

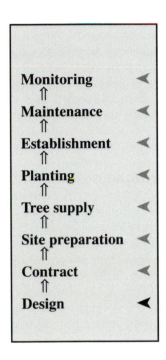

Monitoring ◄
⇑
Maintenance ◄
⇑
Establishment ◄
⇑
Planting ◄
⇑
Tree supply ◄
⇑
Site preparation ◄
⇑
Contract ◄
⇑
Design ◄

- It need not be difficult to achieve excellent survival and growth when trees are planted in urban areas.
- This requires attention to the needs of the tree at the eight different stages in the development of a tree planting scheme.

  1. Design: focuses on the requirements of the tree as well as the potential of the site.

  2. Contract preparation: to specify all the details that will ensure that the tree is properly cared for.

  3. Site preparation: to ensure that the site conditions will be suitable for tree growth.

  4. Tree supply: to provide healthy appropriate material.

  5. Planting: to ensure that the tree is given first class conditions both during and after the operation.

  6. Establishment: anticipates and attends to problems such as water shortage, competition from weeds, and damage from people and vehicles.

  7. Maintenance: continues this aftercare when it could be erroneously believed that the tree could survive on its own.

  8. Monitoring: provides a continuing watch on the tree in case new problems and stresses arise.

- Cost/benefit analyses of what has to be done at each of these stages can lead to radical reconsideration of normal approaches to tree planting.
- Although trees have remarkable resilience and capacity to sustain themselves, successful establishment of trees demands both careful planning and a long-range perspective.

From what has been said in the previous chapters, it will be apparent that a number of conditions have to be fulfilled if a tree is to grow successfully. In this sense planting trees is not so very different from constructing bridges or buildings. Engineers and architects are well aware of the care needed in design and construction if what they build is not to fail. As a result their failures are very few.

There are many fine trees in our cities, in public and private places, and excellent recent planting schemes. But in contrast to engineering products, failures in trees planted in cities are very high. The average failure of about 10% per year needs to be pondered over. Although the individual deaths are not as noticeable as a collapsed bridge or building, the cumulative effect represents a great waste of money – £10 million per year in Britain at least. It also represents missed opportunities, because of the time wasted before the replacements achieve the same effect. There is also the problem of poor growth among those trees that do not die. Twenty-five per cent of trees do not put on any growth in their first year, and increments within a single species can vary from -50 cm to +75 cm.

It is not difficult to achieve excellent growth. In a trial to compare different approaches, planting was carried out on two different urban sites by different contractors. In each case the contractor concerned was asked to follow normal practice, and to provide normal aftercare. At the same time, more of the same material was planted by an independent person in accordance to the recommendations given in previous chapters. In both trials there was approximately a 30% difference in survival and a five fold difference in growth between what the contractors achieved and what could be achieved (Figure 17.1). The performance achieved by the contractors was similar to that which could be found in wider surveys (discussed in Chapter 2). However, some contractors achieve excellent results.

Against this evidence it is worthwhile considering how poor performance is accepted if better performance is readily attainable. Partly this is because individual trees are of relatively low value: but cumulatively, they can be worth a great deal. Partly it is because we have accepted that this is the way it is, in the same way that breakdowns in early motor-cars were accepted as a fact of life: but as technology has improved, it has become clear that car failures are not inevitable, and reliable makes now dominate the market. Partly it is because, with those trees that belong to local authorities, we accept that management responsibility is bound to be complicated. Partly it is because trees have a remarkable ability to recover from initial set-backs, and can turn into swans from ugly ducklings: but even so delays in achieving design objectives remain.

This suggests that it is the ability to recover that makes trees different from manufactured goods and buildings, and encourages us to take an imprecise approach to tree planting. The ability of trees to recover is something we should

Figure 17.1
A comparison of the growth achieved in trees newly planted on two urban sites by contractor using standard practice and by an independent person following the recommendations made in the previous chapters (Dutton, 1991).

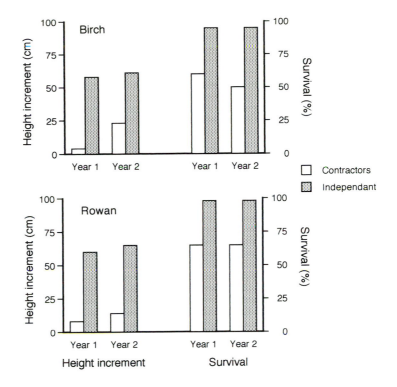

value. If, however, the ability of trees to tolerate bad handling, bad management and bad conditions did provide a full solution to our problems, there would be no need to write this book. But it does not, and steps must be taken to ensure good performance.

These steps are not difficult. The different chapters of this book have shown the individual problems and how they can be overcome. Many of the problems are the subject of on-going research, the results of which are now being more regularly published than in the past, in conference proceedings and in the Research Notes of the DoE Arboricultural Advisory & Information Service. When all this information is taken in combination, success may sometimes look difficult to achieve: there are so many things to get right, and so many operations needing precision and care. Yet the precision and care required to construct a car, a bridge or a building are considerably greater, and there has been no difficulty in achieving success in these. The critical ingredients are awareness of all relevant research, followed by careful planning and equally careful execution.

Successful tree planting depends on the same ingredients. The results of research must be known and understood. There are, then, the same two phases, planning and execution, each of which must be carried out scrupulously. But since trees are alive, and not inanimate, their special needs must be understood, with the realization that if these needs are not met, the trees will grow poorly or die. In the production of a successful tree planting scheme there are a series of stages, divided between the planning and execution phases, all of which are critical (see end papers).

17.1   *Planning*

Any scheme will be as good as the care and attention given to general biological and practical principles. At the beginning of this book these principles were treated separately, implying perhaps that they are a set of things to know about for academic reasons, but otherwise are individually only likely to be important occasionally. Yet subsequently they were used as the basis for action. If, therefore, the planning phase has not embraced careful consideration of each major principle in turn, and integrated the conclusions, failure is highly likely. While design flair, in the aesthetic sense, is important for all schemes, it will not stop a scheme collapsing if even only one basic biological or practical principle has been disregarded. So it is critical that the design and the contract which stems from it are thought out carefully, rather than follow blindly what has been done in the past.

17.1.1 DESIGN

In the design stage there are a distinct set of steps to be taken. The flow of work is essentially linear, but there is also considerable integration, since early decisions will affect those taken later (Figure 17.2). At the same time, in every scheme the possibility of feedback must be taken into account. Once a site has been appraised, characteristics of the site which were not immediately apparent may lead to changed decisions on land use or layout. Equally, decisions on species and type of stock, although they are not themselves necessarily determined by previous decisions on land use or layout, may allow useful modifications to design.

In the end all the decisions by which the project is planned must form a coherent, integrated, whole. If this does not happen, a great deal of money may be wasted. Major site reconstruction should not be chosen without considering whether there might be species which would tolerate the site as it is. The choice of a different species may allow a different, simpler, site treatment or a better layout, by which a great deal of money can be saved (Figure 17.3, Table 17.1). The type of stock should not be chosen without relation to site conditions or land use, otherwise standard trees may be chosen blindly for situations where transplants would be better. This will apply to decisions, such as on maintenance, whose implications are entirely in the future and apply only when the scheme is complete. Maintenance may, for instance, be substantially reduced if mass planted whips ultimately to be left to their own devices are chosen, instead of widely spaced standards set in grass, which will always require attention (Figure 17.4).

In setting out design in this form it can be seen that it is not being thought of as a process in which the grand, aesthetic, idea dominates, but rather one in which careful attention has to be paid to a number of different factors and how they can be overcome. In the end the grand aesthetic view will be achieved by the successful growth of the trees which, as in all countryside situations, provide their own aesthetic appeal, in whatever form they appear. Many landscape

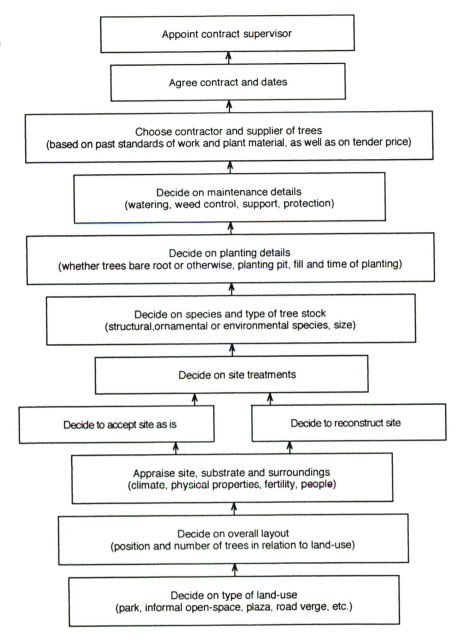

Figure 17.2
The steps involved in the initiation of a successful tree planting scheme. At each step there is need for positive decision.

designers may be worried by such an apparently barbarian approach. But there is no use in having a grand design if the trees fail. Good trees create their own design. Nevertheless such arguments are not meant to imply that design, in the traditional aesthetic sense, has no role, but rather that it is secondary to the design that caters for the needs of the trees.

Figure 17.3
A scheme in which ecologically appropriate species have been planted direct into brickwaste. A great deal of money can often be saved by using a different design approach.

Table 17.1   *A comparison of the costs (at 1987/88 prices) of urban reclamation schemes using different design approaches. The Crown Street site is shown in Figure 17.3 (Bradshaw, 1991)*

	Cost per hectare	Maintenance cost †
Engineering approach		
Site: Everton Park (24 ha)		
Grass and extra-heavy standard trees, on complete topsoil cover		
	£188 500	£11 100 (falling to £6800)
Ecological approach		
Site: Crown Street (0.8 ha)		
Grass/clover mix and transplant trees in mass, on brickwaste		
	£15 500	£900 (approx.)
Site: Bamber Street (2.7 ha)		
Grass/clover on brickwaste, transplant trees in mass on topsoil		
	£53 000	£900 (approx.)

† Per hectare per year.

Figure 17.4
Original dense plantings of whips at Warrington New Town. Mass planted material can be left to look after itself.

17.1.2 CONTRACT PREPARATION

The key to the success of any job, once the design is correct, lies in the contract specification, because this defines what has to be done and will be paid for. The implication is that if it is not specified, it will not get done because it will not be paid for. This is a rather extreme statement, because contractors have a great deal of experience and common sense in knowing what has to be done to ensure the success of a scheme. But they have to work to tight margins, so that they normally carry out only what is specifically required.

The contract specification must therefore define precisely what has to be done. Because success depends on a large number of operations being carried out correctly, the preparation of a good contract may appear a difficult task, involving the specification of such things as stock quality, planting time, handling methods, watering, staking, weed control, etc. Most of these items, however, are standard for many jobs, and a basic specification can be used. A check-list of the items which have to be considered are given in Table 17.2. Any contract is bound to have considerable detail, but proper execution of the operations leading to success cannot be relied on without this.

Some system which ensures that contracts are met has to be built in. Normally this will be by penalties levied by the withholding of later payments. This requires a careful timing of payments, integrated with an effective system of inspection. The latter will require time and trouble taken by the client, for the inspection must be able to check carefully that what was specified has been accomplished. So tight integration is needed between the planning and the execution phases.

Table 17.2   *The items that need to be covered in a contract if success is to be assured. The specification needs to cover many items in considerable detail*

	Chapter
Tree stock	
Size	7
Shape	14
Origin	7
Supplier	7
Transplanting/undercutting	7
Bare root/root balled	7
Transport and handling	7
Species	8
Site preparation	
Site substrate analysis to assess:	
pH and lime requirement	6
nutrient status	6
organic matter content	6
Quality of imported topsoil	6 and 11
Type and rate of application of ameliorants	6
Drainage provision	6 and 9
Identification and avoidance of services	9
Relief of compaction	6
Planting	
Method	9
Pit preparation to include:	
size of pit	9
loosening of pit sides and base	9
protection of pit	12
Planting pit fill	9
Planting pit:	
ameliorants	10 and 11
fertilizers	11
Protection of trees during planting	9
Water	
At planting	10
Timing and amount of subsequent irrigation	10
Support and protection	
Staking	12
Ties and protective pads	12
Guards	12
Aftercare	
Weed control:	
mulch	13
herbicide	13
area	13
Inspection of support and protective measures	12
Replacement of dead or poor specimens	2

17.2   *Execution*

The actual execution of any scheme involves a series of stages which must be carefully integrated. But the situation is more complicated, because there are now two parties, the client and the contractor, each with their own responsibilities (Figure 17.5). The success of the scheme depends on the competence of both parties, and the interaction between them. It is imperative that the client understands the underlying principles, has produced a good design, knows what

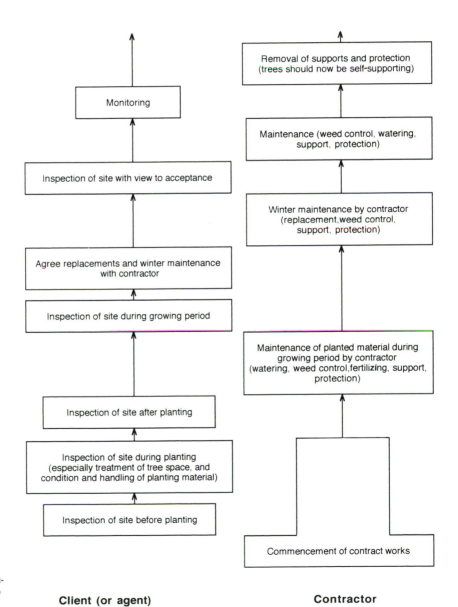

Figure 17.5
The steps involved in ensuring that a tree planting scheme is carried out successfully and establishes well. Regular inspection is important while a scheme is being established.

he/she is expecting, and provides good supervision. A good contractor appreciates this, and a poor contractor will have to be kept up to standard.

It is also important to map out the way that shared responsibility will continue for the life of the tree. Although separate stages can be recognized, the tree will only prosper if there is a continuity of care and appreciation of its needs. It is easy for private owners to achieve this. But within local authorities, which are responsible for such a large proportion of the trees in our immediate suuroundings, such continuity is much more difficult.

17.2.1 THE SITE PREPARATION STAGE

Trees are remarkably tolerant of site conditions. Nevertheless there are site conditions, especially compaction, drainage and toxicity, which can prejudice the final growth of the trees. It is no use forming a planting site so that surface water drains into it if nothing is done about pit drainage. Ground compaction can inhibit root development. These matters have to be dealt with properly. However, importing topsoil is not the only solution; many urban materials, such as brick waste, are excellent for trees providing that their characteristics are understood. Topsoil of poor quality is a waste of money. However good topsoil spread in wet conditions and badly compacted it is likely to be very hostile to tree roots. All site work must be carried out to a high standard and well supervised.

17.2.2 THE TREE SUPPLY STAGE

If stock is of poor quality, complete failure or poor growth is likely. Yet failures due to this factor are commonplace. They can originate at the nursery, or in the storage and transport involved in bringing the material to the site. It is therefore important that the well-established rules for ensuring stock quality are observed. The great problem is that stock is raised away from the planting site, usually by a different contractor. The only way to ensure that stock is being raised properly is to visit the nurseries involved, and then to inspect the material on arrival before it is unpacked from the lorry. With bulk purchases, a sample should be lined out carefully in good conditions by the customer as a matter of routine, to check tree performance in practice.

Type of stock and species are an important decision. The species must have ecological and growth characteristics appropriate to the site, because these will determine the long-term success of the scheme. So will choice of stock type, except that it does not follow that investment in large expensive stock is a guarantee of success, rather the reverse as has been argued in this book.

17.2.3 THE PLANTING STAGE

This could be the stage in which the least number of problems occur, because it should be under the complete control of the contractor. Yet this is not necessarily true; trees continue to be planted badly. The major faults seem to be poor ground preparation, planting too late, excessive exposure during planting, and badly formed and filled planting pits. On top of this is the vexed problem of

Figure 17.6
The results of good specifications and good supervision. The average failure rate achieved by the authority responsible for this scheme was less than 2%.

watering. This should be integrated into the whole operation; if the planting has been carried out properly and at the right time there should only be a need for watering in very dry seasons. Watering, weed control and all the other matters of immediate aftercare should be properly specified and covered in the contract. If problems still occur, either the contract or the supervision are inadequate. When the contract specification is well drawn up, the contractor is well chosen and the supervision good, failures can be less than 2% (Figure 17.6).

17.2.4 THE ESTABLISHMENT STAGE

The operation does not end when the planting is complete. Maintenance is essential, particularly weed control and watering when necessary. Whatever the responsibility of the contractor for maintenance, it is imperative that the client watches over the progress of the trees and looks not only for failures but also for poor growth and its likely causes. The contractor's responsibility for these can then be properly directed.

17.2.5 THE MAINTENANCE STAGE

At some stage, usually at the end of the first or second year, the contractor's responsibility terminates. It is essential that properly directed maintenance arrangements are then made. These must understand the aims and objectives of the original scheme and ensure that progress to their achievement is maintained.

In the second to the fifth year the trees should be growing well and becoming more and more independent. But there will still be need for care, particularly in relation to weed control, support and protection. It is disappointing to see trees which have established well and are well supported, becoming strangled by tree ties and finally losing their heads in an autumn gale. It is equally disappointing to see trees planted in good materials and growing well in their first year, dying from weed competition in a dry period in their second year. Continuity of care is imperative.

17.2.6 MONITORING

Trees have a long-term existence. Care for them must continue for the whole of their lifetime. It is here that often the greatest weaknesses in tree management lie. After a year or two all responsibility for the newly planted tree often evaporates. Most trees in public ownership end up as orphans. This is not the best way to ensure good results.

In present-day circumstances trees are continually being subject to new stresses. The recent increase in the use of salt is taking a considerable toll on trees long established in places of major importance, such as on the Embankment in London (Figure 17.7). The constant need to replace old and provide new underground services can cause major root damage to established trees. Air pollution due to SO_2 may have decreased, but that due to ozone is increasing. The possibility of new diseases coming in from abroad is a very real threat. Continued monitoring is essential, even if only on an annual basis.

17.3   *Cost/benefit analysis*

In deciding on a planting scheme many factors are involved. It may be that the prime need is to achieve a major landscape contribution as quickly as possible. In this case the extra costs involved in using extra-heavy stock may be justified. But it must not be forgotten that there will be other costs beside the tree and its planting costs; in particular it will be important to provide it with reliable irrigation and drainage during its establishment phase.

For most schemes the crucial requirement will be good establishment and rapid growth at minimum cost. Economy may be essential to reduce expenditure or to allow a greater amount of landscaping. So it is important, when deciding on a large scheme or on planting a single tree, to look carefully at what will deliver the required end-product most successfully, and at what price. The following are some examples.

Figure 17.7
Long established plane trees on the Embankment in Central London dying from excessive use of salt. New stresses can appear against which firm action must be taken if trees are to survive.

1. Perhaps the most important analysis that can be made is in the choice of material, for instance between planting a whip (needing only a small pit and no staking; total cost about 0.12 tree units) and planting a standard (total cost about 2.5 tree units). Both will deliver an excellent tree and the whip will grow faster than the standard and perhaps catch it up. But the whip is less than 1/20 the cost of the standard. Although the standard will be necessary in formal areas, there are innumerable open situations where it would be more sensible to plant whips, perhaps planting groups of five or so to achieve an effect that can never be achieved by a single standard. In forest areas transplants will be even more economical.

2. The next analysis is what should be done to achieve the end-product of a healthy vigorous tree. Standard trees, costing about 2.5 tree units each, are liable to a 10% annual death rate. About 30% of these deaths can be attributed to weed competition (Figure 5.1) even with present control measures. So weeds are responsible for a loss at least equal to 0.075 tree units per year per tree. A herbicide treatment can eliminate this loss at the cost of 0.02 tree units or less. At the same time, left out of this equation is the fact that until the tree is replaced its contribution to the landscape is missing. For those not wanting to use herbicides, a bark mulch would cost about 0.2 tree units but unfortunately is not nearly so effective.

3. Various types of stress account for about 25% of deaths. Much of this is due to water shortage. Watering at a cost of 0.8 tree units does not seem worthwhile unless the landscape contribution is important, or the cost of watering can be reduced. But the introduction of a soil amendment may be worthwhile.

4. Vandalism accounts for about 15% of deaths and is very localized. It does not seem worth spending over 1 tree unit on a tree guard for damage costing less than 0.04 tree units, except in special situations. It must also be remembered that the tree guard itself will cause over 10% of deaths.

5. Good soil conditions are often provided by 15–20 cm of topsoil, at a cost of 0.4 tree units per tree (per m^2). Yet trees can root excellently in building rubble and have their nutrients provided by fertilization for 3 years at a cost of 0.06 tree units per tree.

These few examples suggest that it is worthwhile making cost/benefit analyses for all the operations that may be involved in tree planting operations. They have already caused many tree planting authorities to radically rethink their methods. The most conspicuous change in approach is the wide use of whips, planted directly into unimproved soils provided with fertilizer and herbicide. But other operations can also be called into question, such as the provision of tree guards. Important operations such as weed control by herbicides are being given far more emphasis.

17.4   *The need for a long-range perspective*

The decision to plant trees brings with it the need for both a short- and a long-range perspective based on performance and economics, and an acceptance of a long term as well as a short term commitment. In the normal course of events the responsibility for trees planted by public bodies can change several times (Figure 17.8). The fact that trees have a remarkable ability, unlike inanimate objects, to sustain themselves, has meant that it has often seemed that in the long term trees can be left to their own devices, in a way which is inconceivable for houses, roads and other elements of cities.

If we believe that trees are to be a critical component of our cities, then decisions on tree planting must include decisions on the system of supervision which will not only operate at the planting and establishment stages, but also afterwards at the monitoring stage. In some countries, for instance in Wiesbaden in Germany, the maintenance of all trees over a certain size, whether public or private, becomes the responsibility of the city, no matter who is the owner. To ensure that no tree is overlooked, and becomes an orphan, the city is overflown at regular intervals, and the tree population and the health of individuals is assessed by false-colour infra-red photography (Figure 17.9). Any trees which appear in poor health are then inspected by the city's tree maintenance team and restorative action taken. In Britain inventories of public trees are being made by some local authorities, and computerized recording methods are being developed.

It is a reflection on the attitude to trees in this country that lamp standards are listed and numbered while nearly all street trees go unrecorded. A good arbori-cultural service is an essential responsibility of every local authority. City land-owners with considerable numbers of trees on their land should ensure that they have a permanent system for them. Private landowners have mostly understood this need.

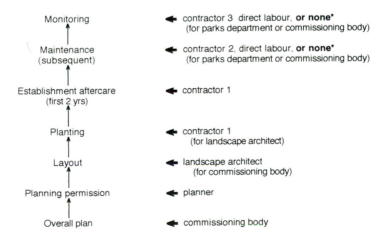

Figure 17.8
The changes in responsibilities which commonly occur during the planning, execution and maintenance of public amenity tree planting schemes in the UK This is a serious factor limiting success (modified from Bradshaw, 1991).

Figure 17.9
False-colour infra-red surveys used in the city of Wiesbaden in Germany in order to monitor the health of the city's stock of trees (de la Chevallerie, 1986). The performance of individual trees can be followed in detail.

Such monitoring and maintenance cannot be carried out without cost. But it can save substantial expenditure by reducing the need to replace trees which would otherwise have failed. What is more important is that it will ensure that our heritage of trees is maintained, not just for ourselves, but for our children and all those that will succeed us.

References

Bradshaw, A.D. (1991) Arboriculture: the research need, in *Research for Practical Arboriculture* (ed. S.J. Hodge), Forestry Commission Bulletin **97**, HMSO, London, pp. 10–22.

de la Chevallerie, H. (1986) The ecology and preservation of street trees, in *Ecology and Design in Landscape* (eds A.D. Bradshaw, D.A. Goode and E. Thorp), Blackwell, Oxford, pp. 383–98.

Dutton, R.A. (1991) Analysis of the critical stages in urban tree establishment, PhD thesis, University of Liverpool.

Other reading

Bernatsky, A. (1978) *Tree Ecology and Preservation*, Elsevier, Amsterdam.

Carpenter, P.L. and Walker, T.D. (1990) *Plants in the Landscape,* Freeman, New York.

Handley, J.F. (1986) Landscape under stress, in *Ecology and Design in Landscape* (eds A.D. Bradshaw, D.A. Goode and E. Thorp), Blackwell, Oxford, pp. 361–82.

Hodge, S.J. (ed.) (1991) *Research for Practical Arboriculture*, Forestry Commission Bulletin **97**, HMSO, London.

Thoday, P.R. (1983) Tree establishment in amenity sites, in *Tree Establishment* (ed. P.R. Thoday), University of Bath, Bath, pp. 12–23.

Appendix

ARBORICULTURE RESEARCH NOTES:
INDEX OF TITLES AVAILABLE JANUARY 1994

48/83/PATH D. Lonsdale, A definition of the best pruning position, Apr. 1993

50/89/SSS W.O. Binns, H. Insley and J.B.H. Gardiner, Nutrition of broadleaved amenity trees. I. Foliar sampling and analysis for determining nutrient status, Oct. 1989

53/90/W.S. P.B. Lane, Chemical weeding – Hand-held direct applicators, Feb. 1990

54/89/SILS D. Patch, M.P. Coutts and J. Evans, Control of epicormic shoots on amenity trees, Mar. 1989

55/84/ENT M.R. Jukes, The Knopper gall, Jun. 1984

56/88/SEED P.G. Gosling, Dormant tree seeds and their pre(sowing) treatment, May 1988

57/93/EXT P.H. Sterling, The Brown-tail moth, Jun. 1993

58/93/PATH R.G. Strouts, *Phytophthora* root disease, May 1993

59/89/ARB R.J. Davies and J.B.H. Gardiner, The effects of weed competition on tree establishment, Jun. 1989

60/88/ENT T.G. Winter, Oak defoliation, Jun. 1988

63/87/SILS J. Evans and C. Shanks, Tree shelters, May 1987

64/86/SILN P.M. Tabbush, Rough handling reduces the viability of planting stock, Feb. 1986

66/86/EXT D.N. Skinner, Planting success rates – standard trees, Sep. 1986

67/87/ARB R.J. Davies, A comparison of the survival and growth of transplants, whips and standards, with and without chemical weed control, Mar. 1987

68/90/PATH D.R. Rose, Lightning damage to trees in Britain, Mar. 1990

69/87/SILS R.J. Davies, Do soil ameliorants help tree establishment?, Apr. 1987

71/87/ARB R.J. Davies, Black polythene mulches to aid tree establishment, Aug. 1987

72/87/ARB R.J. Davies, Sheet mulches: suitable materials and how to use them, Aug. 1987

74/90/ARB R.J. Davies and H.W. Pepper, Protecting trees from field voles, Jul. 1990

75/88/ARB R.J. Davies, Alginure root dip and tree establishment, Jan. 1988

76/88/SSS A.J. Moffat, Sewage sludge as a fertilizer in amenity and reclamation plantings, Sep. 1988

77/89/ARB D. Patch, Stakes and ties, Apr. 1989

78/89/PATH D.R. Rose, Marssonina canker and leaf spot (Anthracnose) of weeping willow, Jun. 1989

79/89/PATH D.R. Rose, Scab and Black canker of willow, Jun. 1989

80/89/ENT T.G. Winter, Cypress and juniper aphids, Jul. 1989

81/90/ARB J.E.J. White and D. Patch, Ivy – boon or bane?, Jan. 1990

84/90/ARB S.J. Hodge and J.E.J. White, The ultimate spread of trees commonly grown in towns, May 1990

85/90/SILS J.E.J. White and D. Patch, Propagation of lowland willows by winter cuttings, Jun. 1990

86/90/ARB S.J. Hodge, Organic soil amendments for tree establishment, Jun. 1990

87/90/EXT K.N. Patrick, Watermark disease of willows, Jul. 1990

88/90/SILN J.D. McNeill *et al.*, Inoculation of alder seedlings to improve seedling growth and field performance, Jul. 1990

89/90/WILD B.A. Mayle, Bats and trees, Sep. 1990

90/90/ARB S.J. Hodge, The establishment of trees in new hedgerows, Oct. 1990

91/90/ARB S.J. Hodge, The establishment of trees in existing hedgerows, Oct. 1990

92/90/ARB S.J. Hodge and T.J. Walmsley, The use of water retentive materials in tree pits, Nov. 1990

93/90/ARB S.J. Hodge, The influence of nursery spacing on outplanting performance of amenity trees, Dec. 1990

94/91/PATH R.G. Strouts, Dieback of the Flowering cherry *Prunus* 'Kanzan', Jan. 1991

95/91/EXT H.J. Read, M. Frater and I.S. Turney, The management of ancient beech pollards in wood pastures, Dec. 1991

96/91/PATH M.C. Dobson, Diagnosis of de-icing salt damage to trees, Apr. 1991

97/91/ARB S.J. Hodge, Amenity tree planting with bare-root stock, May 1991

98/91/ARB S.J. Hodge, Cell-grown broadleaved stock, May 1991

99/91/PATH M.C. Dobson, Tolerance of trees and shrubs to de-icing salt, Jun. 1991

100/91/PATH M.C. Dobson, Prevention and amelioration of de-icing salt damage to trees, Jun. 1991

101/91/ENT T.G. Winter, Pine shoot beetles and ball-rooted semi-mature pines, Sep. 1991

102/91/ARB S.J. Hodge, Improving the growth of established amenity trees. Site physical condition, Nov. 1991

103/91/ARB S.J. Hodge, Improving the growth of established amenity trees: fertilizer and weed control, Nov. 1991

104/92/ENT C. I. Carter, Lime trees and aphids, Jan. 1992

105/92/PATH B.J.W. Greig, Occurrence of decline and dieback of oak in Great Britain, Jan. 1992

106/92/EXT C. Hawke and D.R. Williamson, Japanese knotweed in amenity areas, May 1992

107/92/ARB D. Patch and A. Denyer, Blight to trees caused by vegetation control machinery, Jul. 1992

108/92/EXT P.G. Biddle, Tree roots and foundations, Jul. 1992

109/92/PATH D. Lonsdale, Treatment of tree wounds, Nov. 1992

110/93/EXT D.R. Helliwell, Water tables and trees, Feb. 1993

111/92/PATH J.N. Gibbs, Bleeding canker of Caucasian lime (*Tilia* x *euchlora*), Dec. 1992

112/93/ARB S.J. Hodge, Nutrient injection into trees, Feb. 1993

113/93/ARB S.J. Hodge, Compressed air soil injection around amenity trees, Mar. 1993

114/93/ARB S.J. Hodge, Trials of organic backfill amendments on trunk road sites, May 1993

115/93/ARB S.J. Hodge, Using steel rods to assess aeration in urban soils, Sept. 1993

116/93/PATH D. Lonsdale, A comparison of 'target' pruning, versus flush cuts and stub pruning, Oct. 1993

117/93/PATH D. Lonsdale, Choosing the time of year to prune trees, Nov. 1993

118/94/PATH R.G. Strouts, Fireblight of ornamental trees and shrubs, Jan. 1994

119/94/PATH J.N. Gibbs, De-icing salt damage to trees – the current position, Jan. 1994

Further information available from
Arboricultural Advisory and Information Service, Alice Holt Lodge,
Wrecclesham, Farnham, Surrey, GU10 4LH.
Telephone: 0420 22022. Fax: 0420 22000.

Index

Entries in **bold** indicate lists describing species